The RISE and FALL of an OFFICER CORPS

The RISE and FALL of an OFFICER CORPS

The Republic of China Military,
1942–1955

Eric Setzekorn

UNIVERSITY OF OKLAHOMA PRESS : NORMAN

Publication of this book is made possible through the generosity of Edith Kinney Gaylord.

Library of Congress Cataloging-in-Publication Data

Name: Setzekorn, Eric B., author.
Title: The rise and fall of an officer corps : the Republic of China military, 1942–1955 / Eric Setzekorn.
Other titles: Republic of China military, 1942–1955
Description: Norman, OK : University of Oklahoma Press [2018] | Includes bibliographical references and index.
Identifiers: LCCN 2018002611 | ISBN 978-0-8061-6118-1 (hardcover) ISBN 978-0-8061-9120-1 (paper)
Subjects: LCSH: China. Lu jun—History. | China (Republic : 1949–). Lu jun—History.
Classification: LCC UA837 .S38 2018 | DDC 355.00951249/09044—dc23
LC record available at https://lccn.loc.gov/2018002611

The paper in this book meets the guidelines for permanence and durability of the Committee on Production Guidelines for Book Longevity of the Council on Library Resources, Inc. ∞

Copyright © 2018 by the University of Oklahoma Press, Norman, Publishing Division of the University. Paperback published 2022. Manufactured in the U.S.A.

All rights reserved. No part of this publication may be reproduced, stored in a retrieval system, or transmitted, in any form or by any means, electronic, mechanical, photocopying, recording, or otherwise—except as permitted under Section 107 or 108 of the United States Copyright Act—without the prior written permission of the University of Oklahoma Press. To request permission to reproduce selections from this book, write to Permissions, University of Oklahoma Press, 2800 Venture Drive, Norman, OK 73069, or email rights.oupress@ou.edu.

Contents

List of Figures • vii

Acknowledgments • ix

Abbreviations and Acronyms • xi

Introduction • 3

1. The Development of the Chinese Army, 1850–1927 • 16

2. A Party Army, 1927–1942 • 39

3. Americans and Officers, 1942–1945 • 55

4. A National Army for China, 1945–1949 • 84

5. Refining the Army Profession, 1950–1953 • 117

6. Restoring the Party to Dominance, 1953–1955 • 139

Conclusion • 161

Notes • 175

Bibliography • 207

Index • 233

Figures

Army officers in the late Qing Dynasty • 76

Senior officers in the 3rd Division, Qing Imperial Army • 76

Generalissimo Chiang Kai-shek • 77

U.S. instructor with Chinese mortar regiment • 78

U.S. Army instructors conducting machine-gun training for Chinese troops • 78

Lt. Gen. Joseph W. Stilwell inspecting Chinese troops in India • 79

Generalissimo and Madame Chiang Kai-shek and Lt. Gen. Joseph W. Stilwell • 79

Gen. Sun Li-jen on the front lines in Burma • 80

Gen. Hsiung Shih-fei and Gen. George Marshall • 80

Garden party at Dumbarton Oaks, Washington, D.C. • 81

Chiang Kai-shek meets with Gen. Albert C. Wedemeyer • 82

Maj. Gen. William Chase • 82

Ambassador Karl Rankin in Taiwan • 83

Troops of the Republic of China Army • 83

Acknowledgments

It is a great pleasure to recognize some of the special people who have helped, supported, and assisted with my research over the past several years.

Beginning almost two decades ago at UC Berkeley, Robert Middlekauff and Wen-Hsin Yeh were tremendously helpful and provided a great example for an undergraduate. At UC Irvine, Kenneth Pomeranz and Jeffrey Wasserstrom were exceedingly patient as I engaged with graduate coursework after five years away from academia.

At George Washington University, my PhD dissertation committee has been exceedingly helpful throughout the research, writing, and revision process. My primary adviser, Edward McCord, has been a pillar of wisdom and reviewed draft after draft of my work. Since I began my studies at George Washington University in the spring of 2009, he has overseen every aspect of my academic progress and supplied encouragement or a kick in the pants as necessary. Thomas Long, Gregg Brazinsky, and Daqing Yang were also vitally important for keeping my energy and interest high.

The U.S. Army Center for Military History (CMH), the Smith-Richardson Foundation, Peking University, and the Ministry of Education for the Republic of China all generously supported my research.

Lastly, I want to thank Janice for her understanding of the baffling existence that is graduate school. My absence on long trips to dusty archives and numerous beautiful weekends spent indoors poring over forgotten books is at best eccentric behavior. Her patience and support made this project a reality.

Abbreviations and Acronyms

AIDC	Aerospace Industrial Development Corporation
AMMISCA	American Military Mission to China
CAI	Chinese Army in India
CBE	Commander of the Order of the British Empire
CBI	China-Burma-India
CCC	Chinese Combat Command
CCP	Chinese Communist Party
CEA	Chinese Expeditionary Army
CGSS	Command and General Staff School
CIA	Central Intelligence Agency
CINCFE	Commander in Chief, Far East
CMA	Central Military Academy
CRC	Central Reform Commission
CTC	Chinese Training Command
CYC	China Youth Corps; Anti-Communist Youth Corps
DoD	Department of Defense
DPP	Democratic Progressive Party
FBI	Federal Bureau of Investigation
IDF	indigenous defense fighter
JCS	Joint Chiefs of Staff
JUSMAG	Joint U.S. Military Advisory Group
KMT	Kuomintang (Nationalist Party of China)
MAAG	Military Assistance and Advisory Group
MAP	Military Assistance Program
MND	Ministry of National Defense

NCO	noncommissioned officer
NSB	National Security Bureau
PCC	Political Consultative Conference
PLA	People's Liberation Army
PRC	People's Republic of China
ROC	Republic of China
ROTC	Reserve Officers Training Corps
SACO	Sino-American Cooperative Organization
TGC	Taiwan Garrison Command
TRA	Taiwan Relations Act
USTDC	United States Taiwan Defense Command
VMI	Virginia Military Institute

The RISE and FALL of an OFFICER CORPS

Introduction

During the twentieth century, civil wars, foreign invasion, and the repeated use of military power against civilians by authoritarian governments wracked China. In spite of this bloody history, the study of the military as an institution and its role in Chinese history has been extremely narrow. This is surprising because contemporary China (the People's Republic of China) is a military anomaly in that it is the only large country in the world that does not possess a "national" military, instead relying on a military responsible only to a political party, the Chinese Communist Party (CCP, zhongguo gongchandang).

While clearly political parties, whether the CCP or the Kuomintang (KMT, the Nationalist Party of China), have been tremendously powerful, military officers do have the ability to influence and shape their role in government and society. The subject of this work is the officer corps of the Republic of China (ROC) military from 1942 to 1955 and the development of military professionalism. The core historical argument presented is that during this period ROC military officers were able to leverage political and social currents favoring a depoliticized military, foreign partnerships, and technical expertise to create a true "national" army for the first time in Chinese history. This period also initiated American military involvement in "army-building," a process of encouraging nations to develop stable military institutions. During the Cold War, the lessons that American military officers took from the Chinese experience would influence global programs of developing military allies throughout Asia, South America, and the Middle East.

Between the years of 1942 and 1955, the Republic of China military created a professional, apolitical military force, led by a cadre of highly trained, nationalistic, and cosmopolitan officers. Building on fifty years of Chinese military thought, this group incorporated foreign ideas to develop a concept of an army structured to represent aspirations of China as a world power. Chinese military officers during the 1940s and 1950s had extensive global connections, and perceived their role to be similar to that of American, British, and French officers who were responsible to the nation as a whole, not to a one-party state. The failure of this "army-building" project was not due to a failure of intellectual or professional development as an idea or norm, but because of a renewed politicization of military forces and a purge of key military leaders in 1955 by the KMT. The end of an apolitical, independent professional identity for military officers in the ROC was a result of the power of the KMT to remove, arrest, and, in some cases, kill military officers who objected to KMT party control of the ROC military.

In addition to shining a light on the military history of modern China, this work also highlights broader patterns of military change. Embedded within the narrative of military development from 1942 to 1955 is an exploration of military change, which reaches a conclusion that military change was not pushed on China by foreigners, nor did defeat in 1949 significantly impact ROC military values and beliefs. The most prominent factor driving the ROC military toward the concept of a professional national army was the desires and attitudes of the military officers. Throughout this work, "professional" describes an organization with a high degree of administrative insulation from outside pressures, personnel assignment based on occupational efficiency, significant barriers to entry, a sense of shared identity, and a belief in a special status within society. Increased professionalization was attractive to Chinese military officers because it provided for higher social status, increased political insularity, and improved organizational security.

The ROC officer corps is an ideal subject for academic research because the officers' organizational role placed them in a power-brokerage position between high-level political policy makers and the common soldiers or the Chinese civilian population. In addition, the power and influence of the Nationalist officer corps was especially salient from 1942 to 1955 because military officers acted as the primary partner for an extensive intergovernmental partnership between the United States and the Republic of China. This partnership provided Nationalist officers with access to educational opportunities and technological transfers. In the complex political and cultural environment of mid-twentieth-century China, military officers were a focal point where foreign ideas, political demands, social pressures, and institutional structures were interpreted, contested, and negotiated.

From this central position, military officers sought to redefine their role as apolitical technocrats and "managers of violence" that served in a "national" army. This new role gave military officers greater social prestige because they could portray themselves as patriots serving the nation rather than lackeys of an unelected single-party government. Although the organizational strategy of professionalization offered status advantages to military officers, an environment characterized by poor logistical support, low levels of government capacity, and a contested political space all challenged professional ideals. Specifically, the gap between KMT/ROC political goals and officer professional goals resulted in systemic problems in controlling territory or mounting sustained military operations.

To develop this historical narrative, I will use several interconnecting threads. First, I examine the tension between the professional aspirations of military officers and the political desires of Chinese political leaders in the early twentieth century who sought to use military forces in domestic political struggles. Warlords were an initial obstacle to military officer aspirations, but a more difficult challenge was presented in the idea of a "party-army (dangjun)," introduced by Sun Yat-sen.

Second, I present a thorough examination of the military partnership between the United States and China from 1942 to 1955. Beginning prior to the Japanese bombing of Pearl Harbor, the United States and China initiated a massive program of arms transfers, professional military training, and organizational restructuring. This partnership was motivated by American desires to create a reliable security partner in East Asia, and Chinese political desires to increase their military power and global status. Within the Chinese officer corps, the partnership presented an opportunity to adopt American structures and methods that supported their long-held professional aspirations.

Last, the party-army concept, represented most directly through the Soviet-inspired "political officer" installed in military units, was a direct intellectual challenge to a professional military by placing Party loyalty, political objectives, and ideological conformity above military competence. The fluctuating role and influence of political officers from 1942 to 1955 provides a contrast to professional officer identity, highlighting the process by which officers developed their profession.

At times, this narrative, which focuses on military officers during a frantic period of military change and adaptation, might be difficult to understand at the individual level. To provide a more accessible microcosm of the sometimes-abstract changes described, as a final thread I will follow the life of Sun Li-jen (Sun Liren), a major figure of the 1942–1955 period, whose life story encapsulates both the promise and the peril of military identity in modern China. Sun's life span covers the period of this study and his rise to military prominence during the 1940s and

1950s represents a breakthrough of the professional military over the party-army identity. Sun was also one of the main personal beneficiaries of the Sino-American partnership, parlaying his American education and military skills into a rise to power. Analysis of Sun's life offers the possibility of examining the normative and political forces of the era on a more human scale than the institutional scope presented throughout the work.

The Military as a Profession of Arms

This work examines military officers and the military as a coherent collective group, forced to adapt to technological, social, and political changes to survive. In addition, officers are members of an institution, which shaped their motivation and determination to adapt. While technology is a major factor and the adoption of advanced weapons has sometimes fundamentally altered the battlefield performance of military forces, most military historians have moved toward a cultural approach to military change, and I share this cultural approach.[1]

Traditional historical analysis of military change has emphasized realist conceptions of dynamic competition. The irreducible fact that armed conflict can result in the injury or death of its participants would seem to imply that militaries should be highly motivated to minimize their vulnerabilities and seek advantages. Realists cite this competitive dynamic as the driving force of military change with a regular adaptation of "best practices" from a range of options based on rational evaluation. Military historian John Lynn summarizes the realist argument for adaptation: "War is a matter of Darwinian dominance or survival for states, and of life or death for individuals. When an army confronts new or different weaponry or practices on the battlefield, it must adapt to them, and often adaptation takes the form of imitation."[2]

Contemporary historians have broadened our conception of military change to emphasize "change in the goals, actual strategies, and/or structure of a military organization."[3] The cultural turn in military studies has resulted in multiple studies that have compared military organizations across cultures, times or technological eras, and have stressed the centrality of organizationally coherent, well-motivated forces of military professionals at the center of both battlefield and strategic success.[4]

Regrettably, for military historians the study of organizational change in China is still in its infancy due to a scholarly focus on political rather than social organizations. Only after the intense civil society/public sphere debates of the early 1990s, which were driven by a desire to understand the failure of the Tiananmen movement to produce more lasting political effects, did historians look at public organizations in detail.⁵ Recent works on business associations, police forces, city government factions, and criminal networks have created a more nuanced picture of Chinese society and government during the Republican period.⁶

This work's analysis of the Chinese officer corps from 1942 to 1955 links two main areas of change: organizational and professional. The idea of culture as an important and dynamic concept driving change in the Chinese officer corps might appear counterintuitive in a hierarchical and rule-based occupation like the military, but cultural analysis offers potential insights into civil-military relations, violence, and organizational behavior.⁷ Cultures are systems of belief that participants of a group hold in common. Cultures are valuable because they provide a purpose, morals, and values on which to base behavior.⁸ Within professional and military structures, culture is only one of several factors, including coercive, legal, and remunerative factors, but culture is often an important force in translating official policies into real-world outcomes because it bridges the divide between theory and practice.

During the 1940s and 1950s, the ROC military was often the only core functioning institution of the ROC government, retaining personnel and funding priority throughout wars and changes in policy. The military, a judicial apparatus, and a central state administration are core organizations that all effective states must possess. While none of these organizations is directly analogous to the state itself, taken collectively they are the backbone by which states extract, coerce, and coordinate.⁹ For a state to succeed in maintaining its territorial integrity, policy efficacy, and administrative autonomy in the long term, these state organizations must institutionalize their programs and procedures so that they are able to reproduce the essential skills necessary for their success. Organizations—and their more durable forms, institutions—are important because they provide services to the state above them, but they also directly influence the identity and behavior of individuals inside their domain. Institutions influence society by providing actors, either groups or individuals, with greater degrees of certainty about the present and future behavior of other actors. While the more permanent nature of institutions offers greater security and clarity, which might promote "buy-in" by actors, the desire to have clear, set procedures can make it difficult for institutions to reform themselves to changed circumstances due to social opposition and internal inertia.¹⁰

Fortunately, analysis of the ROC military in the 1940s and 1950s can draw from advances in organizational studies that have given historians new perspectives on groups and their behavior. The study of institutions has expanded in the past several decades with the rise of "new" (neo) institutionalism studies in the fields of political science and sociology. Recent scholarship has focused on the instrumentality of institutions. Drawing from more critical sociological theories, neo-institutionalist scholars argue that rather than a value-neutral project designed to "solve" problems, groups attempt to institutionalize their roles and behaviors because of the social status and legitimacy that derive from a more formalized structure.[11]

In the past two decades, political scientists, historians, and international relations scholars have been highly involved in exploring why military organizations and cultures change, and why military forces around the world have increasingly adopted very similar structures and behaviors. A common term used to describe independent development of similarity in organizations is isomorphism. When cultural factors drive change and the adoption of similar structures, it is "normative" isomorphism.[12] Changes through normative isomorphism occur when groups or individuals are motivated by a desire for social status and legitimacy. This type of isomorphism arises from the desires of groups and individuals within an organization, among which is the desire for professionalization of their organization's occupational role.[13] The case of ROC military officers in the 1940s and 1950s shares many of the hallmarks of this type of change, particularly a desire for legitimacy and respect. Normative isomorphism may include formal instruction within the organization, the power of charismatic leaders, desire for social benefits such as respect, and feelings of organizational insecurity. A common feature of normative isomorphism is change that emphasizes "high status" functions that are both better paying and more socially respected. The creation of new norms encompasses both constitutive functions, which define and give meaning to actors and provide context, as well as regulatory functions that define acceptable behavior.

Two factors are especially salient in normative isomorphism and its applicability to the Chinese military from 1942 to 1955: education centers and member networks.[14] The development of a coherent and systematic set of ideas is vital for the organization's claim to distinctiveness and importance. A formal, university-type education that attempts to link professional training to pre-existing education can solidify a core set of ideas and develop doctrine. Second, the development of networks emanating from educational nodes allows for the development of a sense of identity, uniform codes of conduct, and regular feedback between educational functions and experiences encountered through practice.

From 1942 to 1955, Chinese military officers created a sophisticated identity and culture based on a comprehensive school system and professional networks defined by journals and military publications. The late Qing Empire had created a formal military school system and despite the political transitions and funding issues during the 1910s and 1920s, military schools continued to function. Military schools expanded massively with the assistance of American military aid and advising during the 1940s and in the 1950s on Taiwan.

An extensive system of professional journals reinforced identities developed at military schools and provided a vital space for in-group communication about new techniques and military skills. Like military schools, military journals first flourished in the late Qing period, and during the 1910s and 1920s they expanded their scope of analysis and critique, gaining great influence. Chinese military journals commonly featured three types of articles, all of which helped develop crucial aspects of the military socialization process begun at military schools. First, a large portion of the military articles detailed foreign military developments in tactics and equipment. These articles helped accentuate officers' occupational claims to a status as skilled professionals with a shared worldview. Second, journal articles encouraged a socialization based on continuous improvement and education. Last, officers serving in command positions or within tactical units (i.e., not in a school assignment) wrote a high proportion of articles, providing vital feedback to schools and officers in training. In the aggregate, this network of schools and professional journals created a coherent worldview among Chinese military officers, who had clear ideas about their role in Chinese society and their own internal values. This worldview helped to provide Chinese military officers with a sense of distinctiveness in terms of their profession, technical skills, and an ethos of obligation to the nation.

A key theme of this work is the development of Chinese military officers as professionals, who valued service to the state, rather than to a political party, and actively sought specialized roles. In this work, professions are semi-exclusive groups of individuals that utilize abstract knowledge, which is necessary for the functioning of society. Military officers are sometimes not considered true professionals because they are "unfree," that is, tied directly to the state, and can only operate in a corporate structure, as opposed to functionally independent lawyers and doctors. Nevertheless, military officers share most of the hallmarks of a profession. First, they possess highly specialized skills, grounded on a foundation of abstract knowledge of tactics and strategy. Possession of this specialized knowledge provides a barrier to entry for competitors. Furthermore, the ontological structures of this professional knowledge are determined from within the profession. Military officers decide what differentiates an infantry officer from an artillery officer, in the same way doctors classify and police the boundaries between an anesthesiologist and a pediatrician. Second, most officers are subject to juridical control through military codes and law that are not enforced by civil administration. Officers are responsible to military courts. Third, military professions receive social approval of their exclusive status and special privileges in return for the provision of intangible goods of social utility. The operation of social norms also polices the professional behavior of military officers, with officers operating in an arbitrary, independent or capricious manner dubbed mercenaries, soldiers of fortune or, in the case of China, warlords.

Academic interest in the role of professionals in China has focused almost exclusively on "free professionals," (ziyou zhuanyezhe) such as doctors and lawyers, who operate independent of any larger organization and interact with the public on a personal basis. The study of professions as a socially recognized and internally structured institution is very limited and only one work, Xu Xiaoqun's *Chinese Professionals and the Republican State: The Rise of Professional Associations in Shanghai, 1912–1937*, takes a detailed look at international dynamics and the social role of professions.[15] Xu details the role of the three "classic" professions—medicine, journalism, and the law—as they struggled to suppress local competitors, such as traditional Chinese medicine, and achieve a privileged position within society.

Unlike the case of "free professionals," a crucial aspect of the professionalization process for Chinese military officers was the desire to adopt bureaucratic structures. Military forces are often bureaucracies because of the advantages a bureaucratic system offers in coordinating large numbers of personnel. Bureaucracies are distinguished from other types of organizations by the high degree of formalization in regulating the activities of its members.[16] During the 1940s and 1950s, Chinese military officers increasingly exhibited a universalist mentality that sought to homogenize the officer corps, and were hostile to special treatment of officers with political or family connections. In addition, the ROC officer corps sought to create a system based on defined metrics of education and training rather than on subjective evaluations of performance.

Studies by A. J. Dray-Novey and Julia Strauss have looked at bureaucratic issues of the Republican era and found that developing accountable and systemic bureaucracies was difficult, but not impossible. Strauss examined the unique role of the Salt Inspectorate in providing revenues to the Republican administration, and determined that organizational success developed from the ability of supporting state organizations to achieve political insularity from the national government, and from the ability to create an impression of competence.[17] Both of these two criteria are congruent with the scope of the professionalization project of KMT military officers.

A key element of professionalization is the attempt by an occupation to define a more rigid and clear jurisdiction of their responsibility and authority. Andrew Abbott developed the notion of jurisdiction in his seminal work, *The System of Professions: An Essay on the Division of Expert Labor*.[18] Abbott articulates that ongoing occupational competition shapes the functions, structure, and responsibilities of professions, and that success is achieving jurisdiction over their desired functional areas. Jurisdiction rests on recognition by society of a monopoly over the cognitive structures of knowledge, rights of self-discipline, and control over professional training, recruitment, and certification. Abbott states, "This control means first and foremost a right to perform the work as professionals see fit. Along with the right to perform the work as it wishes, a profession normally also claims rights to exclude other workers as deemed necessary, to dominate public definitions of the tasks concerned, and indeed to impose professional definitions of the tasks on competing professions."[19]

In this conception, the role of a profession is a contested space defined by competition in multiple arenas. A key area of competition is deciding which group controls the ability to recruit, train, certify, and discipline its professional members.[20] Often public opinion decides on successful claims to jurisdiction, which can result in social and cultural authority for professionals. Professional groups can seek to influence public opinion by presenting idealized portrayals of their claimed duties; stories, songs, television, and movies can all accomplish this objective. The promulgation of simple, persuasive norms, such as the Hippocratic Oath for doctors, or claims by military officers to represent "the nation," can be disseminated within society to cultivate public support.

The United States and Military Advising

The United States emerged as the key foreign partner of the ROC military after 1942. Beginning with small transfers of weapons to fight a mutual enemy, Japan, the relationship quickly grew into a massive program that included American military advisers working with ROC units, the retraining of Chinese personnel by American NCOs, the assignment of ROC officers to U.S. military schools, and the translation of American military textbooks into Chinese. Although the United States had supported the training of small forces in the Philippines, the military relationship that developed between the United States and the ROC was unprecedented for American military officers.

By 1944, when supplies and personnel became available in large numbers, the American support and advisory mission had shifted from improving combat abilities to institutional development and "army-building." This program sought to dramatically restructure the ROC army along the lines of the U.S. Army, with increased reliance on tactics and firepower. Although reoccurring problems with cultural misunderstandings and language difficulties created tensions, the overall relationship was never seriously questioned by either side.

Increasing access to archival material and a resurgence of nationalism in China has resulted in a deluge of new works on the 1937–45 war, but few deal with the administrative, policy, and organizational challenges of military partnerships. Much of the recent scholarship on the war has emphasized civilian suffering, Chinese victimization, and Japanese brutality—topics that are politically useful for the CCP but that understate Chinese military agency and push the history of KMT military activity into the background.[21] Sadly, the dominant work on the military cooperation during the period is the badly dated *Stilwell and the American Experience in China, 1911–1945*, by Barbara Tuchman, which was written at the height of the Vietnam War.[22] Professional historians have attacked the book for moralistic assertions and shoddy research.[23]

The Sino-American partnership stalled in the postwar environment of the late 1940s due to diplomatic and policy concerns, but after the outbreak of the Korean War in June 1950 it was easily and efficiently renewed. For the remainder of the Cold War, Taiwan would be a bastion of U.S. defense policy in East Asia and a model for security assistance, and while the Cold War political relationship has been intensively studied, the military-to-military connections are unexamined.

Understanding the development of American military assistance and advising is vital not only for placing the China theater of World War II in strategic context, but also for understanding American policy during the Cold War. The Truman and Eisenhower administrations would use Military Assistance and Advisory Groups (MAAGs) in South Korea, Japan, South Vietnam, and throughout Europe and the Middle East to bolster allies threatened by Communism. Study of the Sino-American military partnership highlights the enduring challenges but also the long-term successes of military advising.

Party-Army (dangjun)

One of the most complex and important aspects of civil-military relations in 1940s and 1950s China and Taiwan was the interaction between ROC military officers and the KMT party. The ebb and flow of power, between technically oriented military officers and political officers oriented toward KMT party guidance, defines the period from 1942 to 1955.

For many general readers, and even some scholars of military affairs, the concept of single-party control of armed forces in the twentieth century appears anachronistic. Both the KMT and the CCP have been very successful in framing analysis in two ways. First, they have created a notion that a party-army was somehow inevitable after 1924. Historical studies of the ROC military commissioned in Taiwan during the 1960s and 1970s, a period of martial law and rigid KMT dominance, presented party control as natural and inevitable, leading readers into a convenient fable where party control of the military had no alternatives.[24] While the ROC Army in the 1940s and later decades clearly drew some of its organizational structure from the military created by the KMT at the Whampoa Academy in 1924–1926, the majority of officers in the ROC Army during the war against Japan, the Civil War, and in the 1950s on Taiwan had not attended military schools controlled by the KMT. The ROC military drew from many sources, and attempting to trace a clear line from Sun Yat-sen and Whampoa in 1924 to the ROC Army in Taiwan is intellectually difficult. Second, the KMT and particularly the CCP have been very successful at hiding their power and authority behind mundane bureaucratic titles, while military officers with high rank have little actual authority as leaders of a "national" army. For example, the CCP maintains a Ministry of Defense for the People's Republic of China, which conducts meetings with foreign visitors and has a prominent position on government organizational charts. In practice, the CCP Central Military Commission headed by the Communist party general secretary wields the real power, such as personnel decisions and policy guidance.

English-language analysis of the history of the party-army is limited. In the 1950s, historian F. F. Liu traced the origin of the KMT "party-army" concept to the aftermath of the 6 June 1922 mutiny by forces nominally loyal to the KMT, after which Sun Yat-sen sought to create a politicized army. Liu highlighted the formative role of the KMT-founded Whampoa Academy, which started its first class in May 1924, and its hybrid six-month program of instruction in military training and political ideology. Richard Landis, among others, highlighted the patterns of political loyalty and education inculcated when Whampoa was in operation, and Martin Wilber and Julie How supplied detailed analysis of the prominent role of Soviet advisors.[25]

The vital role of "political officers," used by the KMT and CCP to exert control of military forces and integrate military operations into party policies, has been almost ignored in the historiographical record. A notable exception is Hsiao-shih Cheng's excellent, *Party-Military Relations in the PRC and Taiwan: Paradoxes of Control*.[26] A deeper understanding of the role of Leninist political parties in shaping military structures is vitally important for understanding the 1942–1955 period, as well as Taiwanese and Chinese history. Analysis of the party-army as a working concept also highlights the tremendous difficulty of maintaining single-party dominance because it directly contradicts the aspirations of military officers to serve the nation.

Sun Li-jen

In an effort to make organizational and intellectual changes more personal and relatable to the reader, the life of Sun Li-jen will be examined as an illustration of major developments within the officer corps. Sun Li-jen played an influential and direct role as an important commander of Chinese forces during World War II, and after 1949 he emerged as the most important military figure on Taiwan. Sun's identity blends the themes of this work because as a devout nationalist and aloof supporter of the KMT, he was more indicative of rank-and-file officers than many other party-appointed senior commanders. Sun was also an exceptional example of the possibilities of military partnerships during the early twentieth century, with his education at the Virginia Military Institute (VMI), training in India, and extensive World War II combat experience fighting alongside American commanders like Gen. Joseph Stilwell.

Little known outside of Taiwan and China, Sun Li-jen, who was critical in rebuilding the ROC army from a defeated and disorganized gaggle into a competent and disciplined force, is not widely appreciated. This oversight is not accidental, and research into Sun's career was limited while he was under house arrest in Taiwan from 1955 through 1988. Taiwan's President Ma Ying-jeou's formal apology to Sun's family and the opening of his house as a memorial and museum is a hopeful and long overdue indication of increasing respect for Sun's life and his significance during a critical period of military conflict and change.

Outline

This work presents a chronological narrative that covers a large part of the twentieth century, and emphasizes the period from 1942 to 1955 as vital for defining the ROC military identity and evaluating the impact of new ideas and practices on the military as an institution. Chapter 1 begins in the last years of the Qing dynasty, when the precursors of an institutionalized military that was based on a technically proficient, bureaucratically organized officer corps began to take shape. Chapter 2 examines the creation of a party-army system by the KMT from 1924 through 1942. Chapters 3 and 4 examine the crucial developments in the 1940s, when a group of young, well-educated officers began to reshape the KMT military from within, using American military aid and advisory programs to catalyze the development of a politically independent officer corps defined by functionally specific military roles. Chapter 5 covers the period from 1950 to 1953, after the retreat of KMT forces to Taiwan, when the professionalization process continued to increase the civil-military bifurcation of roles and responsibilities and the professionalizing endeavor of ROC military officers achieved its highest point. Chapter 6 covers the years from 1953 to 1955, when a political backlash from the KMT and Chiang Ching-kuo led to a politically motivated purge of ROC officers and the reintroduction of "political officers" in the ROC military. The last chapter provides an epilogue discussing the military situation in Taiwan after 1955; it is followed by a brief conclusion.

1

The Development of the Chinese Army, 1850–1927

Military power has always been a decisive factor in Chinese political and cultural hegemony in East Asia. Successive Chinese dynasties employed varying political policies to ensure a large army remained effective in maintaining internal security and conducted offensive operations against regional powers such as Vietnam, Mongols, or Central Asian Zunghars. Universal male conscription under the Qing dynasty, quasi-feudalism during the Tang, and mercenary forces used by the Ming were effective strategies against the threats of their eras, but the Qing dynasty (1644–1912) was the most successful in expanding their territory and maintaining internal control.

After conquering the Ming dynasty and gaining power in 1644, the Qing had almost two centuries of consistent battlefield success. Only in the mid-nineteenth century was the Qing military forced to change its organizational structures, recruitment patterns, and military training programs. Military reforms that began in the 1850s, and strongly accelerated after 1895, acted as the precursors to the creation of a distinct and professional officer corps in the 1942–1955 period. This nascent development of military professionalization from 1850 to 1911 was stalled with the fall of the Qing dynasty but was unchallenged intellectually until the advent of the party-army concept developed by Sun Yat-sen in the early 1920s.

Qing Dynasty Traditions

The tremendously successful campaigns of Qing forces in Central Asia, South China, and Tibet expanded the territory controlled by a "Chinese" dynasty to its greatest extent, but by the mid-nineteenth century, the Qing military faced a wide variety of organizational challenges. The Qing military was an ethnically divided structure with a further subdivision into "military" units, which functioned as constabulary forces responsible for suppressing riots and small uprisings, and a more traditional military force. The hybrid police/military and Han Chinese/Manchu/Mongol force was organizationally complicated but successfully maintained large military forces at relatively low cost throughout the dynasty. The hybrid structure also prevented internal Manchu opposition to the Imperial family or large-scale revolts by military trained ethnic Han officers.

The core of Qing strength was the "Bannermen" (baqi), descendants of the original twenty-four units (banners) formed in the early seventeenth century by Manchu leader Nurhaci. They were instrumental in conquering China and establishing the Manchu-ruled Qing dynasty in 1644. The twenty-four banner units were ethnically subdivided into eight Manchu, eight Mongol, and eight Han Chinese units, and all Manchu were officially enrolled in one of the eight Manchu banners, with recruitment being hereditary.[1]

Until the destruction of Central Asian Zunghar forces in Xinjiang during the 1750s, a large portion of the Qing banner forces, particularly the elite Manchu cavalry units, had been engaged in ongoing military operations or garrisoned in spartan frontier outposts.[2] The century-long peace that followed saw increasing numbers of Manchu Bannermen moving to the capital region and a steady loss of martial traditions. By the mid-nineteenth century the banner organization, and the Manchu forces that were its core strength, had degenerated so much that a British observer reported, "The majority of the so-called troops of the 24 banners are utterly without organization, as their division into banners is of no value from a military point of view."[3] A visiting American general concurred: "The bannermen are seldom required to drill, and, when they are called out, muster with rusty swords, bows, spears, and weapons of various descriptions. Receiving but a small pay, they are permitted to engage in various kinds of business and traffic. . . . As soldiers they have long since ceased to be useful, and until reorganized and disciplined, they must remain but profitless pensioners of the Government."[4] Military training, when conducted, consisted of parade ground drills involving gongs, firing flintlock muskets into the air, and large numbers of flags to simulate enemy positions, which created a fanciful scene that one foreign observer described as military "burlesque."[5]

Vastly more numerous than the Bannermen was the "Green Standard Army" (luying), made up of ethnic Han Chinese. The Green Standard Army was the organizational remnant of ethnic Han Chinese forces that had switched sides in 1644 to support the Manchu, but by the nineteenth century their effectiveness was limited. The Green Standard Army, numbering hundreds of thousands of men, occupied hundreds of small garrisons as a constabulary force rather than a strictly military organization.⁶

The Green Standard command structure meshed military officers with local officials. While this system hindered decisiveness, it was a further check on independent military action.⁷ By the mid-nineteenth century the Green Standard forces had become militarily obsolete, with many troops only notionally carried on personnel books and performing no real functions. Rather than military drill or police (gendarme) functions, many Green Standard posts became comfortable sinecures for local notables. A contemporary observer noted, "These troops [Green Standard] ordinarily render merely nominal service, having purchased from their officers, in consideration of their pay, the privilege of engaging in all kinds of commerce."⁸

Training and promotion of officers was not standardized or bureaucratic, with successive emperors placing emphasis on Manchu retaining their "martial virtues" by promoting hunting expeditions, encouraging the glorification of military heroes and maintaining, a distinct Manchu culture linked to physical prowess.⁹ Promotion within both the Banner forces and Green Standard was politically determined, with a bare minimum of military qualifications. Candidates for officer positions were required to pass an archery test, demonstrate proficiency with a sword, and be able to lift heavy stones.¹⁰ By the 1850s most Manchu families had not taken part in a major military campaign in over one hundred years, and hereditary residence in garrisons adjacent to major urban centers allowed substantial cultural crossover between Chinese society and Manchu lifestyles.¹¹

Imperatives for Change

The defeat of Qing military forces by western powers in 1842 and 1860 was embarrassing to the dynasty but did not threaten the underlying economic or political foundations of Manchu rule. The Taiping Rebellion, which began in 1850, was a much larger, more systemic threat to the Manchu dynasty, not only by seizing the economic core of the empire, the Yangtze (Yangzi) River valley, but also by directly challenging the ideological system that legitimized Manchu rule.¹² The ability of the Taiping to mount sustained operations by hundreds of thousands of troops was beyond the capacity of the degenerated Banner or Green Standard forces to control.

Ethnic Han elites responded to the need for protection against the Taiping by creating localized, functionally independent military forces. Drawing on local and regional networks of the Chinese "gentry," officials in the Yangtze region recruited officers from among holders of civil degrees.¹³ The two largest local raised forces, Zeng Guofan's Xiang Army (Xiangjun) and Li Hongzhang's Huai Army (Huaijun) both numbered over 100,000 men and commanded the authority and taxes of province-sized military regions. These military forces would begin the movement toward increasing technical specialization and increased autonomy over training and promotion from the government.[14] Training for these regional military forces depended on the skill and initiative of the officers, many of whom had little military experience. Tactics culled from classical Chinese literature, combined with simple but effective military drills, were sufficient to fight the equally untrained Taiping rebels, and by the conclusion of the rebellion in 1864 these locally raised forces had become the most experienced in China.[15]

A small but innovative component of the Huai Army of Li Hongzhang was a mixed foreign/Han Chinese brigade of five thousand men formed in the summer of 1861. This new force included both local Han Chinese recruits and the remnants of the defunct Foreign Army Corps raised by nervous foreign residents of Shanghai as the Taiping approached. A Chinese commander, Wu Xu, shared leadership with Frederick Townsend Ward, an American adventurer, and this small force, dubbed the "Ever Victorious Army" (changsheng jun) after battlefield successes, sought to utilize imported organizational structures, create a small staff system and introduce foreign weapons.[16] Foreign officers and noncommissioned officers (NCOs) conducted training, with British logistical and personnel support being crucial. Although some local commanders such as Zeng Guofan rejected the importation of foreign military equipment, Li both encouraged arms imports and took steps to establish arsenals to support his forces.[17] Although small, Li's foreign-trained and equipped brigade represented a fundamentally different approach to military organization and development than either the traditional Qing system or the ad hoc local forces developed in the 1850s.

During the late nineteenth century, the most effective portion of the Qing military forces, Li Hongzhang's Huai Army, was redeployed to the Beijing capital area, and was subsequently labeled the "Beiyang Army" (Beiyang jun). To keep his forces up to date Li created new patterns of military education and weapons development. He established a military academy in Tianjin, which was designed to teach practical subjects like mathematics, military drill, military engineering, surveying, and so forth, and which represented a sharp break with the Manchu traditions of physical ability or Chinese literary examinations.[18] In conjunction with increasing the technical skills of the army, Li supported the importation of large amounts of weapons, primarily Krupp artillery. By 1884, Li's forces possessed over seventy Krupp 8-cm field guns and a battery of quick firing four-pounders.[19]

Nonetheless, the diversity of foreign weapons used by Li's forces included German Mausers, American Winchesters, Russian muskets, and British Martini-Henry rifles, making training and logistics difficult.[20]

Evaluations by foreign observers described Li's forces in positive terms: "Li hung-chang's army is probably the best [in China]. It is armed principally with the Mauser rifle. They are a fine body of men, and are drilled on the German system; but they are badly officered, and as shown by their conduct in Corea in 1882 when they committed grave offenses, they are not sufficiently under control."[21]

In spite of the promising but uncoordinated reforms initiated by Li in North China, the battlefield performance of the Beiyang Army in the 1894–95 Sino-Japanese War was poor. Japanese conscript forces were able to outmaneuver more numerous Chinese forces and capture heavily fortified positions at Pyongyang and Lushunkou (Port Arthur), with minimal losses. Although research into Chinese strategy and tactics in the 1894–95 Sino-Japanese War remains woefully understudied, preliminary research has suggested that poor officer leadership and extremely loose battlefield discipline among Chinese forces was a major factor in their defeat.[22] The defeat of Chinese army and naval forces by Japan in 1895, which was unexpected by foreign observers, created a strengthened desire for military change among senior Manchu leaders. On 8 December 1895, the War Council recommended the creation of a new military force in North China that would incorporate foreign military innovations in organization, weapons, and tactics. The edict read, "China, in experimenting with the training of foreign-style troops, has in general used Western methods only in part. Those who will be trained this time will solely imitate the German regulations."[23] Yuan Shikai, who had served in Korea prior to 1894, and whom many blamed for instigating the political disputes with the Japanese that led to war, was selected as the commander of this force, which was dubbed the "Newly Created Army" (xin jun). Yuan was a strong supporter of wholesale military change. After the Chinese defeat in 1895 he remarked, "The basic reason for our military setbacks, though due to poor direction, could also be traced to our defective organization. If we do not make a drastic reorganization adopting western methods and introducing a system of thorough military training, then I would really shudder to face any further repetition of our early reverses."[24] In spite of the small size of the new force, roughly seven thousand men, Yuan was able to use his political connections to ensure funding for a full range of supporting organizations, such as a German language school to translate books and a full staff component, which featured a foreign military intelligence section.[25]

This small force represented China's most professional and coherent military organization in the nineteenth century. Adequate and consistent pay, standardized weapons and integrated training exercises made it a model force in the eyes of foreign observers.[26] In spite of the potential utility of Yuan's forces in a conflict with a foreign power, the majority of Chinese forces remained in traditional organizational patterns and continued to focus on internal security rather than external threats. Another barrier to systemic change was a continuing xenophobic attitude to adopting foreign practices by military officers and men. A British observer noted that "to be smart [in Western-type military drills] is to be like a hated foreigner and to lose caste [face].[27]

The death of Li Hongzhang in 1901 allowed for the promotion of Yuan Shikai into the position of viceroy of Zhili. Yuan's forces incorporated Li's troops and adopted their name, the Beiyang Army. In theory, the Beiyang Army would be the core of a new "national" army of China, which would include thirty-six divisions, but financial problems hindered the plan.[28] Financial problems also stalled Yuan's effort to develop an arsenal controlled directly by the military, which would have given military officers greater control over weapons acquisition.[29]

Reforming military education was a major component of Yuan's program. Removing the obsolete physical tests for officer recruits in 1901 and the abolition of civil examinations in 1905 broadened the pool of potential officer recruits and more closely aligned military requirements with technical skills taught at civilian schools.[30] To train officers in specialized military skills, Yuan established a military academy in the strategically located city of Baoding, one hundred miles outside of Beijing. The Baoding Military Academy (Baoding junxiao) was the largest military training facility in China from its founding in 1902 until 1927, and the majority of the officers of warlord armies during the 1910s and 1920s, as well as substantial elements of the Nationalist army officer corps, were trained in its German/Japanese style education system.[31] In 1908, total enrollment in Chinese military academies was roughly 4,500 cadets, with 1,000 to 1,500 commissioned every year, and Baoding represented the majority of these officers.[32] The military reputation developed by Baoding officers would carry over after graduation, and during the 1930s and 1940s Baoding graduates would compose the majority of the Chinese generals, but they rarely made it to senior general rank due to a lack of political connections.[33]

The original design of the Qing military education reforms had called for the establishment of military primary schools in every province to train youths aged fifteen through eighteen. By October 1905, all but two provinces, Gansu and Henan, had fulfilled the government requirement, but with no standardized curriculum or established training procedures, the quality of the military education varied tremendously.[34] After graduation, promising cadets would attend one of four regional military academies for a two-year course, followed by a six-month assignment to an army division. Cadets who proved capable would then spend a final two years at the Baoding military academy before receiving officer commissions.[35]

Although this was a coherent plan, in reality the desire to create a large force quickly was subject to financial limitations and provincialism, which hindered the development of an integrated military education system. The pressing need for junior officers led to the creation of abridged courses at Baoding ranging from one and a half to two and a half years depending on the cadets' military experience.[36] Many NCOs, such as future warlord Wu Peifu, became officers after these abbreviated courses, which successfully filled personnel requirements at the expense of standardized training, and slowed the development of a solid NCO corps in army.

Expanding the military education system also encompassed a greatly enlarged program of sending Chinese cadets overseas. Li Hongzhang had begun a small program of sending Chinese officers to Germany for military training in the 1870s, but language barriers, the high cost of foreign training, and a lack of Chinese volunteers limited the program to only seven cadets.[37] After 1900, hundreds of Chinese cadets began to study abroad, with most attending Japanese institutions because they were cheaper, closer to China, and had a good military reputation after Japan's victory over Russia in 1905. In 1906, 691 Chinese military officers and cadets were attending Japanese schools, compared to only fifteen in Europe and three in the United States.[38] Although foreign-trained officers were statistically insignificant in terms of China's total military forces (less than 2 percent of officer strength), in elite units, and especially the Beiyang Army, they represented a significant share of the total officer strength.

In conjunction with a new openness toward foreign training and instruction, the last decade of the Qing Dynasty saw a pronounced cultural shift in favor of martial values that was encouraged both by the Qing state and anti-Manchu Han nationalists. School textbooks and imperial decrees both attempted to raise the status of the military profession. One textbook, the 1904 *New National Reader*, stated bluntly, "[S]oldiers are the foundation of a strong country," and repeatedly linked national greatness to military valor.[39] Reformist intellectuals such as Liang Qichao and Kang Youwei argued for a reinvigoration of China's martial culture as a politically necessity to combat foreign powers, but also as a way to cultivate social discipline.[40] Cai E, an anti-Qing military leader and later warlord, argued that military organizations inculcated precisely the kind of values, behavior, and spirit required to solve China's problems, stating that "to train a good soldier is actually to train a good citizen."[41] Decrees also referred to cultivation of "the military spirit" as an aim of a balanced and "realistic" education. This cultural shift raised the status of military forces, especially officers, which made recruitment of talented men easier. But the desire of many Chinese to turn the army into a laboratory for creating citizens or reforming Chinese character clashed with needs for military specialization and combat training.

Foreign observers were quick to note this cultural transition. Robert Hart, head of the powerful Maritime Customs Bureau, remarked on the new regulations and martial spirit: "[H]enceforth the soldier will be respected, and with her immense population and resources, the Chinese army of the future will count for something in the world's doing."[42] British journalist G. E. Morrison shared this sentiment, writing, "The Chinese soldier of today is a wholly different man from his fellow of even ten years ago. A remarkable reversal of sentiment has come over the nation about the Army. Formerly the soldier was despised. Only the lowest class would enlist, and the officers secured their appointments in the hope of profit from 'squeeze.' This is being changed. The status of the soldier has been transformed."[43]

Professional Military Thought in the Late Qing Dynasty

In conjunction with the establishment of the Beiyang Army, a War College for senior Chinese officers was established in Beijing. In 1911, the college launched a new military professional journal, *Junhua*, which published several volumes in 1911. The first issue included its mission statement: "[T]his journal is for the study of military issues and to encourage the study of military thought."[44] The publication of *Junhua* represented a key event in the development of the Chinese military as a profession, because it served as a mechanism to develop group identity and norms among its officer readers.[45]

After the New Army reforms began during the late Qing dynasty, a series of military journals were created by officers. Returning students from Japanese military schools used journals to retain a shared sense of identity after their return to China, but also to advocate for military changes and political reforms. Between 1895 and 1911 numerous military-related articles were included in popular publications such as the Shanghai newspaper *Da Tong Bao*, the *Dongfang Zazhi*

(*Oriental Times*), and the *Dongya Bao* (*East Asia Times*).[46] Jiang Baili, future head of the Baoding Academy and a renowned military intellectual, started his writing career as a frequent contributor to the journal *Zhejiang chao* (*Zhejiang Tides*) after he returned from Japan's Imperial Army Academy. He used his articles to advocate for the overthrow of the Qing dynasty in addition to substantive military reforms.[47] Commercial publishing houses in Shanghai also offered detailed military journals, often featuring translations of Japanese and European military articles and textbooks.[48]

Military journals were established at many of the provincial military schools, but the premier journals were published in Beijing where the War College (lujun daxue), the highest level of Chinese military education, was located. Originally founded in 1906 by the Qing dynasty, the War College was the capstone of a three-level military education system. The three-level structure included military schools at the primary level located in all provinces for students aged fifteen to eighteen, four secondary-level military schools at Nanjing, Xi'an, Wuchang, and Beijing for students aged eighteen to twenty-one, and the War College in Beijing as the "university"-level military school.

The impetus for creating the War College was Chinese analysis of the changing nature of warfare after witnessing the conflict between Japan and Russia in Manchuria from 1904 to 1905.[49] The massive number of troops involved, more than half a million Russians and 300,000 Japanese, in addition to the tremendous logistical difficulties involving railway transport and commercial shipping, highlighted the increasing need for sophisticated staff work by modern armies.[50] Unlike the provincial and regional military schools, the War College included the study of foreign military operations and tactics, the review of foreign wars, and the examination of new technologies. The War College had extensive foreign-language training facilities and employed foreign instructors, normally Japanese or German officers.[51]

The War College produced the military journal *Junhua* with articles on new equipment, tactics, and the introduction of new techniques such as statistical analysis in military affairs.[52] *Junhua* had many competitors, with the Beiying Army producing its own military journal, *Beiyang bingshi zazhi* (*Beiyang Military Journal*) in 1910, which covered more practical and day-to-day military issues.[53] Other military schools, such as the Nanyang Military Academy, founded in 1907, also began producing professional journals for military officers.[54] In the case of *Junhua*, the approach to the study of military science was from an impersonal and highly technical perspective. Throughout the journal, there are few references to the Qing political leaders, civilian politics, or social forces. Instead, the topics are highly focused on military operations, military history, tactics, and organizational development. One of the most common features of *Junhua* was the listing of new regulations, laws, and announcements of promotions, demotions, and assignments for officers. Although mundane, these listings served to accelerate the integration of widely dispersed Chinese forces around common bureaucratic policies, as well as making the enactment of military policies more transparent. Another common feature of *Junhua* was detailed analyses of key concepts, such as defensive tactics, normally paired with examples depicting a Chinese location to illustrate tactical principles in a real-world setting. Last, every edition of the *Junhua* journal featured news on troop strengths, technological developments, and military actions from around the world.

The introduction of every edition of the *Junhua* journal featured a list of seven topics that it defined as "key problems," on which it invited articles and discussion. The first and most important topic was Chinese military planning and peacetime preparation for mobilization and war. Less important but vital problems included the analysis of current social trends and their effect on military affairs, together with topic number three, civilian education and its relationship or comparison with military education. These topics suggest an awareness of the social context of military reforms. Military education practices, methods, and principles were the fourth key problem and were a frequent topic of discussion. The fifth key problem, identifying reasons for the slow rate of military progress in China, reflects the high degree of self-criticism expressed in military journals. Officer training and officer assignments in relation to military development was identified as the sixth issue but was rarely discussed in the short timeframe of the journal. Last, the use of aircraft in modern warfare, a seemingly incongruous and advanced topic in 1913, was issue number seven.[55]

Much of the content of *Junhua* consisted of information about the Chinese military itself, in order to encourage an understanding of national policies, doctrine, and organizational structures. In modern military affairs, the development of "standards and practices" is a major element of officer training, and necessary for the functioning of a complex, bureaucratically organized structure. These announcements highlight the transition of the Chinese military from a network of individual military units with localized, ad hoc methods into a centrally administered, institutionalized force. For example, in a presentation of the military schools system in *Junhua*, the article presents how the school system is structured, what is studied, and how the system will shape the careers of students around areas of functional expertise, such as engineering, infantry or artillery.[56] For even easier comprehension, a graphic depiction of the military school system was included for officer to study.[57]

Chinese officers writing in *Junhua* used a highly technical perspective to study the military as a science rather than a traditional military emphasis on the military as an art. For example, in the second volume of *Junhua*, professor He Deng from Baoding military academy analyzed the financial system of the Chinese army, and argued that substantial difficulty in coordinating the military forces in north and south China resulted from a lack of rolling stock for railroads and poor financial support for operational training.[58] Another article from the same issue, titled "The Relationship between the Military and Statistics," detailed the number of military personnel of every major power together with the financial cost necessary to support military operations under conditions of wartime mobilization.[59]

During *Junhua*'s brief lifespan, the subject of military aviation was consistently included among the list of topics covered and was part of the "key questions" included in the introduction to every addition. The first issue included a prominent article, "The Future of Military Aviation," which noted that "[t]he Twentieth Century's most thoughtful observers of military technology are focused on the use of aircraft by the military."[60] The article systematically explored the possibilities of aircraft for both air and naval operations and compared them to dirigible airships in both their cost and effectiveness. The emphasis on what was high technology in 1911 appears incongruous with the reality of China at the time, but continuing emphasis on "advanced" or "future" weapons highlights the degree to which Chinese officers were in the process of linking themselves to global norms and practices.

Strategically, *Junhua* focused on China's military posture along its borders with Russia and Japan, with several articles analyzing the military lessons of the 1904–1905 Russo-Japanese War. It is indicative of the high level of international contact that *Junhua* published translated articles from Russian military journals to gain a more international perspective.[61] Chinese attention to Japanese developments was nuanced, with regular features on Japanese military training and equipment. In the third volume of *Junhua*, an organizational chart of the Japanese military shows a level of detail that obviously required Japanese language skills and an extensive experience with the Japanese military.[62]

The development of the military journal *Junhua* represented the final evolution of the Qing military structure away from an ethnic or personality-based organization guided by *military art*, and towards a more impersonal, rationalized bureaucratic structure designed to utilize *military science*. The sophisticated organizational structure developed in the last years of the Qing dynasty served as a point of reference for Chinese officers trained between 1905 and 1911, and represented a breakthrough for the development of military modernity in China.

The last decade of the Qing dynasty saw the increasing divergence of senior Manchu leaders from the new military forces, which were almost exclusively Han Chinese. The cultural disconnect between the emperor and these new officers, trained at specialized military schools at home and abroad, became increasingly salient during the last few years of the Qing dynasty. Historical scholarship has pointed to heightened concern among senior officials about the ability of the Qing central government to control the new military forces, and they sought to recentralize military command under Manchu general officers.[63] The transfer of Yuan Shikai and Zhang Zhidong, a senior Han official responsible for New Army forces in central China, to positions on the Grand Council was technically a promotion but in reality removed them from positions of power.[64]

The increasing unpopularity of Manchu rule after 1905 led to numerous rebellions, revolts, and political opposition movements rooted in China's growing population of cosmopolitan urban elites but crucially instigated by newly trained officers. The Wuchang Uprising (Wuchang qiyi) in October 1911 by ethnic Han officers of a New Army unit began a series of military and political maneuvers that would eventually lead to the end of the Qing dynasty on 12 February 1912.[65]

Following the end of the Qing dynasty and the short-lived national government of Yuan Shikai as president of the Republic of China, Chinese military forces lacked a central command authority. The 1911–27 period, the "warlord era," was characterized by military governments in a politically divided China. The expansion of military organizations into direct administration of governments, and the role of military officers in positions of political leadership, was a result of both opportunism and extremely weak and divided civilian political systems.

The shady past of many prominent warlords (e.g., Zhang Zuolin was a former bandit), makes it easy to stereotype the Chinese military in this period as degenerating into mindless thuggery. Academic scholarship similarly portrays Chinese military forces of the period as venal, coercive, and often in the employ of foreigners, an interpretation that is politically useful for both the KMT and CCP.[66]

In spite of political uncertainty, major aspects of the Qing military program continued to function after the downfall of the dynasty. Some military academies, particularly the Baoding Military Academy, remained open and even expanded their training programs after 1911.[67] Between 1912 and 1923 the Baoding Military

Academy graduated almost nine thousand officers, who formed the backbone of the warlord armies and later the KMT army.[68] Two of the four mid-level military schools, in Xian and Nanjing, closed, but the two in Qinghe and Wuchang continued to train cadets and send graduates to Baoding Military Academy for final training throughout the early warlord period.

The Yunnan Military Academy (Yunnan lujun jiangwu tang), which had been founded in 1909 during the late Qing reforms, also continued to train hundreds of officers. The Yunnan provincial government, which had many military officers in senior positions, supported the school through regular appropriations and a highly competent officer education program that continued through the 1910s and 1920s. Like other military schools, the Yunnan military academy produced a professional journal, *Yunnan junshi zazhi* (*Yunnan Military Science Journal*), which continued to study and analyze strategy and international relations and served as a forum for military officers to exchange professional views.[69]

During the 1910s and 1920s, young Chinese continued to pursue military education abroad. Increasingly, Chinese students began to study in Europe and the United States. By 1925, several dozen Chinese cadets had trained at West Point, the Virginia Military Institute, and Norwich University in the United States.[70] Following their studies, these cadets generally returned to their home region but could join any of the warlord factions. These students brought their training in military affairs back to China, and in addition to diverse military journals, the 1920s saw an increase in the translation of foreign military books. In bookstores in Beijing and Shanghai, military intellectuals could choose from translations of French Socialist Jean Jaures's *Democracy and Military Service*, which opposed national conscription, or the hawkish Friedrich von Bernardi's *On War of Today*, which argued that war is a biological necessity.[71]

International cooperation with Chinese military forces in equipment and training continued during the warlord era but with a change in the foreign partners. The Sino-German relationship, which dated back to the 1860s, diminished in importance after the 1911 Revolution and was completely severed with the start of World War I.[72] The pressing security needs of France and Britain in Europe during the war opened the path for increasing Japanese involvement in China, particularly by supplying the northeastern warlord Zhang Zuolin with equipment and military instructors.[73] International diplomatic agreements precluding arms sales to China were signed in 1919 by all major powers except the Soviet Union, but Soviet security interests in Central Asia made it a strong supporter of Feng Yuxiang's Kuominchun (guominjun) army.[74]

In total, the period from 1850 to 1924 was one of constant military change, with Chinese military officers increasingly taking the lead in creating a "modern," bureaucratized military officer profession. Although political difficulties often overshadowed their efforts, military officers had developed a school system, professional journals, and a distinct identity that aligned with international norms. The period from 1850 to 1924 highlights the increasing convergence of the Chinese military system with global norms, especially in terms of its officer corps.

The KMT and Military Power

Contemporary observers harshly criticized the decentralized political situation after the 1911 Revolution, and the rise of military leaders as the real holders of power in China, as a perversion of the ideals of patriotism and national unity. Warlord rule was particularly galling to anti-Manchu forces, who had helped spark the 1911 Revolution but were subsequently blocked from exercising political power. The "solution" to the problems of warlord rule was the creation of military forces loyal to political parties. Although party-armies were reasonably successful in achieving power, the nascent professional military identity begun under the Qing continued within the new party-army structures.

The creator of the enduring party-army model of Chinese military identity was the Kuomintang. First formed after the 1911 Revolution by several of the small anti-monarchy parties, it quickly became the leading national-level political party under the overall leadership of Sun Yat-sen. During the January 1913 National Assembly election, the KMT was able to win a plurality of seats in both the lower house and the Senate, but before it could exercise genuine power is was disbanded by Yuan Shikai in 1914.[75] A KMT-organized military effort in 1913, sometimes called the "Second Revolution," was defeated by Yuan's better trained Beiyang forces in July 1913, and senior members of the KMT were either killed or fled into exile.[76]

The KMT was able to restart its political efforts in southern China during 1916 and 1917, but without military power it was vulnerable to local warlords. Sun noted that political power in China was founded on military strength, observing that "unless we [the KMT] appeal to the force of arms there is no way to settle the present national crisis."[77] During the late 1910s and early 1920s, Sun was also impressed with the glowing reports coming from inside the Soviet Union, which had created a politically dominated "Red Army" during its civil war.[78]

In 1921, Sun signed agreements to create an independent KMT military academy in Guangdong using Soviet instructors and equipment.[79] The mutiny of forces nominally under the control of the KMT, but actually under local military leader Chen Jiongming's control, on 6 June 1922 further crystallized Sun Yat-sen's desire to institute a politicized army under party control.[80]

On 1 May 1924, the Nationalist Party of China's Army Officer Academy, commonly known as the Whampoa Academy (Huangpu junxiao) because of its location downriver from Guangzhou at the Whampoa docks, officially opened. Speaking at the opening ceremony, Sun outlined the political purpose of the military academy, "On inaugurating this school, we hope that we will create a revolutionary army, the nucleus of which will be the students of this school. If the framework becomes reliable and we create a revolutionary army, then our revolution will achieve success. Without a revolutionary army, the Chinese revolution will suffer defeat forever."[81] The KMT was able to attract large numbers of applicants to the academy, and of more than three thousand applicants only a carefully selected 613 students formed the first class of cadets, which began training in June 1924.[82] The demographics of Whampoa recruits highlight a disproportionate number of rural, middle-class cadets from southern China.[83]

The first class only received a rushed six-month training course, but future classes would receive between one year and a year and a half of training.[84] During its existence, the Whampoa Academy trained roughly ten thousand officers, which helped make the KMT the dominant political force in China. The first four classes of the Academy, who enrolled when the KMT was only an isolated and regional force, would form an influential group of trusted senior officers in both the KMT and CCP (Chinese Communist Party) armies into the 1970s.

Drawing on both Soviet experience and military education techniques developed by Chinese instructors trained at Baoding or the Japanese Military Academy, Whampoa training encompassed infantry, artillery, and staff training. Until the delivery of eight thousand rifles and ammunition in October 1924, the Whampoa Academy had only thirty functional rifles and no ammunition for training of any kind.[85] Coordination of Soviet and Chinese instructors was difficult due to language differences and only the simplest of infantry tactics—suppressive fire, flanking maneuvers, and assault rushes—were taught, and even then only through demonstration, not practical exercise.[86] Only during the fourth class, March 1924—October 1925, were unit exercises at the platoon, company, and battalion levels conducted.[87]

As the incubator of Sun's new "revolutionary army" (gemingjun), the Whampoa Academy curriculum included a large amount of political and ideological indoctrination, using rote instruction rather than critical thinking. Classes and instruction given to officer cadets at Whampoa emphasized loyalty and obedience to party leaders, senior military officers, and revolutionary principles at the expense of intellectual creativity.[88] Soviet advisers and members of the Chinese Communist Party played a major role in the establishment of the Political Department, which drew from Soviet techniques in its use of ideological education by featuring stories of revolutionary martyrs, including extensive anti-imperialist propaganda, and emphasizing deference to party authority.[89] The Political Department produced ten theses of behavior and conduct, which stated explicitly that, if necessary, all cadets should "sacrifice themselves for the sake of their party and their country." Moreover, "cadets must be taught that the duty of a revolutionary soldier is to sacrifice his freedom to the party."[90] In later year groups, the Whampoa Academy offered classes specifically for "political officers," but the curriculum for this group of cadets was similar to that for normal military cadets, with occasional special lectures on "theory" from senior Party officials such as Wang Jingwei and Hu Hanmin.[91]

The creation of a political officer role and the Political Department system within the Chinese military arose from several interrelated factors. First, the decision of Sun Yat-sen to adopt Soviet aid and re-shape the KMT as a Leninist party entailed the adoption of Soviet organizational models of military control and supervision. Soviet advisers introduced the Political Department system as part of a strategy of military control in conjunction with military aid and training. Second, the contemporary experiences of warlord depredations and brutality during the 1910s and 1920s made exercising strict control over military forces politically essential for the KMT. Third, creating a disciplined ideological force would also give the KMT a politically useful distinction from rival warlords, portrayed in propaganda as venal militarists opposed to enlightened KMT patriots.

The role of the political officer in modern China differed sharply from the original conception of "political officers" (représentants en mission) during the French Revolution, who focused on restoring discipline to the formerly Royalist Army, or from the Soviet commissar position (politruk), which sought to control the behavior of Tsarist military officers.[92] The KMT political officer sought to ensure discipline and political allegiance, but also acted as an enabler of military activity by providing logistical support and collecting intelligence. In addition, the political officer acted as a bridge between the KMT military and larger civilian society. The lack of adequate civilian administrative capacity to conduct basic functions such as taxation, infrastructure development, and the provision of legal order meant that political officers were often required to interact with local communities to procure food and billeting. This administrative challenge was also an opportunity for KMT political officers, because they could act as a focal point for KMT involvement in and penetration of local society.

Within the KMT, and later the ROC military structure, political officer duties included *Party* work and *Political* work.[93] Party work entailed the development, maintenance, and discipline of party members and the party structure within the military, as well as the surveillance of military personnel. Political work involved a much broader variety of tasks including the general education of troops (although with a heavily political subtext), attention to soldiers' welfare, and interaction with local communities. Political work also included large amounts of moral and spiritual (jingshen) education. During periods of Party inactivity, political officers reverted to political work and performed functions similar to chaplains or regular officers. However, in periods of intense political mobilization, often in response to top-down programs initiated by the larger party organization, party work became more important.

Party work was difficult to sustain in the ROC military because it functioned in opposition to military norms of unified command and unqualified command authority. At the most basic level, party work involved the routine recruitment of party members from among military personnel and the holding of regular meetings and educational activities to build cohesion within the party structure.[94] Ideally, many officers and NCOs would be party members, but the ratio varied from a low point during the Sino-Japanese War to high party membership within the military in Taiwan after 1953. Party members within the military reported to political officers about the operations and morale of their units, and the political officer had broad authority over personnel assignments. Instructor Liu Zhi summarized the division of instruction thus: "Party and political education tells students why they are here, moral education tells them what to do, and military training teaches them how to do it."[95]

Political work tasks were often related to the party but dealt with issues that were personal to soldiers. Education was the most basic political task in China, due to a very low level of literacy among army recruits. Improving the education level of soldiers increased their military utility, but also was a major benefit to larger society after their military service. Political officers might also be involved in personal issues, such as solving a soldier's financial problems, finding employment after military service, and even helping in finding a spouse. After 1950, many political officers spent significant time dealing with the retirement of old soldiers who had no family on Taiwan and no employment prospects. In wartime, political work would include propaganda aimed at the enemy population, and in the event of success, political officers would guide a period of temporary military government.

The establishment of the Whampoa Academy in May 1924 began the process of integrating political officers into the KMT through the creation of a hybrid military-political training program designed to develop ideologically sound officer candidates. The Whampoa Academy training, developed with the advice of and precedents outlined by Soviet advisers, separated students into two overlapping course programs for military and political officers respectively.[96] Political training for military officers included more than two hundred hours of instruction in general principles, but political officers, referred to as "party representatives" (dang daibiao) received 550 hours on more detailed activities such as propaganda operations and organizational techniques.[97] After graduation, the political officers were assigned to all levels of military units, with a formal rank slightly lower than the military commander but with a separate chain of command within the political officer system.[98]

Once attached to a military unit, political officers had four primary internal tasks.[99] First, they were to develop the party organization within military units, many of which were former warlord forces that had switched sides. This entailed developing party cells down to the platoon level and recruiting military personnel in key positions or with leadership skills into the party. Second, the political officer emphasized the concept of party supremacy to all military members through education, cultural activities, and personal interaction. Third, the political officer worked to encourage discipline and unity within the KMT army. This task conflicted with military concepts of a commander's authority, so in this area the political officer had to work closely with the military commander, who might grant him full authority over military discipline or might deny the political officer any role, depending on their relationship. Last, the political officer looked out for the welfare of the soldiers, many of whom were very young, poorly educated, and far from their home districts. This could take the form of personal counseling, basic education, coordinating the sending of soldiers' pay back home to their families, or writing letters if they were illiterate.

A key aspect that would distinguish political officers during the 1924–26 Whampoa period was the separate chain of command, which limited the influence military officers could exert on political officers.[100] With a separate chain of command, the next higher level within the Political Department determined personnel policies and promotions for political officers, and military officers could not order the political officer to perform any duties. This process required military officers to coordinate with the political officer as an equal. The separate chain of command provided both protection from military cooptation and the means by which the central Political Department headquarters could maintain operational and ideological control over their officers.

During the Northern Expedition of the KMT in 1926–27, political officers acted in a hybrid role, maintaining supervision over military efforts to ensure they were in accordance with KMT political decisions as well as mobilizing local populations, coordinating with local governments, and distributing a wide range of pro-KMT propaganda.[101] Within the military specifically, political officers undertook several key tasks: monitoring military officers' orders, developing party committees at all levels, recruiting new party members from among military personnel, and promoting party authority in matters of personal conduct and behavior.[102] Although this system was militarily useful, and had been a key element in the KMT army's ability to defeat much larger warlord forces, the purge of the CCP members from the KMT in January 1927 disproportionately affected the ranks of the political officers, many of whom were also CCP members.

From the very beginning of Sun Yat-sen's introduction of a Soviet inspired party-army concept, there was an intellectual tension between the party ideology and military procedure. The tone of the political training appears to have conflicted with the more purely military instruction at Whampoa, with a split between school commandant Chiang Kai-shek (Jiang Jieshi) and the Soviet advisers. Chiang had studied at the Baoding military academy before enrolling in the Imperial Japanese Army Academy (Shikan Gakko) in 1907, and he appointed fellow alumni of Japanese military academies to three of the four department head positions.[103]

Rather than appeal to ideology, Chiang argued that grueling military training and attention to the rigors of military discipline were vital to "be a man" (zuo ren) and that the military ethos carried into daily practice will cause cadets to "act like a man."[104] In 1925, Chiang's obsession with collective military discipline, the personal honor of an officer, and unwavering obedience to senior commanders was highlighted by the publication of a new military law for the KMT forces. This legal code highlighted the tension between party control and internal military procedural autonomy that was already apparent during the first class at Whampoa. The most radical element of the new regulations was the "Military Law of Collective Responsibility," which updated a ruthless system of individual punishment first outlined by the Chinese general Qi Jiguang in the sixteenth century. The regulations stipulated that in cases of cowardice by officers, "[i]f the platoon leader retreated with his platoon without orders, he must be executed . . . and so forth, the same death penalty must apply to commanders of battalions, regiments, divisions." The law also applied to enlisted men in that "[w]hen the squad leader did not retreat, but his entire squad retreated without orders, thus causing the death of the squad leader, then all the privates of the squad must be executed."[105] The effect of these new military regulations was to move military justice outside the range of direct party control. The harshness of the regulations and the terms of conduct outlined expressed the idea that personal honor and responsibility to fellow soldiers was the highest standard of behavior, and violating these principles had the most extreme punishments.

At the Whampoa Academy the KMT received intellectual and material support from the Soviet Union. One Soviet political adviser to the KMT, Michael Borodin, was crucial in establishing the initial plan for the Whampoa school and coordinating the delivery of military equipment to the fledgling army.[106] The Soviet role in the day-to-day operations of the Whampoa Academy focused on the political training rather than the military component of the course. At its peak, the number of Soviet instructors at the school was eighteen, but the inability of Soviet officers to speak Chinese hindered their influence.[107] Perhaps most directly, the Soviet Union supplied the overwhelming majority of funding for school operations, including almost all of the start-up capital and a regular monthly stipend for personnel expenses.[108]

By the spring of 1926, the KMT had been able to form multiple army divisions, officered by Whampoa graduates and lightly equipped with Soviet weapons. The death of Sun Yat-sen in March 1925 had allowed Chiang Kai-shek to assume political leadership as head of the KMT, as well as retaining his military role as commander in chief of KMT forces. Chiang then launched a major attack northward from Guangdong into Hunan, Jiangxi, and Fujian, in an attempt to defeat the armies of Wu Peifu and other major warlords. This Northern Expedition (bei fa) of 1926–28 was the first significant operation by the new KMT military, and it was able to achieve notable successes against less cohesive warlord forces. By October, KMT forces had reached the Yangtze River in central China.[109] Continued KMT advances during the winter of 1926–27 brought the majority of the Yangtze River valley, which encompassed a large percentage of the Chinese population and its most economically developed areas, under a unified government for the first time since 1916. Battlefield victories increased political disputes over the spoils of war, and a decisive split between the KMT and CCP in April 1927 ended the partnership, with both sides viewing the other as a mortal enemy, and each side sought to develop their own "party-army."

Although the Whampoa period from 1924 to 1926 was brief, it established the framework of a party-army system that would exist in the KMT army and later ROC army into the 1990s. Despite the nearly immediate attempt of military leaders both inside and outside the KMT to limit the influence of party policy on military affairs, the party-army remained the primary intellectual competitor to the concept of a national army.

Sun Li-jen: Early Years and Education

During the late Qing and early Republic periods, individual military officers had the difficult challenge of navigating an unstable civil-military system and a rapidly changing military organization. Many of the most important and influential military leaders of the 1940s and 1950s were born and raised during this period of dynamic change. Sun Li-jen was born in December 1900, into the family of Sun Huanting, a low-level official assigned to an isolated and poor region of central Anhui. Sun Huanting had successfully passed the imperial examinations in 1887, with a jinshi degree, a status that made him eligible for positions within the government administration.[110] Sun Li-jen spent the majority of his childhood in Shandong, where his father served as a county level administrator after 1906. Shandong was one of the most vibrant commercial and intellectual areas of China, with extensive development of its trade and academic networks due to increasing prosperity and communication.

Beginning in 1906, six-year-old Sun received private tutoring at home in Chinese history and culture. Sun Li-jen began his education shortly after the abolition of the imperial civil service examinations in 1905, which eliminated the lengthy study of Chinese classics and literature as a prerequisite for entry into government service. Nonetheless, in spite of their loss of official authority, Sun's father engaged private tutors and instructed Sun in traditional Chinese material with its strong emphasis on cultivating correct behavior. Despite his apparent traditional inclinations, Sun's father quickly moved to give his son a Western style education, and at age eight Sun began attending the Jinan German School (Jinan dewen gaodeng xiaoxue), which had the most modern curriculum in the region.[111]

As the beneficiary of an excellent education in Shandong and strong family support, Sun gained an undergraduate position at Tsinghua University (Qinghua daxue), one of the most prestigious and well-funded Western-style universities in China. Sun Li-jen's admittance into Tsinghua was also likely helped by his father's new position as a dean in a nearby university in Beijing.[112] From age fifteen through twenty-four, Sun was raised in the cosmopolitan and politically fractious world of Beijing's university district. His academic record during this period is vague, with little impression from his later speeches that he was a serious student. Similarly, Sun's involvement in the student-led opposition movement to the Versailles Treaty, the May 4th Movement (wusi yundong), is unclear. Although he likely supported the movement's nationalist objectives, he was not a politically active student.

By far the most important developments in Sun's life during his undergraduate education were his athletic ability and his leadership skills. Sun spent much of his college years involved in sports: basketball, soccer, and handball.[113] As team captain of the Tsinghua University basketball team Sun led the school to the Far East Games in Shanghai during 1921. The Games were the precursors to the modern Asian Games, and Sun was widely lauded after the Tsinghua team beat the Philippine national team for the gold medal.[114] Sun's experience in the Far East Games was his first overt leadership position, and the personal connections he made with his teammates, most of whom came from the wealthiest and politically connected Chinese families, would help him early in his military career.

A recruiting attraction for Tsinghua University was its preferential access to American universities, which allowed its students to transfer to American schools for tertiary studies. On graduation from Tsinghua in 1923, Sun immediately departed for the United States, where he entered Purdue University as a junior. Sun's education was paid for through the Boxer Indemnity scholarship fund, which was a trust fund established by the United States government to promote Chinese education in American universities by awarding scholarships to exceptional students. In 1925, Sun graduated from Purdue with a degree in civil engineering and worked briefly as a draftsman for the American Bridge Company but had little inclination for engineering as a profession or for permanent emigration to the United States.[115]

Sun entered into the Virginia Military Institute (VMI) as a senior level cadet in 1925. There was little indication that Sun had military inclinations prior to 1925, and his family had no history of military service. In later years Sun claimed that he had always been interested in military affairs but had pursued his civil engineering degree based on his father's judgment, and only due to the increasingly chaotic warfare of the era did he feel compelled to become involved.[116] Although this patriotic narrative is almost certainly embellished, Sun was clearly well motivated while at VMI and survived the brutal hazing given out to new students.

Aside from the education in military skills, organizational techniques, and, for Sun, English language training, VMI appears to have been a formative experience for Sun's conception of military life as a cloistered, self-policing community. VMI's educational program was characterized by a high degree of student leadership, with upperclassmen assuming most of the managerial functions of running dormitories, mess halls, and disciplinary functions such as demerits and inspections. Sun frequently spoke of his time at VMI during his later years with the Chinese army, and the dominant theme he presented was the culture of autonomy or self-control (zizhi) inculcated in cadets.

The VMI class yearbook from 1927 praised Sun's character and optimistically looked to a future China where he would be a source of stability and strength. The glowing description of Sun states, "As to his character, he has many good qualities. He says little but he is kind and gentle, respectful to his superiors, and sincere and friendly to all." In describing the military training undertaken by Sun the yearbook remarks that he has performed well: "Li has shouldered his responsibilities like a man and we do not doubt that he will make an excellent soldier." The laudatory description of Sun included a note of caution that underscores the stark differences in the political behavior of the American and Chinese military systems in 1920. Like American army officers, VMI represented a cloistered, insular environment both geographically and mentally separate from American politics and culture. The conclusion of Sun's yearbook page notes that, "We only hope that he will not use his military knowledge to any more revolutions in his native land."[117]

2

A Party Army, 1927–1942

The massive expansion of KMT military training after the transfer of power to Nanjing allowed for the training of large numbers of officers, who would form the elite of an enlarged KMT army after 1927. During the 1930s, this force was widely recognized as the "national" army of China even though large areas of nominally Chinese territory remained under the control of warlord forces. Diplomatic recognition of the KMT's Nanjing government as the national government of China also allowed for the lifting of the international arms embargo, which enabled the KMT to make large purchases of advanced military equipment from foreign suppliers. The widespread and significant contact between German military advisers and all levels of the KMT military added a greatly needed international context and foreign linkages to aid China's military development. German military assistance coincided with and facilitated Chinese military development, but did not guide its evolution in ways inimitable to KMT leaders.[1]

During the Nanjing decade German military advisers, armaments manufacturers, and economic planners exerted tremendous influence in China, enabling the KMT army to become an increasingly professional and capital-intensive army. Although German expertise was important, Chinese officials and military officers instigated the German military mission, closely scrutinized its conduct, and exerted administrative control over the advising officers at all times. Chiang Kai-shek was personally involved in the Sino-German partnership and had frequent personal meetings with German officers.[2]

With a small initial body of only twenty-five officers in November 1928, the German military mission began an intensive training program at the newly opened Central Military Academy in Nanjing. The Central Military Academy (CMA, lujun guanxiao) was created by transferring the staff at Whampoa to Nanjing in March 1928, and the training program was also significantly expanded in class size and coursework requirements.[3] Unlike Whampoa courses, which could be as short as five months, the CMA program stipulated a strict two-year program, with all potential officer cadets serving a year in the army as enlisted soldiers prior to beginning officer training.[4] The CMA had a purpose-built campus, with its own weapons ranges, obstacle courses, and extensive athletic facilities.[5] The commandant of the school for the 1929–37 period was Gen. Zhang Zhizhong, a professional military officer, but Chiang Kai-shek appears to have been closely involved with all aspects of the school administration.[6] Like many other Chinese military schools since the late Qing period, CMA began publishing its own military journal for military officers.[7]

At the CMA, German officers conducted lectures and training, but also began a structural reform of KMT military forces. The German plan involved creating a model "training division," which would be given six months of intensive instruction in military theory, field exercises, and technical training. The training division would also be equipped with a complete set of new uniforms, small arms, artillery, and supporting equipment in order to gain familiarity with more advanced military weapons.[8] After six months, a new unit would rotate into the training system, and according to KMT plans this rotational training format could create the core of a new professional army within five to six years. By late 1931, three complete Chinese divisions, roughly 30,000 men, had trained under German guidance and had been equipped with uniform, modern weapons.[9]

In the early 1930s, the German advisory effort peaked at roughly fifty officers. New specialty schools for artillery, cavalry, tanks, intelligence, and engineering officers were opened between 1933 and 1935.[10] A major problem that the small number of German military advisers and the one primary officer academy were unable to overcome was the sheer quantity of officers required by the KMT army. With roughly five hundred thousand men in the KMT army, the CMA graduated fewer than 2,500 officers per year.

Observers of the reformed and re-equipped KMT forces had high praise for their increased professionalism and military efficiency. American military attaché Capt. Parker Tenney praised the effect of German advisers: "Chiang's army, down to the rank and file, is showing the results of German tutelage. The men are well dressed, their set-up [logistics] has improved and they are apparently well disciplined."[11] Particularly impressive was the tremendous improvement in staff work, which would have meant both increased coordination of military operations and more effective logistical support for military units.

Sino-German cooperation also extended into military procurement and the development of a sizable armaments industry in China. During the mid-1930s, China was Germany's largest purchaser of arms and ammunition by a wide margin, with exports including basic supplies and sophisticated weaponry.[12] German industrial advisers assisted in the rebuilding of the Nanjing arsenal and a new artillery factory in Hunan. The Sino-German partnership enabled the creation of a reasonably sophisticated military industrial base that could support a small modern army with advanced weapons.

A subtle difference between the Whampoa and CMA training programs was a decrease in political instruction at the CMA. During the KMT move from Guangdong to Nanjing, Wang Jingwei, a prominent KMT political leader and chairman of the National Military Council, insisted on the creation of an independent Central Political Academy that was not under Chiang Kai-shek's control.[13] This bifurcation of school curricula into two separate institutions removed much of the crossover political-military education. The purge of Communists from the KMT in April 1927 also eliminated a major internal party constituency that had argued for close military-political coordination. In addition, unlike the Soviet advisers at Whampoa who had promoted a hybrid military-political organization, the German military officers remained purposefully detached from Chinese politics and internal factions.[14]

During the Nanjing decade, 1928–37, the role of political officers languished due to misgivings by senior KMT leaders, most notably Chiang Kai-shek, who saw political officers as potentially leftist disruptors. At the same time, the political officer role was increasingly subsumed by a larger governmental project to create a new administration that could fulfill the functions performed by the political officer. In a speech during the spring of 1929, Chiang bluntly outlined the criticisms of the political officer system: "Currently in the Kuomintang's Army, you could say that political work and party functions are lacking. . . . Why is this? The main reason is that from the beginning the majority of political officers and workers have been Communists. . . . The second reason is that military commanders don't trust them."[15] Moreover, under the influence of German advisers, a Military Information Bureau was established in 1930, which functioned to collect intelligence and distribute propaganda, further removing one of the political officers' core tasks.[16] Moreover, instead of using political officers to conduct political surveillance over military officers, Chiang Kai-shek promoted the adoption of "officer societies" such as the Officers' Moral Endeavor Corps, the China Reconstruction Society (Fuxingshe), and most famously the Blue Shirt Society (lanyi she) to create social cohesion within the military officer corps.[17]

Following the CCP purge in 1927, a series of administrative changes changed the title of the political officer system from a "party representative system" to a much more constrained "political training department" (zhengzhi xunlian chu) within the KMT military.[18] Moreover, because the KMT was eager to present itself as the "national" government of China during the 1928–37 period, membership in the KMT by students at the military academy was not mandatory, although 75 percent were members.[19] After 1927, political officers' separate political chain of command was abolished. The relegation of political officers to being part of the military staff drastically reduced their authority, and they were often labeled the "commander's concubine," because of their lack of independence or personal authority.[20]

After the CCP–KMT split, the formal training of political officers was disrupted, and for the next twenty-three years there was no dedicated training center for KMT political officers. During the Nanjing decade, political officers received only two weeks of classroom training before assignment to military units.[21] In place of classroom education, Chiang Kai-shek attempted to influence the political officers through frequent conferences and meetings where the emphasis was on understanding KMT policy rather than developing robust skills. In addition to decreasing quality, the quantity of political officers also decreased during the Nanjing decade, with only 3,616 official political officers for a total force of over 2 million men spread out over two hundred divisions, compared to roughly 1,500 political officers for a total of only 250,000 men during the Northern Expedition.[22]

Military officers trained at the CMA did receive instruction on the role of politics in military affairs, and the term party-army continued to be used in the school curriculum. Textbooks noted that, despite the success of the KMT in achieving military and political victory, continued political control of the military was important for two reasons. First, victorious revolutionary movements often succumbed to factionalism and leaderless opposition, and the example used was the Paris Commune, a not very subtle attack on the Communists. The second rationale given for continued party control of the military was the need to ensure that groups such as the remaining warlords and Communists were unable to coerce the government.[23]

The ad hoc nature of post-1928 political officer education, and the emphasis on training for specific tasks rather than a broader education, carried over into the Sino-Japanese War era from 1937 to 1945. In addition, political officer efforts within military units most often took the form of short-term programs of instruction rather than long-term development of organizational structures. This preference for short-duration, mission-specific training (xunlian), was exhibited in all KMT government departments and was driven by wartime necessities to increase morale, but also by a failure of the KMT to develop coherent and durable organizations.[24] Analysis of KMT military journals and publications shows that many of the political officer efforts were little more than patriotic pep talks, devoid of any significant ideological content or policies.[25] A typically inane and poorly written passage from the era reads, "Implementing political education within the military is particularly important in our war against Japan. Why? For one reason, our Army is a Revolutionary force . . . for another reason, because our war is a people's war."[26] An emphasis on patriotism rather than party was part of KMT efforts to portray itself as a national government, but the downplaying of the role of the party seemed to have hindered the development of a solid party structure within the army.

The establishment of a quasi-national government by the KMT in 1928 initiated a boom in military journals, with dozens of provincial- and national-level military journals published after 1928 and throughout the war with Japan. Between 1928 and 1937 a wide range of specialized military journals appealed to distinct occupational fields. A prime example of this trend was the publication *Junyi zazhi* (*Military Doctor Magazine*), but the subdivision of military journals also included the development of branch-specific air force and navy journals such as *Kongjun yuekan* (*Air Force Monthly*) and *Haijun qikan* (*Navy Journal*). Difficulties in arranging for the national distribution of publications, increased numbers of technical military skills, and persistent regional military variations all limited the development of a comprehensive national military journal. Many of these journals, especially those produced in provinces outside of KMT party control, such as *Junshi yuekan* (*Military Monthly*) produced in Yunnan, contained views that deviated from KMT party rhetoric.[27] The KMT produced a wide variety of military journals, such as *Junshi weiyunhui gongbao* (*Military Affairs Committee Bulletin*) or *Junzheng xunkan* (*Military-Political Review*), which featured political articles and analysis that dealt with the role of the army within a larger party organization, rather than focus on purely military affairs.

During the Nanjing decade and into the first years of the Sino-Japanese War, the only journal to have consistently sophisticated and relevant articles was the *Huangpu yuekan* (*Whampoa Monthly*). The *Whampoa Monthly*, first published in 1930, took its name from the Whampoa Academy, which by this point had transferred its students and faculty to Nanjing and had been renamed the Central Military Academy. As an official product of the primary officer training center of the KMT, which had become the de facto "Chinese" government after 1928, the *Whampoa Monthly* was required reading for military officers. In addition, senior political leaders often wrote articles or had speeches posted in *Whampoa Monthly*, which, while normally focusing on military issues, often included a broad range of political, economic, and social commentary.

A typical issue of *Whampoa Monthly* consisted of fifty to sixty pages of dense text with few visuals. The first section of the journal always included two or three articles devoted to KMT policy and political issues. Typical topics might include discussions of government policy on transportation development, especially railroad construction essential for troop movements, government subsidies to industrial development, or the principles composing "Sun Yat-senism."

An underlying tension running throughout the journal's publication was a subtle difference in the tone of discussion between political leaders and military officers on the degree to which China should be a status quo power. During the Nanjing decade, the KMT was recognized by major world powers such as Great Britain, France, and the United States as the de facto Chinese government, but substantial elements within the KMT continued to argue that it should remain opposed to global international norms. For example, KMT political leaders fawned over the Indian independence movement, which some of them believed would lead to a new anti-imperialist Asian solidarity.[28] Similarly, the anti-imperialist rhetoric that the KMT had adopted during the 1910s and 1920s lingered in the form of blistering attacks on a vaguely defined "imperialism" for causing Chinese economic problems. This is in contrast to the close, nonideological partnership the KMT military was forging with Germany, a partnership that involved economic transfers of valuable rare earth minerals.[29]

In *Whampoa Monthly*, articles on domestic Chinese economic, social, and political issues were frequently included in the content produced by KMT officials, but article contributors drawn from military officer ranks never approached these topics. Even within the articles presented by KMT officials, the Nanjing period's content vacillated between preserving the status quo and advocating change. For example, in a discussion of the difficulties of Chinese peasants, *Whampoa Monthly* acknowledges the problems of high rents but also asserts that the rights and prerogatives of landholders must be respected.[30] The dangers of Communism were frequently noted by political officials, with substantive articles attacking the CCP on the grounds that it sought to fracture Chinese unity and that it threatened stable development.[31] In contrast, none of the articles by military officers suggests that undertaking military action against the CCP was a core function of the military.

CMA commandant Zhang Zhizhong was a frequent contributor to *Whampoa Monthly*. In a typical article, a reprint of a speech he gave to the academy students, Zhang argued that a good officer must pursue a moral and personal path of development to enable him to thrive in his position. Zhang's proscription for moral development included reading the works and speeches of important leaders, learning from biographies of great men, keeping a diary of daily behavior, and critiquing actions and intentions.[32] This increasing emphasis on internal character development for military officers was shared by other senior leaders, and corresponded with many of the tenets of Chiang Kai-shek's "New Life" (xin shenghuo yundong) civic education movement.[33] However, for military officers, character development designed to pursue honor, justice, and honesty was problematic with continued obedience to single-party rule.

Although many of the articles and speeches presented in *Whampoa Monthly* appear to conform to the pattern of party dominance developed at Whampoa, more technical military discussions were included in the back pages of the journal. Beginning in the first issue of *Whampoa Monthly*, in 1930, global military developments were reviewed in brief expository segments, followed by short one- or two-paragraph assessments. The reviews focused on technological and organizational changes in Europe, and carried on the professional focus of journals first established at the end of the Qing dynasty. In one example, the development of air forces and the possibilities of strategic bombing, a trend far removed from Chinese capabilities in 1930, was a subject of intense interest.[34]

Despite the KMT involvement in Nanjing-based journals, military officers could choose from alternative professional military journals that had no party controls. *Junshi Xunkan (Military Affairs)*, published in Beijing during the 1930s, maintained a highly technical and cosmopolitan approach to military topics.[35] With little or no analysis of domestic political issues or leader personalities, *Junshi Xunkan* devoted its dozens of pages every month to understanding tactics and new weapons developed by major world powers.

While military officers and KMT party officials were most heavily involved in civil-military debates and discussing the degree of party involvement in military affairs, civilian newspapers and magazines were part of the public discussion. Civilian commentators frequently argued that the KMT's campaign to create a central government needed to transition from a party to a national system of government, with a nationalized military serving the entire country. In a 1935 edition of *Huanian* magazine, an article titled "National Defense and Military Nationalization" (Guofang yu jundui guojiahua) argued that reform was vitally important because in an era of increasing foreign threats, "military nationalization was a prerequisite condition" for a solid national defense.[36] A 1936 article in *Tongyi Pinglun* (*Unified Discussion*) argued that the educational system of the military needed broadening, with an increased role for civilian engagement to nurture "character" in soldiers.[37] While these public criticisms did not carry the weight of inter-army and inter-party discussion, it is an indication that KMT party control over the ROC military was contested, and that professionalization had a constituency outside of military officers themselves.

By the late 1930s, discussion of the principles and practices of a national army had even crept into military training manuals. Materials from the CMA itself used the term "constitutional state" (lixian guojia), and noted that the conduct of military officers needed to be regulated by a robust system of military law.[38] Notably missing from this framework was a place for a single-party system.

War with Japan, 1937–1941

The beginning of the second Sino-Japanese War in July 1937 resulted in the first large-scale combat operations by the KMT military against the armed forces of another nation. The decision of Chiang Kai-shek to respond to Japanese military operations in North China by attacking Japanese forces in Shanghai was determined in large part by the presence of the majority of Chiang's elite German-trained units in the lower Yangtze region. Although initial operations were successful and the KMT army performed better than expected, the lack of trained reserve forces meant the eventual exhaustion of Chinese units, followed by a skillful Japanese amphibious landing, routing the Chinese forces in the Shanghai area. The destruction of the majority of the KMT's best-equipped and best-trained units during the first months of the war was a major blow to the cohesiveness of the Chinese army as an organization.

The continued retreat of Chinese forces during November and December 1937 led to the evacuation of the capital, Nanjing, and the relocation of the central government to the interior city of Chongqing. The capture of Wuhan on 25 October 1938 marked the end of major Japanese offensive operations and the beginning of the Chinese strategy of avoiding battle, which led to a pause in significant combat operations.[39] Chinese military forces did not significantly oppose Japanese offensives in North China during the summer of 1940 and the occupation of Hong Kong in December 1941.

During the course of the war, there was a steady decrease in the quality of military training and education within the ROC military. In spite of tremendous efforts during the Nanjing decade to train competent military officers and create a system of military academies, China was still largely unprepared for wartime demands. In 1936, the total number of commissioned officers was 136,474, and roughly half of the 25,000 officers trained at the Central Military Academy between 1929 and 1937 were killed during the first four months of the war.[40] During the war years, roughly 190,000 new officers received some form of training, although the quality of instruction was poor. For comparison, the United States trained 162,000 reserve officers through its ROTC program in 1939 alone.[41] The result of chronic under-manning of officer positions was that, by the later years of the war, only 15 to 25 percent of officer positions were filled, leaving most lieutenant and some captain positions unoccupied.[42]

As the Japanese advanced, the instructors and some instructional materials from the major military academies in Nanjing and Baoding relocated to interior regions. The Central Military Academy moved to Chengdu, in Sichuan province, but suffered from a lack of teaching materials and instructors.[43] Reduction of class times to a maximum of twelve months and lowered admission standards enabled the academy to graduate 34,430 officers between 1937 and 1946, but the quality of training was poor.[44] Nine additional branch campuses, established during the war, graduated an additional 80,000 officers, and refresher courses attempted to improve the quality of already serving officers, but officer education failed to keep pace with high rates of attrition.[45]

The rate of battlefield casualties among KMT officers was not uniform; the majority of officer casualties were junior officers educated at the Central Military Academy in Nanjing with relatively few losses among the Whampoa generation, who by 1937 had advanced to senior military positions. In 1936, the percentage of KMT general officers who had been educated at Whampoa was only 7 percent, compared to 31 percent for general officers educated at the non-KMT controlled Baoding Military Academy. By 1947, Whampoa graduates composed over 35 percent of total general officer strength, while the ratio of Baoding alumni had dropped to 8 percent.[46] Whampoa-trained officers also became the dominant demographic within active command positions, and by 1944 42 percent of division commanders and 36 percent of army commanders were Whampoa alumni. The natural career progression of many of the still-young Whampoa graduates probably accounts for some of this increase, but overt political favoritism of officers seen as loyal to the KMT likely played a major role in accelerating Whampoa graduates' advancement.

Assessments of the performance of Chinese military varied wildly. Many observers pointed to significant problems in logistics and training, but senior, politically appointed KMT military officers developed a reputation for incompetence and venality. American general Joseph Stilwell, chief of staff to Chiang Kai-shek from 1942 through 1944, commented, "The junior officers respond readily to direction. Battalion and regimental commanders show considerable variation, but there are many good ones. It would be easy to sift out the efficient in these grades, and the resulting promotion would have a good effect on morale. Division and Army commanders are a great problem. They seldom get up to the front and they very rarely supervise the execution of their orders."[47] This divided opinion between competent junior and poorly performing senior officers was a common feature of American military reports and was shared by Chiang Kai-shek, who routinely criticized his senior officers.[48]

Another factor undermining officer performance was the problem of filling technical fields such as military engineering, communications, and medical services with officers either intellectually unprepared or unable to leave combat operations for training. Gen. Tang Enbo commented, "[M]ost of the officers in various ranks did not have the training relevant to their present responsibilities. Those trained in engineering might be asked to command infantry units, and ordinary citizens could be asked to coordinate military supply. One finds all kinds of similar examples in the registers, and basically most officers did not have the appropriate training."[49]

KMT attempts to strengthen the cohesiveness of its military forces relied on both ideological appeals and brute coercion. Throughout the war, Chiang promoted conceptions of loyalty, nationalism, and ethnic solidarity to military officers through speeches at army training facilities, meetings, and special "education" sessions. A frequent method used by the KMT was the promotion of patriotic military martyrs who died fighting the Japanese, in addition to praising the heroism of successful generals.[50] A more coercive method of promoting loyalty was through public executions of officers who had failed in their duties. Only months into the war, the Military Affairs Commission ordered the execution of two army majors for cowardice in the line of duty.[51] Less than six months later, eight high ranking officers were executed on charges of cowardice, looting, rape, and failure to obey orders.[52]

The outbreak of the Sino-Japanese War and the Second United Front between the CCP and KMT allowed for the creation of a reformed political work system in February 1938.[53] Headed by KMT stalwart Gen. Chen Cheng, the renewed political effort stressed patriotic education more than purely political initiatives, in keeping with the spirit of the United Front.[54] After less than two years in the position, Zhang Zhizhong replaced Chen as director of the Political Department in September 1940. Zhang attempted to increase the number of political officers from roughly seven thousand to over 25,000 in less than twelve months, but with a further decrease in the quality of instruction given to political officer candidates. Many of these hastily recruited and poorly trained political officers were students and office workers displaced by the Japanese advance, who had little to no military training.[55] Zhang also initiated a rotation program designed to cross-train military officers at political officer schools and vice versa, but at the unit level military commanders resisted this program and it was never fully implemented.[56] Political training at the military academy, relocated from Nanjing to Chengdu during 1937, appears to have similarly atrophied due to a lack of interest from officers and directions from senior officials.[57]

Faced with problematic domestic politics, financial constraints, and logistical difficulties, the KMT attempted to utilize foreign support to buttress its military efforts. The end of the German military mission due to changing German foreign policies, which now favored Japan, left a large void in advisory capacity and industrial supply. Japanese diplomatic and military pressure limited the purchase of supplies from British-controlled Hong Kong or by rail from French Indo-China.[58]

During the first three years of the Sino-Japanese War, Soviet assistance in personnel and equipment was the KMT's primary source of foreign support. Sino-Soviet rapprochement during 1937 was a marriage of convenience rather than principle. Chiang Kai-shek's violent purging of Communists from the KMT in 1927, and subsequent anti-Communist campaigns, made a full alliance impossible, but the signing of a Sino-Soviet Non-Aggression Pact (zhongsu hu bu qin fan tiaoyue) on 21 August 1937 allowed for extensive military cooperation. Soviet military aid to China promised USD $20 million worth of equipment, enough for twenty-four divisions, but actual deliveries likely totaled less than ten divisions' worth of supplies.[59] The bulk of Sino-Soviet equipment transfers were in aircraft, with over eight hundred planes sent to China, where Soviet pilots trained Chinese crews and conducted operations against the Japanese under the guise of a Soviet volunteer group.[60] Roughly five hundred Soviet military officers were directly attached to training facilities or headquarters units in the

Chinese army.⁶¹ Language difficulties, the low quality of many of the Soviet officers (following Stalin's extensive purging of Soviet officers during the late 1930s), and Chinese distrust of Soviet intentions meant that Soviet advisers never had the same influence as earlier German officers.

From 1937 to 1942, the quality of Chinese military journals declined due to the occupation of the major military training facilities and publishing centers in east China by the Japanese, but several journals continued to function from interior provinces. The journal of the Central Military Academy, *Whampoa Monthly*, resumed publishing after relocating to Chengdu, but content suffered due to a lack of research facilities and the dispersion of faculty.

During the initial fighting between Japanese forces and the Chinese army in 1937, *Whampoa Monthly* devoted the majority of its content space to short, succinct summaries of battlefield developments, interspersed with speeches by political leaders. The tone was optimistic, pointing to the successful defense of Shanghai as a positive example and discussing the possibility of imminent foreign intervention.⁶² After the Japanese destruction of much of the German-trained elite in the Yangtze River valley and the occupation of large areas of China, the tone of *Whampoa Monthly* coverage shifted sharply away from decisive battles and toward long-term strategies. In February 1938, a special issue of *Whampoa Monthly* was devoted towards the "long war." A series of articles detailed the need to rely increasingly on political and economic strategies rather than military action to oppose the Japanese and exhaust their resources. Noted military theorist Jiang Baili argued that, faced with a clear disadvantage in weapons and skills, China could only rely on its sense of nationalism to wage a populist "race war."⁶³ A similarly themed article by Shen Qingchen, a senior KMT official, argued in 1938 that the world was merging into two groups, with Germany, Italy, and Japan opposed by the remainder of the world.⁶⁴ In his analysis, China needed to remain engaged with the world and active while these developments played out.

While the strategy of prolonging the war and engaging in asymmetric tactics was no doubt valuable to Chinese political leaders, the lack of content in military journals from Chinese military leaders suggests the policy might have been less popular among military officers.

Sun Li-jen and the Nanjing Decade

After Sun's graduation from the VMI in 1927, he traveled briefly in the United States and Europe before returning to China. His European trip included visits to military academies in Great Britain, France, and Germany, and the battlefields of World War I.⁶⁵ When Sun had left China to study at Purdue in 1923, the warlord era was in full swing with decentralized, military governments across the country. When Sun returned to China in 1927, a nascent national government under Nationalist Party leadership had been established after the military conquest of the crucial Yangtze River valley during the Northern Expedition (bei fa). Sun had no previous connection to the Nationalist party and while likely sympathetic to their cause, he did not return to China in 1925, after studying at Purdue, to join the KMT military. Sun's decision to study at VMI had given him unique military training experiences, excellent English language skills, and a deep understanding of American and European culture, but also meant that he had missed the opportunity to study at the Whampoa Academy in Guangdong.

In spite of a period of national optimism surrounding the new KMT government, Sun attempted to find a direct military commission in a local warlord force. Through a former basketball teammate, who had a relative looking to recruit junior officers, Sun was given an officer's commission in a cavalry unit in Changsha, Hunan.⁶⁶ Unfortunately for Sun, the unit was largely imaginary, with recruitment and supplies hindered by poor local finances. Sun left Hunan and enrolled in the Nationalist Party School (zhongyang dangwu xuexiao) in Nanjing.⁶⁷ This Nationalist Party School trained both political cadre and military officers for service in government administration, but did not require students to be KMT members.

Sun's period of study at this school set the pattern for an enduring tension in his military career, with his academic and real-world experiences often being overlooked in favor of more politically reliable KMT members. At the school, Sun noted that the students in the military track, of which he was one, were divided into three factions. Officers who had trained at the Whampoa Academy were the dominant faction and had a clear political advantage through their party connections. Next were officers who had trained at Japanese military academies. They represented a large percentage of the students and they had considerable military skills. Lastly, a third faction was composed of students like Sun who had been educated either at elite Chinese or foreign universities, which meant they were often the most well educated but had little military experience or political influence.⁶⁸

In 1929, Sun took a position at one of the military training schools established in Nanjing as part of the German military advisory program, even though Sun's direct contact with German officers was slight.⁶⁹ Sun's duties focused on trainee behavior, physical training, and administration, not military theory and academic teaching. For three years Sun had multiple positions at several different schools but was not assigned to the prestigious Central Military Academy. The four years from 1928 to 1932 were largely a fruitless period in Sun's life, with no career advancement or significant accomplishment.

The rapidly deteriorating Sino-Japanese relationship during the late 1920s and early 1930s slowly began to shift the KMT army's focus, from internal operations against warlord and Communist forces toward repelling Japanese invasion. In January 1932, a series of attacks on Japanese civilians and property in Shanghai led to the outbreak of widespread fighting between Japanese troops and forces of the Chinese 19th Army, which, although nominally loyal to the KMT, was under the control of its former warlord commander Cai Tingkai. After six weeks of fighting that devastated large portions of the Chinese-administered section of the city, the 5 May cease-fire agreement (Songhu tingzhan xueding) made Shanghai a demilitarized zone, with only small police forces allowed within the city and its environs.

As the center of China's international economy, banking, and cultural life, Shanghai was too important and valuable to the Nationalist government to leave unprotected, so a large "tax police force" (tuojing tuan) was formed to evade the cease-fire restrictions. Although the tax police force was under the Ministry of Finance administration, it functioned as a miniature army in the Shanghai region. Rather than patrol cars and nightsticks, the tax police units had several dozen small tanks, a fleet of armored cars, and heavy machine-gun units. By the mid-1930s this force had grown to over 25,000 personnel divided into six regiments.

Although the creation of a miniature army of tax police was a deliberate "creative fiction," it was necessary to give command to officers outside of the KMT military. Moreover, because military officers in the KMT often had long-established personal connections to their units and strong financial incentives, such as skimming payroll funds, for remaining in their units, it was necessary to promote unaffiliated officers to the tax police units. Sun Li-jen's limited identification with the regular KMT army and lack of a pre-existing command position made him an ideal choice for assignment to the new force. This was a major opportunity for Sun, giving him an official rank of a colonel and his first major command, over a regiment of five thousand men.[70]

Over the next five years, Sun remained in command of one of the six tax police regiments and created a strong personal relationship with T. V. Soong (Song Ziwen), who was Sun's boss as minister of finance but also the brother-in-law of Chiang Kai-shek. Sun's time in the tax police was notable because it allowed him to spend half a decade assigned to the most cosmopolitan region of China, with the only duty being the training of his troops. Sun never participated in the anti-Communist encirclement campaigns of the 1930s or anti-warlord operations. The KMT army, created by Sun Yat-sen in 1923, had now become an institutionalized force with a comprehensive education system, command structure, and a history of near-continuous fighting against internal Chinese opponents. Sun's relative isolation in Shanghai pushed him further into a role as an outsider in Chinese military circles, with none of the collective experiences of other KMT officers.

In response to aggressive Japanese behavior in North China during the spring and summer of 1937, Chiang Kai-shek decided to deploy Chinese army units to the Shanghai area in the hope of negotiating from a position of military strength. The shooting of Lt. Gen. Isao Oyama by Chinese paramilitary forces on 9 August quickly ignited a full-scale conflict between Chinese and Japanese forces. Sun's 4th Regiment of the tax police force acted in concert with regular KMT army units and engaged the Japanese in brutal, close-quarters urban combat.[71] The Chinese forces' lack of artillery and poor tactical mobility allowed the Japanese to wear them down and out-maneuver them, leading to a collapse of the Chinese position in early October. During this grinding battle, Sun was severely wounded by shrapnel and was evacuated to Hong Kong for more sophisticated medical care.[72]

Sun spent four months convalescing in Hong Kong before returning to duty in February 1938. By this time the KMT army had been decimated, with heavy casualties to its officer corps, and had been pushed out of the capital at Nanjing. In spite of a critical need for well-trained military officers, Sun lacked the military connections to get a transfer to a KMT army unit. Sun was technically still assigned to the Ministry of Finance forces, and he was transferred to an anti-smuggling paramilitary force in Guizhou.[73] Sun was placed in charge of a training camp in Duyun, where he trained forces reporting to the Ministry of Finance. These forces acted to suppress the operations of warlords and smugglers in the region who had violated the Salt Monopoly, which was one of the main bases of KMT revenue. For three years, from December 1938 through December 1941, Sun's career again stalled, with his functions reserved to routine training duties in an isolated, rural province.

In summary, by the end of 1941 a rough balance of the ideas of a professional versus a party-army had taken shape within the KMT military. Real-world concerns about military effectiveness gave technically proficient officers a great advantage, and the training of the Beiyang Army, Baoding Academy, and German influence remained in the army organization. However, faced with tremendous political uncertainty and a lack of military institutions, the party-army concept remained, and provided the KMT military with a degree of cohesion and purpose. This balance of power between the two competing strains of Chinese military modernity was radically altered by the Japanese attack on Pearl Harbor. The subsequent effect of United States military cooperation, training, and logistical support would drastically alter the organizational leverage of Chinese military officers seeking to develop a professional military.

3

Americans and Officers, 1942–1945

The entry of the United States into the war against Japan profoundly changed the balance of power between officers desiring to be military professionals and those who were adherents to a party-army system. During the 1942–45 period, the United States Army became the most important foreign partner of China and the major supplier of equipment, ideas, and training that would shape the Chinese Nationalist Army identity. United States Army cooperation with the Nationalist Army was larger in scope—involving thousands of officers—than any experience in military cooperation by either the Americans or the Chinese up to that time. Materially, the partnership resulted in a massive transfer of arms and equipment, fundamentally reshaping Chinese military strategy away from wars of attrition fought by infantry and toward offensive action by mechanized forces. Intellectual transfers of U.S. Army doctrine and tactics through an integrated military school system helped shift the military culture of China away from command relationships based on political or personal loyalty and toward a system characterized by military professionalism. During the 1942–45 period, Chinese officers used American support to revitalize the concept of a professional officer corps and entrench its tenets in military schools and journals. Most important, Chinese officers with technical military expertise but few party connections, with Sun Li-jen being the prime example, used the American support during the 1942–45 period to rise in rank and influence.

The start of the close partnership between the KMT army and the United States Army was not the result of prolonged contact, institutional affinities, or personality. Throughout the late nineteenth and early twentieth century the United States had become involved with China on multiple levels—economic, educational, and political. However, military contact was nonexistent. In spite of extensive American private involvement in Chinese universities, hospitals, and religious organizations, the U.S. government role was highly constrained. The United States took a back seat politically to Great Britain in Chinese politics, and its economic interests focused on small-scale exports of consumer products to Chinese customers in port cities.

Aside from a motley collection of American adventurers like Frederick Townsend Ward, who had assisted the Qing during the Taiping Rebellion, the American military had little contact with the Qing, warlords, or the KMT or CCP forces. After the violence of the 1911 Chinese Revolution, a small U.S. garrison, consisting of the 15th Infantry Regiment, was assigned to Tianjin in 1912 under the terms of the Boxer Protocol to protect diplomats, and several small U.S. Navy gunboats patrolled the Yangtze River, but the general atmosphere of these forces was quiet neglect. During the twenty-six years that the 15th Infantry Regiment was in Tianjin, the most serious issue faced by its officers was the constant bureaucratic infighting between the State Department, the Marine Corps legation guard commander, and U.S. Army officers for primacy in organizational status.[1]

The primary activities of American officers and enlisted men in the 15th Infantry were drinking, souvenir shopping, and rifle marksmanship. Like the stateside U.S. Army at the time, training emphasized close-order drill, map exercises, and long-range marksmanship with the Springfield rifle. Realistic training opportunities in the interwar era of austere budgets were nonexistent, and the center of unit life was athletic competitions: baseball, football, and boxing. Although the Army sent its best men and officers to the 15th, in an effort to maintain respect among Chinese and foreign observers, the slow pace of life in Tianjin and the garrison mentality of the organization was similar to the larger U.S. Army pattern of half-day, martinet existence caricatured in James Jones's novel *From Here to Eternity*.[2]

The U.S. Army, 1900–1941: Isolated but Professional

The United States Army organization that the Chinese came in contact with before 1941 was a modest and insular force compared to the situation after 1941. The American army officers in China had three distinguishing characteristics, which became important during contact with the KMT army. First, the U.S. military operated as a "cadre" force, maintaining a small strength in peacetime but ballooning in wartime, with volunteers or conscripts filling in the personnel strength. Second, the American army maintained an extensive school system that inculcated a highly technical and military science ethos into officers. Lastly, the

American army sought to remain isolated from political affairs and opposed what it viewed as unnecessary interference by civilian leaders.

Less than forty years before the start of World War II, the United States Army had been poorly equipped and miniscule in size and skills. The brief Spanish-American War in 1898 had been a debacle that revealed major problems in American military logistics, officer training, and organization, with poor coordination of transportation assets leaving thousands of troops sitting in Florida while the crucial battles were being fought in Cuba. In the words of Theodore Roosevelt, who fought in Cuba with the 1st U.S. Volunteer Cavalry, the American war effort was "within measurable distance of a military disaster."[3]

After the war, political leaders like Secretary of War Elihu Root and senior Army officers such as Gen. Leonard Wood created a more centralized and professional organization to handle the mobilization of manpower and war material. Secretary Root was convinced that a highly trained officer corps was vital to American national security: "Our trouble will never be in raising soldiers; our trouble will always be the limits of possibility in transporting, clothing, arming, feeding and caring for our soldiers, and that requires organization."[4] In 1900, Root expanded the number of West Point cadets by over 40 percent, adding more trained officers to the Army. In 1901, the Army War College was founded to train senior officers, and in 1903 a distinct "General Staff" was established in Washington, D.C., to increase strategy coordination and streamline logistics.[5] Root's efforts helped create the organizational framework needed to deal with the mobilization challenges of twentieth-century warfare.

In World Wars I and II, the regular officers and troops of the U.S. Army served as the core "cadre" of a much larger force of conscripted men and temporary officers. The U.S. Army expanded from 98,000 men in 1914 to over 3 million in 1919, only to drop to less than 138,000 during the 1920s and early 1930s.[6] American political distrust of militarism and standing armies meant that the cadre structure created a socially acceptable and cost-effective way to retain military skills during peacetime. This force structure led to a comparatively large number of officers relative to peacetime enlisted strengths, and a large emphasis on officer education because in case of wartime mobilization, temporary promotions would result in junior officers serving in senior positions.

A key element of the interwar American army system, which was especially salient in relations with China and victory in World War II, was an extensive officer education program. When asked to compare the U.S. Army before and after

World War I, Gen. Omar Bradley remarked that the greatest difference "was the school system."[7] Before World War I, the major elements of the U.S. Army school system had been established, with West Point conducting junior officer training, branch schools for infantry, artillery, and so forth, the Command and General Staff School (CGSS) at Fort Leavenworth conducting highly technical staff exercises, and the Army War College for senior officers studying the theoretical issues of war. Prior to World War I, these schools had been small and the quality of instruction poor, but after difficulties in conducting large-scale operations in France, the curriculum was modernized and the number of students increased. The Command and General Staff school trained only 432 students prior to World War I but during the 1920s and 1930s it operated at full capacity in spite of the small size of the contemporary army, graduating over 3,600 senior officers during the 1920s and 1930s.[8] In 1924 the Army Industrial College was established in Washington, D.C., to improve military understanding of budgets, procurement, civil-military relations, and other areas of expertise traditionally dominated by political appointees in the War Department.[9] In addition to internal schools, the Army also began sending officers to civilian institutions for graduate level degrees. The Harvard Business School was a popular choice, with over two hundred officers from the interwar Army completing the full two-year program.[10] The Army school system benefited from the extremely slow promotion of the period (many officers spent over fifteen years as lieutenants), so competition for school positions was extremely tough because it would help distinguish "fast track" officers.

In addition to conventional professional military education and civilian education in the United States, the U.S. Army prepared a small cadre of officers for foreign liaison duties. The Military Intelligence Division began a Chinese language training program in 1919, to prepare officers for assignments in the Peking Embassy.[11] Often assignment to the 15th Infantry Regiment in Tianjin followed military attaché duty, giving officers a period of five or six years of duty experience in China. Many of the officers selected for the language program and duty in the 15th Infantry Regiment, such as Stillwell, Hayden Boatner, and Frank Dorn, later went on to key positions in the wartime Sino-American military partnership.

A characteristic of the U.S. Army of the interwar period was an aversion to politics, both as a matter of professional ideology and for the institutional security of the Army. Practical difficulties in establishing legal residency where they were stationed prevented many officers from voting, but many seem to have felt that their duty required a sharp divide from political life, with many officers taking pride in not voting.[12] Remaining aloof from politics was also professionally responsible because it avoided providing ammunition to pacifists and populists who had attacked the American involvement in World War I and who fought any appearance of militarism. Army officers assigned to Washington, D.C., during the 1920s and 1930s wore civilian suits. Even Douglas MacArthur, during his time as chief of staff of the Army, wore civilian suits at nearly all official functions.[13]

A New Partnership

During the Japanese invasion of Manchuria in 1931, the Shanghai conflict between Japan and China in 1932, and the Japanese invasion of China in 1937, the American public had been supportive of China in general and Chiang Kai-shek in particular, but very little direct political or military support was provided by the United States government. Influential writers such as Pearl Buck, newspaper publisher Henry Luce, and political leaders like Henry Stimson sought to keep China in American hearts and minds, but the U.S. Army did not share this affinity. Intelligence reports, many of them written by Joseph Stillwell, American military attaché to China from 1935 to 1939, pointed out a wide variety of fundamental problems within the Chinese army in areas of command and control, unit training, and basic tactics.[14]

American public sympathies and an effective Chinese lobbying campaign eventually resulted in economic aid, beginning with two loans from the American Export-Import Bank in 1939, but no arms sales.[15] Only in 1940, after the inclusion of China in the list of countries covered by the Lend-Lease Act, did the United States begin large-scale arms transfers, with P-40 fighters and 2½-ton trucks being priority requests.[16]

In order to coordinate arms transfers, advise the Chinese on military training, and plan for future joint operations, the American Military Mission to China (AMMISCA) was formed in August 1941.[17] Led by Gen. John Magruder, AMMISCA established offices in China's wartime capital Chongqing and in Washington, D.C., as well as branches at major supply ports such as Rangoon. AMMISCA studies of the Chinese army expressed a clear pessimism about the utility of arms transfers to the Chinese army without systematic reform of the Chinese military structure. After three years of war and the destruction of the Nationalists' most capable forces, American observers found Chinese forces to be politically fractured, poorly trained, and tactically passive.[18]

After a brief survey of Chinese military units and practices in late 1941 and early 1942, AMMISCA produced a damning report on Chinese military practices. General Magruder was highly critical of the glowing praise of the Chinese military produced by the "China Lobby" and argued against providing more material support without increased supervision of the use of arms provided to China. He wrote, "It is a known fact that the Chinese are great believers in the world of make-believe, and they frequently shut their eyes to hard and unpleasant actualities, preferring rather to indulge their fancy in flattering but fictitious symbols, which they regard as more real than cold facts. . . . As instances of this deceptive symbolism, I may adduce many reports emanating from Chinese diplomatic sources abroad, referring to the marvelous achievements and abilities of the Chinese army."[19]

Following the Japanese attack on Pearl Harbor on 7 December 1941, American military leaders were skeptical of direct American military involvement with the Chinese army but political leaders, including President Franklin Roosevelt, desired a symbolic American presence in China. With no interest among senior American officers in being assigned to China, Gen. George Marshall nominated an old friend, Joseph Stilwell, for the still vaguely defined position of commander of American forces in the China-Burma-India theater. On paper, Stilwell's appointment seemed an ideal choice. During the 1920s and 1930s Stilwell served multiple tours in the 15th Infantry Regiment in Tianjin and was fluent in Chinese. Moreover, during his assignment as military attaché in Beijing, Stilwell had observed at firsthand Japanese military operations and the tremendous internal problems of the Chinese military.[20]

The American original operating concept was that military aid and "strategic coordination" would be sufficient to revitalize the Chinese army, worn down by four years of war, and allow it to take the offensive. Stilwell's authority was hindered by a highly ambiguous mission statement, which lacked clear objectives or metrics. War Department orders vaguely stated that Stilwell was to "increase the effectiveness of United States assistance to the Chinese government for the prosecution of the war and to assist in improving the combat efficiency of the Chinese Army."[21] Even more confusing was Stilwell's assignment as Chiang Kai-shek's *Allied* chief of staff while Gen. He Yingqin served as chief of staff of the regular Chinese army.[22]

Establishing the Template: Ramgarh Training Center and Liaison Officer, 1942-1944

From the very beginning of Stilwell's tenure, his personal goals of assisting and developing the Chinese army were not limited to the immediate wartime situation but looked ahead to a period after the war when China would need to assume a role as one of the "Four Policemen" of a new world order alongside the United

States, Soviet Union, and Great Britain. American ambitions for China to become a responsible great power in the world, based on a large competent military force, would be an enduring problem throughout the 1941–49 period, with long-term political ideals often taking priority over near-term military practicalities.

Stilwell clearly stated his objectives to his staff:

1. Long-Range Objective: A powerful independent China, with a modern well-organized Army, in a position to back up all legitimate demands, and with close ties of interests and friendship with the United States. (Under these conditions, peace in the Orient could be assured, and China would take the lead in the organization of an Asiatic League of China, Indo-China, Siam, Burma, and India.)
2. Immediate Objective: Re-organization, equipment, and training of the Chinese Army, including the Air Force. The 30-Division Plan can be adapted to the units of the Y-Force, concentrated in Yunnan, where they are accessible for training and supply.[23]

The Japanese seizure of Burma in the spring of 1942 disrupted Stilwell's grandiose vision of re-organizing the entirety of the Chinese army, cutting China's last road access to the outside world. With inadequate airlift capacity to supply forces within China, Stilwell proposed to train 100,000 Chinese troops at the Ramgarh camp in northeast India, using American methods. Chiang Kai-shek tentatively approved this plan on 27 April 1942, but troops did not arrive in strength until September.[24] This force, code-named the "X Force," was planned to encompass two complete Chinese armies, each with three divisions, in addition to special training for separate engineering, field artillery, and medical detachments.

While at Ramgarh, Chinese officers remained in administrative control over their men, but the United States and Great Britain provided all supplies and equipment. Chinese soldiers assigned to Ramgarh were designated the "Chinese Army in India" (CAI) with General Stilwell as commander. Subordinate to Stilwell were two of the most well educated and capable division commanders in the Chinese army: Sun Li-jen and Liao Yaoxiang. Both Sun and Liao personified a trend in Chinese officer promotions after 1941, with the rise of young officers who thrived in the American system displacing less adaptable, often older, Chinese officers. Sun Li-jen, in particular, would parlay his popularity with Americans and advanced military skills into a series of increasingly senior positions, culminating in his appointment in March 1950 as commander of the Army of the Republic of China.

The American instruction force at Ramgarh included over 250 American officers and 500 senior enlisted personnel for only two divisions of the KMT army, which enabled a large amount of close, hands-on instruction. The American training program included a wide range of instruction, ranging from bayonet and hand-grenade training to automotive maintenance and tank driving.[25] In addition to American instructors, American liaison personnel were directly attached to Chinese units. The direct "supervisor" (Chinese troops technically remained under Chinese command) of the CAI, Brig. Gen. Hayden Boatner, had received Chinese language training as an attaché at the Peking Embassy from 1930 through 1934, and had earned an MA degree in Chinese history at Harvard before the war, but was under no illusions about the difficulty of the military partnership.[26] In instructions to new liaison officers, Boatner commented, "You are taking up a very, very difficult assignment. . . . It will tax your initiative, ingenuity, tact, and spirit of cooperation to the utmost," and offered the practical advice to always think of situations from the point of view of their Chinese officer counterparts.[27]

With the Ramgarh training center firmly established by the fall of 1942, Stilwell sought to begin forming a second offensive force, based in China's southwestern Yunnan province, which would attack into Burma and link up with the units driving east from India. This force was designated the Chinese Expeditionary Army (CEA), code-named the "Y Force." While the Chinese Army in India was built through a military school system, the American role in the Y Force would be built around small groups of American liaison teams operating with Chinese units. Although the addition of American advisers allowed for better integration of American air support with Chinese ground operations, and provided specialized skills such as engineering elements to Chinese units, the Y Force failed to meet military needs or create a viable core with which to revitalize the Chinese military. The experience of the Y Force demonstrated the difficulties of Chinese army reform without solid logistical support, and highlighted the debilitating effects of China's convoluted domestic politics on military reform.

After months of wrangling over supply requests, Chinese troop contributions, and operational roles, the first U.S. instructors began arriving in Kunming in January 1943. The commander of the Y Force American training and supply program was Col. Frank Dorn, a longtime "China Hand" who had served as an attaché at the Peking Embassy and a confidant of Stilwell. However, Chinese troops remained under direct Chinese command at all times. In contrast to the Ramgarh program, which took almost eighteen months to make Chinese troops fully certified for combat operations, formal training for Y Force units was limited to brief, six-week courses designed to familiarize the Chinese with American methods but not fundamentally retrain them.[28]

The Y Force benefitted from the administrative and cultural familiarity gained by Americans and Chinese at Ramgarh, but practical details involved in establishing a large training program in China hindered the program. Unlike in India, where the Chinese had occupied preexisting military facilities at Ramgarh, the establishment of military schools near Kunming required building new facilities. Construction contracts provided an opportunity for corruption in the form of kickbacks paid to Chinese officers by local contractors, and builders frequently used poor quality materials, pocketing any savings. In poor, rural areas imported electric power generators also proved tempting to Chinese residents, and American reports related numerous occasions of the power grid going down because of attempts by local Chinese to tap into overhead wires.[29]

Among the Chinese students, prolonged malnutrition, poor levels of education, and inadequate numbers of students limited the effectiveness of early training classes. Improving the quantity of meals, increasing the number of interpreters, and altering the curriculum overcame many of these issues, but without a senior Chinese political or military patron the military school program remained underutilized. Stilwell made attendance of U.S. Army–run schools a requirement for Chinese officers prior to their units receiving Lend-Lease supplies, but enthusiasm was often lacking.[30] Col. Walter Wood, a senior U.S. liaison officer, wrote disparagingly, "The sad thing was that it did not teach. No one fired on the ranges. No one maneuvered on the training areas. Haphazard lectures, or to be more accurate, speeches were the order of the day. . . . The feeling seemed to be that, so long as the opening ceremony went well, the student body remained in attendance and the graduation ceremony and banquet went smoothly, then the school was a success."[31]

The experience of many American liaison teams was similarly dispiriting, with American officers put in the ambiguous position of supporting Chinese officers but having no authority to lead Chinese soldiers even in cases of battlefield expediency. Liaison officers often withheld American supplies in order to influence Chinese officers, but withholding supplies could lead to tensions between Chinese and American officers. Liaison officer Frank Lilley wrote that in his Chinese unit, "the Chinese battalion commander is poor [in quality]—he runs around in his jeep with singsong girls and cares nothing about training," to which he could only respond by cutting off the supply of gasoline to curtail his joy riding.[32]

Only after the Cairo Conference in November 1943 did Chiang fully support developing the Y Force and assent to its use in attacking Burma. By February 1944, the Y Force had expanded to fifteen divisions spread over two group armies. Although significantly under strength with only 72,000 men assigned to it, the Y Force, the Chinese Expeditionary Army, was the largest and best-trained offensive force in China. In addition to infantry and artillery schools, American weapons had been laboriously air lifted over the Himalayas. Large numbers of sub-machine guns, rocket launchers, mortars, and small howitzers, for offensive operations in mountainous terrain, were transferred to the Chinese troops.[33]

On 12 April 1944, the Y Force began attacking into Burma, attempting to link up with the Chinese Army in India. American liaison forces remained with Chinese troops during combat operations to advise, assist in supply operations, and coordinate air force support. Increasing numbers of Americans in the China theater allowed for the expansion of U.S. liaison units down to the regimental level, with teams of officers ranging from six to twenty assigned to regimental units, depending on mission requirements. American portable surgical units and field hospitals supplemented the rudimentary Chinese army medical services.[34] American assessments of the Y Force effectiveness were mixed, with praise for the conduct of junior officers and soldiers but sharp criticism of the senior officers.[35]

Wedemeyer and the Shift to a "Big Army" Program

By the spring of 1944, General Stilwell and the fully retrained, American-equipped Chinese Army in India (X Force) and the Chinese Expeditionary Army (Y Force) in Yunnan province were both engaged in offensive operations in northern Burma. Although the basic framework and crucial procedures for assistance and advising had been established, progress in changing the performance of the overwhelming majority of China's 300-division army had been minimal. The excellent performance of the Chinese Army in India and the less successful Y Force experience still encompassed less than 200,000 men from a total Chinese army strength of roughly 2 million soldiers.[36]

In April 1944, after almost two years of near stasis in its military operations in China, the Japanese army began a series of large-scale offensives designed to systematically cripple Chinese military capability. Operation Ichi-Go (yihao zuozhan) targeted key rail links, vital food producing areas, and airfields used by the American 14th Air Force to bomb Japan. Further Japanese attacks in East China during the summer and fall of 1944 alerted Chinese leaders to their military weakness, and only through massively increased logistical support—provided by streamlined air transport over the Hump, the colloquial term for the eastern end of the Himalayan mountains, and the reopening of road communications by the retaking of the Burma Road—was the Japanese offensive blunted.

The political fallout from the disastrous Chinese military performance in Ichi-Go resulted in increased pressure on Chiang Kai-shek, from previously supportive American leaders and from inside the Chinese military command, to undertake military reforms based on American guidance.[37] General Stilwell, whose discussions with Chiang were becoming increasingly acrimonious, directly applied the growing American pressure on Chiang. American political and military leaders, including President Roosevelt, demanded that Chiang make Stilwell his chief of staff and give him authority over the Chinese army.[38] Chiang's rebuttal conceded the need for a direct American presence as his chief of the General Staff, but Chiang stated that he would accept any American general except Stilwell. Rumors that China might sign a separate peace with Japan led President Roosevelt to accept Chiang's terms and recall Stillwell.

Stilwell's replacement, Gen. Albert Wedemeyer, perceived his role in China as an organizer and coordinator rather than as a battlefield leader, skills he had developed as one of the key architects of American strategic planning, helping prepare for a ground campaign in Europe during the first two years of the war.[39] Wedemeyer's experience and talent for organizational planning, as well as the successful conclusion of the north Burma campaign, resulted in increased supplies of American equipment for China, allowing for the creation of an integrated plan to reform the Chinese army for the first time. Wedemeyer's program for the Chinese army, code-named "Alpha," envisioned a gradual shift from defensive to offensive operations in Southern China, with the end goal being the taking of a port on the Chinese coast (Operation Carbonado), in September or October 1945.[40]

The backbone of the Alpha Plan was the creation of thirty-nine combat divisions of the Chinese army. The organizational and administrative framework for the planned Alpha divisions was based on the experience of the Chinese Army in India. Compared to a regular Chinese division with roughly 2,400 men, an Alpha division would have over 6,100 personnel assigned to it, with a regular system of replacements for combat losses.[41] All Alpha divisions were classified as infantry formations, although independent armor and motorized regiments would be assigned to operate with divisions, to increase their mobility and firepower.

Wedemeyer identified the biggest problem to Chinese army reforms to be a lack of trained, competent officers. Wedemeyer wrote that Chinese officers appeared "incapable, inept, untrained, petty . . . altogether inefficient."[42] One element of improving the performance of Chinese officers was the integration of patchwork Chinese training centers into a comprehensive military school system. The newly formed Chinese Training Command (CTC) was responsible for all schools from basic training to General Officer refresher courses. Headquartered in Kunming, the CTC included training centers for the functional areas of infantry, artillery, automotive, and ordnance specialists, an introductory officer course for lieutenants and captains, and a command and general staff course for senior officers.[43] The combined effect of Wedemeyer's reforms was to unify and rationalize the ad hoc, fragmented training centers established by Stilwell. *Time* magazine accurately noted in 1945 that "[t]hese institutions [training schools] were conceived by General Stilwell and were in existence when Wedemeyer arrived. But Wedemeyer welded them into a cohesive whole."[44]

The largest school was the Field Artillery Training Center, which at its peak utilized over one thousand American personnel training up to ten thousand Chinese at any one time.[45] Lessons learned in the Burma campaign had shown that Chinese commanders frequently used artillery to make up for tactical deficiencies in their units by reducing bunkers and fortifications through lengthy barrages rather than direct attacks. A key element of the Alpha training was a shift to larger 105-mm howitzers, drawn by trucks and used for indirect (non–line-of-sight) firing. This made the Alpha division formations much more powerful in terms of firepower, but necessitated increased American logistical support and training for support units.

The most prestigious of the new training centers was the Command and General Staff School, which provided a three-month course for senior officers. Nicknamed "Little Leavenworth" by American instructors, the program was a direct copy of the U.S. Army Command and General Staff School at Fort Leavenworth, Kansas, but of shorter duration.[46] The school program focused on the leadership of units through staff exercises rather than directly leading combat operations, with the majority of the instruction time being concerned with reports, record keeping, and order formats.[47]

In addition to regular army schools, each Alpha division, with the exception of units from the Chinese Army in India, was designated to go through two thirteen-week training programs as a unit. Chinese officers who had been through the U.S. Army school system led these unit-training programs, with the assistance of the U.S. liaison officers attached to each division. The focus of the initial thirteen-week program was weapons training, because many of the men had no experience with the new American weapons and insufficient training in basic soldier skills like rifle marksmanship. American adviser Col. F. W. Boye noted, "A part of the training time was employed in weapon training. The expenditure of target ammunition was pleasing and amazing to the Chinese; until that time each soldier had been limited to firing three rounds with the weapon with which he was armed."[48] In the second thirteen-week training cycle, units would focus on tactical and operational training, with a variety of exercises in offensive operations.[49] By the beginning of August 1945, all Alpha divisions had started at least the first thirteen-week, program with roughly half completing it prior to the Japanese surrender.[50]

For highly specialized training such as aircraft operations, radar-directed antiaircraft artillery, complex bridging operations, and so forth, Chinese officers were sent to American schools in the United States. By V-J day there were approximately 2,300 Chinese military officers participating in training in the United States, with over 1,200 additional personnel en route.[51] The majority of Chinese personnel sent to the United States were aircraft pilots and crew, with nearly 900 pilots and 250 bombardiers being trained alongside U.S. Army Air Force crews.[52]

In conjunction with a reformed school system, Wedemeyer initiated a massively expanded liaison program under the designation Chinese Combat Command (CCC). In contrast to the small observation teams that had been in China with the Y Force prior to 1944, the new liaison effort planned to encompass over four thousand Americans.[53] Considering that Wedemeyer had only 5,549 troops directly under his command in November 1944, the liaison effort represented both a major expansion in the American personnel assigned to the China theater and the largest portion of American troop strength.[54] Each Alpha division included roughly ten American officers and twenty to thirty enlisted men, with additional air-ground liaison teams attached to Chinese units during combat situations.[55] U.S. advisory teams were specifically instructed not to attempt to take command in any way, and the preferred method of dealing with units that failed to address advisory concerns was through reporting failures to higher headquarters and the withdrawal of American support from noncooperative units. Beginning in early 1945, the U.S. liaison teams produced a steady stream of accurate, timely information on the strengths, weaknesses, and operations of Chinese army units. Each adviser submitted a note card for his assigned unit, keeping a log of key events and grading Chinese performance.

U.S. Army liaison teams were the subject of a significant amount of reporting from American magazines and newspapers, who promoted them as an example of the shared wartime effort. Glowing press reports could not disguise the fact that liaison duty was gritty, exhausting work, which put a great deal of stress on American personnel. *Time* magazine described the teams:

> The smallest knots are air liaison teams, artillery and regimental liaison units. They makeshift as they can. They consist of an officer, one or two enlisted men, a Chinese interpreter and a Chinese cook. This is the nervous system by which control runs up to American headquarters in Kunming and Chungking, 700 or 800 miles away. Each tiny cell of it consists of four or five American boys sitting in a tent or ruined farmhouse, slapping at mosquitoes, coding and decoding messages, trudging through paddies, piling up dirty tin cans beside their tents, living in stinking clothes and incessant squalor.[56]

The stress of combat operations and cultural isolation led to a degree of tension in the Sino-American relationship, which sometimes found expression in heavy drinking and low morale among Americans. Among the major complaints by American personnel were the personal habits of the Chinese, especially Chinese peasants, who often spit and defecated in public view, practices that most Americans considered both repugnant and unhygienic. Another substantive problem was the endemic corruption of the Nationalist regime. State Department attaché Edward Rice wrote:

> Of the substantial number of servicemen with whom I have come in contact, I have found almost all to be adversely and often bitterly critical of China and the Chinese and somewhat bewildered that what they consider to be the true facts about China are not, or in the past were not, available to the American public. Typical American officers and men have mentioned to me such things as follow: seeing few planes on Chinese airfields but many in warehouses near Chengtu; buying from the wife of a Chinese official gasoline assumed by the serviceman to have come to China under lend-lease; and several instances of catching Chinese in circumstances such as to indicate beyond reasonable doubt that they were engaged in espionage on behalf of the Japanese and turning them over to Chinese officials only to have the latter quickly release the culprits.[57]

Assignment to China offered a wide range of temptations to Americans: easy access to alcohol for those under twenty-one (the legal drinking age in most of the United States), widespread prostitution, and a favorable currency exchange rate, which made even lower enlisted soldiers comparatively wealthy. This was not a new problem; when the U.S. 15th Infantry Regiment had been stationed in China before the war it had led the U.S. Army in both rates of alcoholism and venereal disease.[58] Chinese soldiers working with Americans commented that, "For Americans, there was no fun without alcohol," and complained that U.S. personnel would sometimes trade military supplies for alcohol.[59] Crimes against inebriated U.S. personnel were common, although most were robberies rather than violent activities.[60]

Due to rising numbers of such incidents, General Boatner, commander of the Chinese Combat Command, ordered that all Americans under his authority had to attend command briefings on their role in China as "salesmen of American standards of conduct."[61] Boatner also began a program of cultural education, especially language training, designed to eliminate some of the more glaring lapses. His orders state that "it is especially desired that stress be laid upon acquainting the officers and enlisted men of your command with China, the Chinese people and Chinese customs. Elementary and advanced classes in the Chinese language should be instituted, making use of both language officers and interpreters."[62] While never a primary obstacle, the constant frictions highlight the difficulties that military forces, even those engaged in a common effort, frequently encounter.

In spite of isolated cultural difficulties and the lingering problems of coordinating two sharply different military systems, the overall result by 1945 was generally positive, and the first reaction of many observers on the different look and military bearing of American-trained Chinese soldiers was surprise and delight. American consul general William R. Langdon wrote of a recent public ceremony, "These men were from Ramgarh, India, (American-trained) units, most of them veterans of the North Burma campaigns. Sturdy, cleancut, confident, and jaunty, and dressed in khaki woolens and British-type helmets, they looked as unlike their local brothers in Chinese uniform as men of a different race. It did not seem possible that food, good care and training could work such a physical and psychological transformation on ordinary Chinese peasant soldier material."[63] *Time* magazine was similarly glowing in its portrayal of the Alpha divisions during the last months of the war. A report from July 1945 describing the "New" Chinese Army noted:

> On our way back we saw one of the divisions of the new army marching down the road. They had flesh on their biceps, meat on their legs. On their shoulders they carried American Enfield rifles marked: "USA 1917." Their pack bearers had huge spools of telephone wire slung on bamboo staves across their shoulders. When the infantry in this division

goes forward, it will need no runner to carry back reports; it will use American telephones to call the artillery in from the very point of attack, and American howitzers directed by an American officer will bring support down before them at the right place at precisely the right time.[64]

At the end of the war the model of a unified military school system, American liaison teams, and sustained logistical support had accomplished much of the initial goal of reforming the Chinese army and making it more combat effective. Unfortunately for American and Chinese military planners, these efforts relied on political will in Washington, which, after the Japanese surrender, rapidly evaporated.

Paths Not Taken: Alternatives to a National Army

From the very beginning of the American Military Mission to China in 1941, throughout General Stilwell's command and into General Wedemeyer's term, there was a constant American focus on building a "national" army. This emphasis illustrates a clear desire for a large army to attack or at least tie down the Japanese army but also a political desire for China to play a role as a regional power, one of FDR's "Four Policemen."

The alternative to building up a national Chinese army under Nationalist control was the support of Chinese military leaders with a more localized and independent political standing. The decentralized government, military, and political structure in China provided opportunities for American military officers to favor specific Chinese commanders with preferential access to supplies, training, and air support. Systematically encouraging local forces to attack the Japanese would likely have resulted in an intensification of combat operations in a far shorter time span than training entire new divisions. However, sponsoring localized forces would have made coordination of larger offensives difficult.

The U.S. Navy took the localized approach through its partnership with the Nationalist Secret Service, the feared Juntong, led by the notorious Shanghai gangster turned spymaster Dai Li. Capt. Milton Miles collaborated with Dai to form the Sino-American Cooperative Organization (SACO, Zhongmei tezhong jishu hezuosuo), which was organized to provide intelligence, conduct guerilla operations, and sabotage in Japanese-occupied areas. Throughout the course of the war, SACO was continually attacked by U.S. Army officers as a diversion of resources and an ill-advised partnership with the worst elements of the Nationalist government. Stilwell, in particular, was sharply critical of Miles for supporting the Juntong, which he referred to as equal to the Gestapo.[65]

The most obvious potential subject of this regional approach was Gen. Xue Yue, commander of the 9th Military Region, which encompassed most of Hunan and Guangdong. Xue had a strong regional base in South China, being originally from Guangdong and spending most of his military career in the area. Although Xue had studied in the first graduating class at the Whampoa Academy, and had proven himself during both the Northern Expedition and anti-Communist campaigns of the 1930s, he was regarded as insufficiently loyal to Chiang personally. Xue had been appointed to command the 9th Military Region in 1937, had personally appointed the majority of his officers, and operated with little to no oversight by the Nationalist government in Chongqing. Faced with wartime problems of recruitment and logistical support, Xue had also appointed trusted military officers to ostensibly civilian administrative positions within his war zone.

During the summer of 1944, Japan's Ichi-Go offensive cut into Xue Yue's 9th War Zone and directly threatened the American bases in the area. Xue had come to a tacit understanding with Gen. Claire Lee Chennault, and received token material and air support when needed in return for protecting the bases. During Ichi-Go, Chennault officially requested that Xue receive American arms and equipment, but Stilwell denied his requests. Chennault repeated his requests after Wedemeyer had assumed command, but the result was the same. All American military support would go through the Nationalist government in Chongqing.[66]

In the spring of 1945, as American arms and personnel flooded into China, several American officers, who felt that Nationalist corruption, slow progress in training programs, and a lack of political will by Chiang Kai-shek were hindering the war effort, again argued to supply Xue Ye directly. In a top-secret memorandum, an Army observer team recommended that Xue be provided with American liaison teams, that weapons be air lifted to his forces, and that medical support be established in his units. The clear feeling expressed in the report was that Xue was a likeminded, patriotic young officer, eager to fight the Japanese, but poorly supported by Chiang. The report stated, "I am convinced that Hsieh Yoh [Xue Yue] is eager to undertake limited objective attacks to the south or west, provided he is furnished with the means."[67]

In contrast with many American reports that highlighted Nationalist corruption and military passivity, Xue was presented in a highly favorable light. The report stated that, "According to all Americans who have served with him, Gen. Hsieh Yoh [Xue Yue] is a competent, tactically sound, energetic Commander. He is aggressive, progressive and sold on American methods of training."[68]

These reports went unanswered by American headquarters in China and no significant liaison teams, instructors, or weapons transfers took place. The proposal to support local forces cut against the cultural and political norms of the successive American commanders in the region, who likely perceived military leaders such as Xue as legacies of China's warlord past, even if they were nominally heads of Nationalist forces. The political costs of supporting local forces would likely have also made supporting Xue the prelude to a major loss of influence with Chiang Kai-shek.

Sun Li-jen: Rise to Fame

In December 1941, after the destruction of the American fleet in Pearl Harbor, the Japanese moved against Dutch and British possessions in Indonesia, Malaysia, and ultimately Burma. Japanese goals in Burma were initially confined to occupying the vital port of Rangoon, where Chinese supplies were landed and stored before transport by rail to Lashio and ultimately by truck over the border to Kunming. After a relatively easy occupation of Rangoon, the weakness of Allied forces in Burma and further Japanese reinforcements allowed for a Japanese drive northward into central Burma.

To stop the Japanese offensive, which threatened to cut off China's last overland supply route, three Chinese armies and three independent divisions, a total force of roughly 100,000 men, were dispatched into northern Burma in February 1942, to aid the British defense. The severe manpower problems confronting China after four years of war and the quick pace of the Japanese advance meant that the Chinese Expeditionary Force in Burma (Zhongguo yuanzhengjun) contained a random assortment of Chinese divisions. A last-minute addition to the Expeditionary Force was the recently created 38th Division, which grouped all of the anti-smuggling forces into one unit with command given to Sun Li-jen.

The 38th Division had been one of the last Chinese units to enter Burma, and its initial deployment was near the vital transportation junction and oil-producing region of Yenangyaung. On 16 April a force of seven thousand British soldiers and a large number of civilian refugees were cut off in Yenangyaung after the Japanese seized the roads to the north and south. The commander of the Chinese Expeditionary Force, Luo Zhuoying, denied British appeals for the nearby 38th Division to attack and open a line of retreat due to a lack of artillery. Sun Li-jen took personal command of one regiment and attacked the Japanese position with the support of a British armored brigade.[69] By 19 April, the relief column had reached the British forces, evacuated them north, and sabotaged the oil refineries.

The battle at Yenangyaung was one of the few bright spots in an overall disastrous Allied campaign in Burma. In the Chinese press, the victory was hailed as a great victory (ren an guang dajie) and Sun was hailed as a hero. Allied commanders noted Sun's tactical performance, close coordination with the British, and willingness to interpret his orders without relying on a superior officer's orders. During the chaotic Allied retreat into India, British general William Slim interacted frequently with Sun and shared the high praise of the American officers. Slim wrote of Sun, "He was alert, energetic, and direct. Later I found him a good tactician, cool in action, very aggressively minded, and, in my dealings with him, completely straightforward. In addition, he had a great advantage that he spoke good English with a slight American accent, having, as he was rightly proud to tell, been educated at the Virginia Military Institute. The Institute could be proud of Sun; he would have been a good commander in any army."[70] Based largely on Slim's account of the battle of Yenangyaung, Sun was made a Commander of the Order of the British Empire (CBE) by King George VI.

Sun's battlefield performance was an isolated success in an overall failure by the Allies to contain the Japanese offensives during the spring of 1942. By late April, Allied forces were retreating into India, losing much of their equipment and suffering heavy losses due to inadequate food, disease, and Japanese attacks. Sun argued that because of more difficult terrain, lack of logistical support, and poor road networks along the Burma-China border, it would be better to withdraw along with the main body of Allied personnel into India, rather than withdraw back to China's Yunnan province. In spite of clear opposition to the plan by the senior Chinese general, Du Yuming, Sun and two other division commanders led their forces into India, where they regrouped and were supplied by British and American support units. The majority of the twelve-division Chinese force attempted to return to China but inadequate supplies, hostile tribes along the border, and continual Japanese attacks decimated the column, leading to the deaths of an estimated 50,000 Chinese troops.

The Chinese forces that had made it to India in late May and early June 1942 were redesignated the Chinese Army in India (CAI, zhuyinjun) and assigned to Ramgarh for retraining and reequipping. American personnel ran the Ramgarh training center, with funding provided by the British. Most of the classes consisted of basic soldier skills, leaving little for Chinese officers to do. General Slim remarked that, for the Chinese commanders, leaving the training to the Americans was a tremendous loss of prestige or "face." Slim noted that "Sun, I think, especially felt this, but when I advised him to make the best of it and reap the benefit later, he was too sensible not to agree."⁷¹ During the training period, Sun remained the commander of the 38th Division. Then, following the removal of Luo Zhuoying from overall command of the CAI due to his refusal to allow for a direct distribution of pay to his men, a move that would have eliminated his ability to skim a percentage for himself, Sun was designated the senior Chinese officer in India and reported directly to Gen. Joseph Stilwell.

Sun and his troops spent over a year in Ramgarh, training with a complete set of American equipment, integrating replacement troops, and developing an integrated Sino-American command structure, with American advisers and technical troops attached to Chinese units. By October 1943, Sun was in command of 30,000 Chinese troops and had been able to select, train, and mentor a force of over 2,500 officers.⁷² The overall strategic plan for an offensive in Burma called for Sun to drive south from India, down the Hukawng Valley to reach the important road junction at Myitkyina. In spite of the extensive training and close coordination between Chinese and American forces the offensive, which started on 30 October 1943, produced no breakthrough of Japanese lines. The mountainous terrain, poor artillery support, and tough Japanese resistance slowed the advance to a crawl. American commanders were critical of Sun's performance and perceived his slow maneuvering to be overly cautious.⁷³

As the campaign progressed from the fall of 1943 into the spring of 1944, a pattern emerged, with Sun's Chinese forces moving forward to engage and fix the Japanese in their defenses while American light infantry forces moved through the jungle to flank the Japanese positions and cut their supply lines. Sun's maneuvers were slow and deliberate, with American artillery and close air support used in conjunction with Chinese ground attacks. By early June, Sun's 38th Division and was advancing on Myitkyina, but the Japanese had withdrawn behind World War I–style trenches and prepared positions, which Chinese frontal assaults proved unable to overcome. A two-month blockade of the Japanese positions, American artillery, and heavy bombing eventually degraded the Japanese force but almost one thousand Chinese were killed and three thousand wounded by the time Myitkyina was taken on 3 August.⁷⁴

The heavy losses suffered by the 38th Division in the Myitkyina campaign required extensive recovery and reintegration back in India. Replacement personnel arrived from China, but the lengthy retraining process required for raw Chinese recruits meant the 38th Division was largely inactive from mid-1944 through the end of the war. Sun was promoted to deputy commander of the New 1st Army, a formation that was organized around the New 38th Division but included follow-on units that had flown from China to India to be trained at Ramgarh during the long Myitkyina campaign and were now combat ready.

In the fall of 1944, Sun was the primary Chinese ground force commander in North Burma, coordinating the drive south from Myitkyina to open a land route into China. The New Sixth Army under Liao Yaoxiang conducted most of the fighting. A major responsibility was coordinating American and CAI efforts with a Chinese offensive from Yunnan moving southwest. Commanded by Wei Lihuang, this new Chinese Expeditionary Army had received some training and new equipment from American advisers. With a marked superiority in manpower, air support, and artillery, the combined Allied forces slowly drove the Japanese south until, eventually, the two fronts met at Hsipaw on 21 January 1945, with the first truck convoy reaching Kunming on 4 February.

Sun's position and prestige was not affected by the contentious recall of General Stilwell on 19 October 1944. Sun had benefitted from Stilwell's removal of Luo Zhuoying as the senior Chinese commander in India, but Stilwell had criticized a reluctance on Sun's part to attack as aggressively as Stilwell wanted during the Myitkyina campaign. Nevertheless, one day after his recall, Stilwell wrote a glowing farewell to Sun that noted his work over the past two years while encouraging him to complete the transformation of the Chinese army. Stilwell wrote, "You have amply demonstrated the bravery and ability of the Chinese Army, and I am very proud to have had a small part in it. . . . You have laid the foundation for a new and efficient national force, and with this example, China can go on and build up an Army that will make her free and strong."[75]

Generalissimo Chiang Kai-shek lectures at an
officers' training camp during the war against Japan, ca. 1937–43.
Library of Congress, Prints and Photographs Division, Washington, D.C., LC-USZ62-126112.

Opposite, top
Army officers in the late Qing Dynasty, early twentieth century.
*Bain Collection, Library of Congress, Prints and Photographs Division,
Washington, D.C., LC-DIG-ggbain-08618.*

Opposite, bottom
Group photograph of senior officers in the 3rd Division, Qing Imperial Army,
16 October 1911. Notables include Chang Tso Lin (*seated, far left*), and
American officer William "Billy" Mitchell (*seated, second from right*).
Library of Congress, Prints and Photographs Division, Washington, D.C., LC-USZ62-32966.

U.S. instructor with Chinese mortar regiment at
Ramgarh Training Center, India, June 1944.
United States National Archives and Records Administration.

U.S. Army instructors conducting machine-gun training for Chinese troops,
Ramgarh Training Center, Bihar, India, 16 December 1943.
United States National Archives and Records Administration.

Lt. Gen. Joseph W. Stilwell inspecting Chinese troops in India, accompanied by Gen. Sun Li-jen (*far left*) and Gen. Lo Cho-ying.
Library of Congress, Prints and Photographs Division, Washington, D.C., LC-DIG-ds-03107.

Generalissimo and Madame Chiang Kai-shek and Lt. Gen. Joseph W. Stilwell, Commanding General, China Expeditionary Forces.
United States National Archives and Records Administration.

Garden party at Dumbarton Oaks, Washington, D.C., 6 September 1942. Lieutenant Commander Y. C. Yang chats with officers from Norway and the Netherlands.
Library of Congress, Prints and Photographs Division, Washington, D.C., LC-USE6-D-010383.

Opposite, top
Gen. Sun Li-jen on the front lines in Burma, 25 December 1943.
Image courtesy CriticalPast.

Opposite, bottom
Gen. Hsiung Shih-fei of the Republic of China Army, visiting Gen. George Marshall in Washington, D.C., December 1942.
Library of Congress, Prints and Photographs Division, Washington, D.C., LC-USW33-000785-ZC.

Chiang Kai-shek meets with Gen. Albert C. Wedemeyer, 1945.
Image courtesy CriticalPast.

Maj. Gen. William Chase, ca. 1945.
Image courtesy CriticalPast.

Ambassador Karl Rankin in Taiwan, 1953.
Government Information Office, Executive Yuan, Republic of China.
Image from the author's collection.

Troops of the Republic of China Army parade through Taipei, 1955.
Image courtesy CriticalPast.

4

A National Army for China, 1945-1949

The abrupt end to World War II was a surprise and a relief to Chinese and American military officers, but it also disrupted the planned development of the Chinese army into a mobile, firepower-oriented force. During the 1945–49 period, the Sino-American military partnership continued to influence the development of Chinese military identity but to a much lesser extent than during the 1942–45 period.

Within the KMT army, military officers struggled to adapt to a new political climate that led to the development of the Republic of China Constitution of 1947, which stipulated that the KMT Army would become a national "Chinese army." From 1945 to 1949, Chinese military officers in key cultural nodes, such as educational centers and military journals, strongly pushed the idea of a professional military focused on interstate conflict and based on mobile warfare. United States military cooperation during this period stalled due to State Department pressure, highlighting the high degree of active agency among Chinese military officers even without U.S. support. The military identity developed by Chinese officers during this period also displays their concern to adopt global military norms, develop a Chinese military comparable to other world powers, and present a professional, apolitical image to the Chinese public. These inclinations are indicative of normative isomorphism, and show that a desire for social, international, and professional status was a primary motivator of officer behavior.

The State Department and a Stalled Sino-American Military Partnership

In August 1945, the basic framework of Operation Carbonado, which called for a force of American-trained Chinese Alpha divisions to attack and open a seaport in southern China, was still being worked out when Japan surrendered.

The U.S. response to the Japanese surrender was the immediate suspension of all training, liaison, and advising activities in China. A presidential directive dated 11 August 1945 specifically "precludes any assistance except that required to support the reoccupation mission, and therefore does away with any program which, as a program, is designed only to strengthen the Chinese Army."[1] Driven by the political imperative to bring American forces home as quickly as possible, only American logistics and supply efforts continued to function. Throughout the 1945–49 period, the effective model of military assistance and advising developed by American and Chinese officers from 1942 to 1945 was neglected in favor of political strategies advocated from the U.S. State Department. Although this slow process of bureaucratic maneuvering limited American military support to China during 1945–49, the eventual consensus decision to create a military advisory group, focused on introducing American equipment and training techniques, became the template for numerous Cold War partnerships.

Two weeks after the Japanese surrender, the American ambassador to China, Patrick Hurley, notified President Harry Truman that Chiang Kai-shek had requested plans for a peacetime American military advisory board, with General Wedemeyer specifically requested as the head of the mission.[2] The proposed mission would encompass air, ground, and naval forces in the areas of unit training, logistical support, organizational reforms, and military education for the Chinese military over a period of five years. Hurley was enthusiastic about the proposal, which was the realization of wartime plans: "The Generalissimo states categorically that he desires to adopt American equipment, tactics, [and] techniques as well as organization throughout [the] Chinese Army."[3] Chinese initiatives by both Chiang Kai-shek in Chongqing and T. V. Soong, the Chinese ambassador in Washington, sought a massive U.S. presence in China with the assignment of thousands of American adviser officers and equipment for over one hundred divisions. From the Chinese perspective, getting American agreement for sustained advising and equipment transfers would tie the United States government closely to the Nationalist position, with obvious political benefits for Chiang. The initial Chinese request was for a staggering 120 divisions' worth of arms and equipment, in addition to a sizable air force.[4] Moreover, Chiang requested that active-duty American generals be assigned as chiefs of staff to the three proposed postwar military regions, a necessary move in terms of integrating American logistical support but which would have made American military officers complicit in Nationalist military operations.[5]

The dramatic collapse of the Japanese empire and the abrupt halt of American support for the Chinese army left a large gap in the training program of the latter, with different units at varying degrees of completion. Chinese and American military officers in China were supportive of a continued Sino-American military relationship until the Alpha Plan objective of training thirty-nine divisions was completed. In early September, messages from U.S. Headquarters in China argued that "it is our belief that Americans should participate as strongly as possible in assisting the Chinese [military] effort . . . stated bluntly we are today on the ground floor and should not lose [an] existing favorable opportunity to insure full American participation . . . other countries have already made overtures to the Chinese government in this connection."[6] The desire of American military officers to continue that partnership was shared by Chinese officers, who had formed a strongly favorable impression of American organizational abilities and military structure. One Chinese general remarked, "We saw the American system win the war. . . . Any system which won the war must be a good system."[7]

By early October 1945, the broad outlines of the advisory group were being formed, to consist of American officers stationed at Chinese military schools and within Chinese units. The proposed mission of the group was to form "a well-trained and well equipped Chinese national (non-political) army."[8] This repeated emphasis on creating a nonpolitical army, and restricting the American role to a purely training capacity at military schools, with no liaison officer system, was strongly influenced by the State Department, which felt that an overt presence by American military advisers would threaten U.S.–USSR relations. Moreover, the State Department was concerned that "[i]n granting any military assistance to China we should therefore exercise care to give no basis for a suspicion that we are creating a de facto colonial army in China under our official aegis."[9]

Although the War Department was advised of State Department concerns about an overtly close working relationship between the two military forces, the planned Advisory Group was very large in scope, including over one thousand officers and almost three thousand enlisted men.[10] The War Department plan entailed not only a robust Chinese army school system, with Americans directly teaching classes, but also a liaison system of appointing Americans to headquarters units in the field.[11] Although the wartime structure had been an effective model, ongoing clashes between Nationalist and Communist Chinese forces in the fall of 1945 meant that assigning Americans to field forces raised the potential of involving Americans in the combat operations of a Chinese civil war.

The State Department response to the proposed military mission was direct and highly critical, attacking the military conception of the proposed Advisory Group and calling into question its background assumptions about supporting

Chiang's Nationalist government. The director of the Office of Far Eastern Affairs for the State Department, John Carter Vincent, wrote:

> It has been made clear to China on many occasions that we do not intend that military assistance and advice shall be used in support of an administration not in conformity with the general policies of the United States, or in support of fratricidal warfare, or as a threat of aggression. We should have reasonable assurances that an Advisory Group of the size and character proposed would in fact encourage the development of a unified and democratic China . . . if the [Advisory] Group serves simply to encourage Chiang to seek a settlement of his difficulties by means of force and if maintenance of unity in China were to become dependent upon American military assistance in the form of material and advice, we would find ourselves in an unenviable, and perhaps untenable, position.[12]

Secretary of State James F. Byrnes strongly supported Vincent's position and argued that the large-scale War Department proposal "might be construed as a projection of U.S. military power onto the Asiatic continent rather than simply aid to China in modernizing its Army."[13]

The State Department position in favor of a "light footprint" U.S. military presence in China won the bureaucratic battle in Washington, and in December 1945 a new directive was sent to Wedemeyer (who remained the commanding general of the China theater), which neglected to mention any training or advisory effort. Instead, the directive stated that the priority of the U.S. military forces in China was the relocation of Japanese nationals back to the Japanese islands.[14] In early February 1946, the War Department withdrew its plan for a 4,500-plus personnel Advisory Group and proposed a stripped-down initial authorization of only 750 Army personnel.[15] Furthermore, the mission statement given to the advisory group was extremely constrained, focusing on international obligations for peaceful military development rather than assistance with specific Chinese military needs. The bland official mission statement of the advisory group stated that they were to "assist and advise the Chinese Government in the development of modern armed forces for the fulfillment of those obligations which may devolve upon China under her international agreements, including the United Nations Organization, for the establishment of adequate control over the liberated areas in China, including Manchuria and Formosa, and for the maintenance of internal peace and security."[16]

While the American foreign policy bureaucracy had been haggling over the organizational structure of the American advisory group, the Chinese had relocated and expanded the military training centers established by the U.S. Army during 1943–45. The Chinese school network was an exact copy of the American officer training system, with branch schools at the junior office grades, command and staff training at the field grade level, and specialized courses in strategy for general officers. Junior officer education was rapidly developed, and new lieutenants were trained in a comprehensive network of branch qualification schools including infantry, field artillery, cavalry, quartermaster, signal, engineer, and adjutant general.[17] These branch officer-training centers were based on American course schedules, training activities, and equipment, and in many cases the training manuals were direct translations of American materials. Compared to the wartime training programs, these schools were massive in size. The infantry school at one time supported 500 officers, military police 200, and artillery 120, and so forth. In total, the officer branch school program was capable of producing over 1,200 trained officers every six months.[18] Nonetheless, only in May 1946, nine months after the Japanese surrender, did the first group of peacetime American advisers begin their assignments in China to assist the Chinese military education program.[19]

By the summer of 1947, the small size and restricted mission of the Military Advisory Group continued to lag behind U.S. Army objectives and real-world requirements. The War Department's acquiescence to the State Department framework in 1945 had suggested that the 750 personnel were only an initial personnel strength, allowing for a future increase. But over eighteen months after the mission was established there had been no increase in adviser strength. Maj. Gen. John P. Lucas, chief of the Army Mission in Nanjing, wrote about the organizational limitations of the group:

> the core of the problem—the actual modernized training of the combat echelons; the development of adequate administrative, technical, and logistic service in all echelons; and the elevation of the common soldier from the status of a feudal serf to that of a self-respecting and efficiently trained fighting citizen—remains to date untouched. No effective steps in this direction can be taken until the restrictions as to personnel and equipment necessary for training can be removed. Without the removal of these restrictions, further effort on our part can hope to achieve only rapidly diminishing results.[20]

In addition to the small size and limited influence of the military advisory mission, lingering problems of low morale and high levels of alcoholism continued to hinder efforts. In a scathing critique of the Army advisers, the *Chicago Tribune* described daily behavior as "going through the motions at the office and hurrying off to the officers' club where they drown their sorrows at the bar."[21] Prostitution remained a problem, with women frequently reported to be staying overnight in Army barracks. A high level of misbehavior by military personnel led to the imposition of an 11 P.M. curfew for all U.S. forces in China.[22]

Only after the political relationship between the United States and the USSR had significantly deteriorated, and after the loss of significant Nationalist military forces in Manchuria, did the War Department's continued advocacy of a stronger American presence in China lead to a reshaping and redefinition of the U.S. military mission. The Joint U.S. Military Advisory Group (JUSMAG) directive of 17 September 1948 was a direct rejection of the "light footprint" military policy and political neutrality that the United States had attempted to maintain from 1945 to 1948.[23] The first priority for refining the American military role was better integration of the divided American advisory efforts from separate Army, Air Force, and Navy missions into a unified JUSMAG structure under the command of a general officer. Second, the 1948 JUSMAG directive specifically focused on maintaining control over all areas of China, openly acknowledging that a civil war existed in China and that the United States desired a Nationalist victory. Lastly, the JUSMAG directive called for furnishing direct logistical assistance to the Chinese army, entailing American participation in supply efforts.[24]

The renewed military-to-military contact provided by the creation of the JUSMAG was overtaken by events as the Chinese Nationalist Army suffered a series of battlefield defeats in 1948 and 1949. Civilian factors such as weak Chinese political leadership, rampant inflation, and a desire for land reform in the countryside have all been used to explain the underlying cause for the success of the Communist Revolution in China, but the battlefield defeat of the Nationalist Army by Communist forces is the proximate cause of the power transition in 1949.[25]

Sun Li-jen, 1945–1949: Frustration and Failure

With the end of major combat operations in northern Burma, Sun and the Chinese Army in India (CAI) redeployed as a strategic reserve force in southern China and India. During the period from March through August 1945, Americans took the lead in further retraining new personnel in preparation for a planned drive toward the Chinese coast in the fall of 1945, leaving Sun Li-jen with no significant duties. To broaden his military skills, make connections with Allied officers, and as part of the American public relations effort to promote China as one of the big four Allied powers, Sun went on an extensive tour of the European theater in the spring of 1945. Sun visited Allied combat units and reviewed recent operations in Europe, had discussions with Gen. Dwight Eisenhower, and toured captured German arms factories and advanced weapons programs.[26]

Sun did not return to a troop command after his European tour but undertook a wide variety of military diplomatic missions, primarily with the United States. While in the United States, Sun took the politically hazardous decision to visit Gen. Joseph Stilwell, who was still viewed with hostility by Chiang Kai-shek, at his home in Monterey, California. In a long conversation, reported in all major newspapers, Sun presented himself as a devout student of the now ailing Stilwell, which was a direct challenge to the narrative presented by Chiang Kai-shek that Stilwell was an arrogant, isolated leader.[27] The political implications of this overt critique of Chiang's decision likely played a part in the failure of Sun to get command of a unit. The next major task for Sun was his appointment to the Joint Military Staff Committee of the United Nations Security Council, which met in London on 1 February 1946.[28] Sun was part of an international staff of senior military officers on this committee, which was designed to give military advice to members of the Security Council.[29] With the increasing breakdown of international cooperation due to the incipient Cold War, the Joint Military Staff Committee never fulfilled its intended role of coordinating military policies and peacekeeping operations, but it further delayed Sun's return to China.

Sun remained in London or New York through the spring of 1946 and was only recalled to China in late April because of increasingly heavy fighting between Nationalist and Communist units in Manchuria. After Japan's surrender in August 1945, the majority of the American-trained units, such as the CAI and Chinese Expeditionary Army (Y Force), were in South China, and spent the following months moving into areas south of the Yangtze River. Beginning in November 1945, Chiang ordered the elite American-trained units into Manchuria to forestall the entrenchment of a Chinese Communist government in the economically vital region.

Sun was appointed the deputy commander of the Northeast Region in May 1946.[30] More specifically, he was given command of the New 1st Army, which was charged with driving the CCP out of the Siping area. Liao Yaoxiang, Sun's wartime partner in India, was assigned to command the nearby New 6th Army.

Less fortunately for Sun, Du Yuming, a more orthodox KMT general, whom he had disobeyed in the 1942 Battle of Yenangyaung, was appointed the senior commander in Manchuria. By the time Sun reached the battlefield in late May 1946, the major KMT offensive to retake Siping was essentially over and the main military task for KMT forces was garrison duty in the major cities of the northeast.

Between May 1946 and May 1947, the military situation in Manchuria was largely static, with Communist forces regrouping around Harbin and in the countryside. Meanwhile, the ill-fated American peace negotiation led by George Marshall, and internal KMT political conflict, curbed the scope for new operations.[31] In late May 1946 Sun visited Nanjing for a series of conferences, political meetings, and visits with the press. In a rambling interview, a clearly frustrated and angry Sun severely criticized the KMT course of action in Manchuria:

> QUESTION: How can this situation be turned around?
> SUN: In the Northeast the situation is pretty bad, in Siping we really only have one route in and out but Du Yuming doesn't want to do anything about it! Du sits in Changchun and Jilin with all the troops when we could be planning to strike the undefended city of Harbin. The end result is that even though the Siping situation could be settled, Du doesn't have the guts to do it.
>
> QUESTION: If Changchun and Jilin were lost would you be surprised?
> SUN: This kind of question shows that you and Du Yuming think alike, but you are a reporter so its natural, Du Yuming is just a defeatist who is afraid of his own shadow so he wastes every good opportunity.
>
> . . . .
>
> QUESTION: General Sun, why haven't you proposed a plan to attack Harbin to General Du, perhaps he would accept it?
> SUN: Du lacks the guts to do anything. I just don't believe in him. Let me give you an example, on the north bank of the Songhua River I left a small force of three hundred men as a beachhead protecting a vital bridge but when Lin Biao launched an attack elsewhere, Du asked me to redeploy the 300 men to other areas but I refused. If we are going to win in the northeast we are going to have to take Harbin and this bridge was vital.[32]

Shortly after the disastrous interview, which made public the deep-rooted differences in personality and professional opinion between Du and Sun, Sun was transferred to the Army training command.[33] The move was widely perceived as a demotion, and the transfer removed Sun from the troops that had served with him since Burma. Chinese and foreign media reported the news as a great blow to KMT chances for military victory in the northeast. The Chicago *Herald Tribune* reported:

> The New 1st Army is the cornerstone of the Chinese military forces in the northeast, which is the most politically crucial part of China. Several weeks ago, General Sun Li-jen was removed from command and his position assumed by his superior Du Yuming. His [Sun's] new position lacks any real power, the conventional wisdom is that his reassignment is the result of continuing friction between Sun and Du. It has been said that Du has long been envious of the reputation of the New 1st Army. . . . According to the opinions of American military observers the effect of Sun's removal will be immense. The observers noted that this situation has strongly lowered the morale of the New 1st Army, which has always been strongly linked to General Sun.[34]

Sun as Army Builder in Taiwan

Sun's new assignment also relocated him far from the northeast area, which saw large combat operations in the summer of 1947, to the relative backwater of Taiwan. Sun assumed command of the Taiwan Training Command in July 1947, and began to establish a network of army training centers clustered around the southern end of Taiwan. Sun's assignment to military training in Taiwan appeared to be a mistake in mid-1947, but by 1949 as KMT forces fled to the island, Sun's control over the only remaining effective KMT military force made him the de facto head of the army, and, after 1950, the commander in chief of all ROC armed forces.

Shortly after Sun Li-jen's de facto demotion in May 1947, he used his authority in Taiwan to create a military training system for his small forces. Sun arrived in Taiwan on 23 July 1947 with the authority to develop training facilities only for enlisted personnel, but after he personally lobbied Chiang Kai-shek, Sun was given authority to establish a small officer-training center.[35] With this grudging approval, Sun developed a comprehensive system of officer education, training, and development centered on the city of Fengshan, near the city of Gaoxiong.[36]

Sun attracted nearly four hundred young officers, many with overseas education and combat experience with the New 1st Army in World War II, to serve as instructors in Taiwan, including Sun's deputy Gu Youhui, a Stanford graduate. Many of the officers who moved to Taiwan had received training at American military schools, in China during the war or in the United States.[37] During the 1947–55 period, these several hundred officers were able to complete the transformation of the ROC Army into a thoroughly American-style force.

In contrast to most of the Chinese military schools operating during the 1945–49 period, Sun's school system had an extremely strenuous program of instruction. Training days normally lasted for twelve hours or more, with lengthy field training exercises several times a year. A particular emphasis of Sun's training was physical fitness, and all personnel began the day with American-style calisthenics, followed by a 5,000-meter run, often up one of the surrounding hills.[38] Being isolated from effective control by ROC military headquarters in Nanjing, political instruction was discontinued and no class hours were devoted to political or "moral" instruction.[39]

Between November 1947 and July 1951, when the independent Taiwan army-training program merged with the larger ROC training system, a total of over 450,000 personnel passed through Sun's training command.[40] Sun's creation of a stand-alone army training facility, staffed by pro-American officers implementing a depoliticized training program, represented the fruition of the Sino-American army-building ideals first developed in 1942. While this program did not represent the entirety of the ROC military, it provided a firm organizational foundation for growth after the 1949 retreat to Taiwan and dramatically increased Sun's military importance. In combination with ideas of scientific warfare developed in military journals, Sun's training program shows that international, specifically American, norms were embraced by ROC military officers, who pursued reforms during a period without extensive American involvement.

The Idea of a Chinese Army

The end of China's eight-year war with Japan initiated a prolonged phase of intellectual debate and discussion among Chinese military officers on the role, missions, and organization of the future Chinese army. Within the Chinese officer corps, the idea of an army based on loyalty to the nation, a professional military organization insulated from political debates, and a normative belief in restricting military operations to "core" tasks had gained widespread support. This is most clearly shown by examining the military journals and writing from the 1945–49 period.

In professions, journals are a core element of the professionalization process in that they promote a sense of shared identity, which is both continually reinforced by regular intellectual contact "from the top down" through research centers or noteworthy members, but also "from the bottom up" through member participation. Professional journals have become part of the pedagogical process by reinforcing many of the values and skills developed in formal training schools, and also by providing additional education in newly developed techniques, ideas, and procedures that help support a profession's jurisdictional and normative claims as a "learning" occupation. Last, journals provide feedback from professional members working in the field, and institutional members in training centers or research positions. This feedback process benefits the profession by allowing its institutional apparatus to refine the focus of its efforts and procedures.

Within a military, journals are especially important because they provide a unique space for semipublic debate in an otherwise hierarchical work environment. In China, a key element of this space was the ability for all ranks of officers to read and contribute articles for publication. In the late 1940s it was common for low ranking junior officers to have articles published alongside senior generals and field commanders, with rapidly changing technology often making the most recently commissioned officers the most alert to the challenges and opportunities of new equipment and techniques. Chinese military journals almost never identified the rank and position of individual writers, and while some were well-known soldiers or prominent intellectuals, many were unknown junior officers. Military journals also offered a space for substantial criticism of military and civilian personnel, institutions, and policies through attacks on their "ideas." Analysis and commentary in Chinese military journals sometimes included direct and brutal criticism, many using episodes of military history to allude to contemporary folly, a characteristic that was impossible in other public spaces without dismissal of the officer involved.

From a low point in the early 1940s, Chinese military journals increased in quality and scope throughout the remainder of the decade. The increase in quality had several interrelated reasons. First, the start of truly global military operations after the German invasion of Russia in the summer of 1941 and the Japanese bombing of Pearl Harbor in December 1941 meant that China was now part of a global alliance, requiring some understanding of the international military situation by Chinese officers. Second, the pace of military change accelerated throughout World War II with the poorly equipped armies of 1939, reliant on horse-drawn transport and light tanks, evolving into large-scale mechanized formations operating with integrated air and naval support. While Chinese units still were primarily infantry-based, even in 1945, the experiences of other nations provided a wide range of cases for study and analysis. Third, the inclusion of China as one of the "Big Four" Allied powers might have been an empty gesture in 1942, but Chinese officers believed, and were supported in their belief by American officers, that in a postwar world China would be a major power, with security interests throughout Asia. Last, the massive American presence in China from 1942 to 1945 included the development of vastly expanded and increasingly centralized officer training centers, which served as the ideal sites for the production of military journals. American and Chinese officers assigned to these schools as instructors developed military journals as a way to prepare future students prior to arrival, reinforce lessons learned in training, and increase the esprit de corps and collective identity among the officer corps.

In August 1945, the War College began to publish an official journal, *Xiandai Junshi* (*Modern Military Affairs*), with articles on a wide variety of international and Chinese military developments. Under American influence, in late 1944 and early 1945, the War College was comprehensively restructured. The War College had initially been located in Beijing to serve as a national institute of high-level military education, but during the 1930s it had relocated to Nanjing and lost its distinctive identity, becoming one among many KMT military schools in the capital.[41] Drawing on American educational patterns, in late 1944 the Chinese army shifted its military educational structure toward a unified system of officer training in centralized facilities. The War College mission was refocused during the 1942–44 period into a tertiary educational facility, which took mid-career Chinese officers, gave them training in advanced staff techniques, and returned them to their units.

The War College Education Act (lujun daxue zuzhifa) codified the reshaping of the War College, removed many of the basic military training requirements such as marching drill or rifle marksmanship, and streamlined the school bureaucracy around academic studies rather than tactical issues. The school administration was also expanded, with the addition of departments of translation, military history, and international affairs. The overall size of the school was also increased, with student numbers during the late 1940s averaging over 140 officers per class, which was a significant increase from the low point of only sixty per class during the period of neglect prior to World War II.[42]

In addition to organizational changes, personnel changes increased the intellectual rigor and international connections of the War College. Gen. Xu Peigen, a Jiangsu native with close ties to Chiang Kai-shek, was appointed as head of the school. Xu's record as a combat soldier was very brief, but he had graduated from the Baoding Academy and the War College when it was still in Beijing, before studying at the elite Kriegsacademie in Berlin before the war. After 1941, Xu had served as a member of the Chinese military mission to Washington, D.C. Xu was a prolific writer, and during the period from 1945 to 1949 produced several books in addition to numerous articles.

The broad reforms undertaken to turn the War College from a teaching institution to a graduate-level research center were clearly reflected in the production of the premier Chinese military journal of the early twentieth century, *Xiandai Junshi*. Beginning in July 1945, *Xiandai Junshi* would function as China's most articulate and comprehensive military journal. During its brief publication history from July 1945 through August 1948 it included a wide range of articles by senior generals, young commanders with field operations experience, foreign military analysts, and Chinese military theorists.

The clear impression gleaned from close reading and interpretation of *Xiandai Junshi* is that mainstream Chinese military officers believed that scientific and technological progress had fundamentally altered the character of military operations by 1945, and that China needed a highly skilled, standing national army. The purpose of this highly skilled national army was either a large-scale land conflict with the Soviet Union in the near term, three to five years, or an integrated land-sea-air conflict with a resurgent Japan in the long term, fifteen to twenty years in the future. Almost totally lacking from professional military discussions are immediate military requirements involved in fighting the Communists or KMT policies.

The inaugural issue of *Xiandai Junshi*, written in the last days of the war against Japan, exhibits an emphasis on technology and firepower. Gen. Xu Peigen wrote in the first issue's introduction: "Modern military education has undergone great progress and is changing every day. From World War One until our current great struggle, a little over twenty years' time, military technology has rapidly advanced, strategy and tactics have changed tremendously."[43]

During its brief publication history, several key themes were consistent topics of discussion and debate. The most salient topic was the role of the United States in the world, its connections with China, and its function as a military model on which to base Chinese military reforms. During the 1945–48 period, Chinese officers published a wide variety of articles detailing U.S. officer training programs, many of which Chinese participated in, and organizational reforms, such as the integration of the U.S. Army and Navy into the Department of Defense in 1947. Related to discussion of the United States was the prominent role of the atomic bomb in Chinese military thinking. The atomic bomb was regarded as the most direct manifestation of "scientific" warfare, which was felt to be characteristic of the age. Related to both the United States and the atomic bomb was the concept of tactical and strategic mobility, which similarly interested Chinese military intellectuals.

The United States

As China's major strategic partner, and with the experience of a close wartime working relationship, the United States was the subject of frequent discussion and reporting in *Xiandai Junshi*. Chinese military officers had a very favorable impression of the United States. The United States had been able to mobilize, train, equip, and deploy a massive number of troops thousands of miles from its shores. Chinese officers were amazed at the ability of the U.S. forces to deploy against both European and Pacific theaters while maintaining overall strategic coordination. Chinese statistical analysis of the U.S. forces highlighted that almost 50 percent of U.S. personnel served in logistical or support units, with a further 15 percent assigned to the Air Force, leaving only 34 percent of the total U.S. Army strength in ground combat units.[44] The United States was seen as an unrivalled "scientific" power after the defeat of Germany. Although the Soviet Union might have had a larger ground army, U.S. skills in radar, aviation, naval construction, and so forth, were seen as barometers of military power. In addition, during the later stages of World War II, thousands of Chinese officers had studied at American military facilities such as West Point, Fort Leavenworth's Command and General Staff College, and many of the officer branch schools. Last, Chinese officers viewed the United States model as a much better fit for China's cultural and social environment than Soviet or British models.

Like many Chinese officers, Xu Peigen was a strong supporter of a close Sino-American alliance, and he wrote frequently in *Xiandai Junshui* and elsewhere on the "special relationship." His affinity for the United States was broad, with recognition of scientific accomplishments, effective political structures, and integrated air-ground-naval capabilities. Xu was a prolific writer, and two of his books from the 1940s dealt with U.S. defense policy. One book examined economic mobilization and economic warfare, while the second dealt with the impact of the atomic bomb on military tactics and strategy. *American Economic Mobilization and Economic Warfare* (*Meiguo jingji dongyuan jiqi jingji douzheng*) was published in 1945, and *The Effect of the Atomic Bomb on Chinese Military Affairs* (*Yuanzidan duiyu junshi zhi yingxiang*) was published in 1946.

Bai Chongxi, one of the KMT's most senior generals, was a frequent contributor to *Xiandai Junshi* and, from 1946 to 1949, he was China's minister of national defense. Bai wrote knowledgeably about the advantages of the U.S. political system, "The United States has a population of 170 million, and has a great leader in Franklin Roosevelt . . . before WWI they had an army of less than 200,000 men but increased it to 4 million during wartime, before this war they had an army of only 1 million but within a short time after the outbreak of war had over 11 million in the armed forces."[45] Bai elaborated that the stability of the U.S. political system allowed for a high degree of unity among the population, which made it easy to have a large percentage of the population potentially in uniform without significant political opposition.

The U.S. military education system was almost universally praised by Chinese officers, many of whom had studied in the United States at both civilian and military schools. Bai Chongxi commented, "As to the question of the [Chinese] military education system, at present most of the army's equipment is American, the military education and training system need to adopt American methods."[46] A common type of article detailed Chinese officers' experiences at U.S. schools and provided a detailed examination of the school organization and methods. Two aspects that Chinese observers admired in U.S. military schools were the intraschool competitions for academic performance, which helped inculcate a competitive spirit, and the regular rotation of instructors between command and academic posts, unlike in China where instructors often served their entire careers at military schools.[47] On a more philosophical level, Chinese observers felt that basic education for American officers at West Point was successful in inculcating a sense of responsibility and correct behavior in future leaders. Chinese officer Luo Hongyan neglected to describe details of the cadet curriculum but made the concept of "A Soldier and a Gentleman" (junren yu junzi) a key part of his description.[48]

The fundamental problem for Chinese officers was adapting elements that they liked about the United States military model and making them work in a Chinese environment, which had significantly fewer material and human resources. For example, officer training in the U.S. model, with short-term officers trained in ROTC programs at civilian universities, could not be adapted to China because of vastly fewer universities.[49]

In stark contrast to China's relationship with the United States, which was close, broad-based, and revolved around a wide range of Chinese interests, Chinese officers' views of the Soviet Union were quite harsh. While there was some respect shown toward the USSR as a partner in World War II, there were deep suspicions of Soviet geopolitical motives. In the early years of *Xiandai Junshi*, one of the main points of discussion regarding the Soviets was their continual desire for territorial expansion. In a translated article segment drawn from the work of historian R. J. Sontag, the Soviet Union was compared directly to Imperial Russia, with the assessment made that the methods and principles of Soviet and Russian warfare and diplomacy seemed remarkably similar in spite of differing ideologies.[50]

Atomic Bombs and Scientific Warfare

The theme most commonly expressed throughout the 1945–48 period was that modern warfare was "scientific." *Xiandai Junshi* articles consistently repeated the mantra that modern warfare would be decided by science and the skills of officers in managing the application of firepower from airplanes, tanks, and artillery. Although the meaning of what exactly "scientific" meant was vague, the clear impression conveyed was that an emphasis on firepower, technology, and cold-blooded management was now more important than martial spirit.

Bai Chongxi spoke of science as one of the trends of the time: "The modern era is characterized by science, modern warfare is scientific warfare, the entire military has become automated. Today we understand that we must use the most modern equipment and the most modern tactics, in a period where technology changes daily we must always be on our guard."[51] Fan Chengyuan agreed that "[t]he modern era has passed through steam power to electric and now to atomic science, warfare has become dominated by artillery and the tank, on the ground and in the air we have advanced into the era of radar and atomic bomb centered scientific warfare."[52]

One of the strongest supporters of a highly professional army was former Army War College head Yang Jie, who—along with Jiang Baili, Xu Peigen, and Zhu De in the PLA—was one of the preeminent military intellectuals of twentieth-century China.[53] In a 1947 article, Yang strongly argued that future wars would be decided by three factors: 1. scientific abilities, 2. mass production of sophisticated military equipment, 3. high levels of mobility. Yang argued that since 1914, military science had triumphed over individual bravery. "Modern warfare is scientific warfare. This modern age is the age of science and that has been shown in its application in the military. . . . Now that the second world war is over some people say that a third world war is impossible, I say it is possible."[54]

The atomic bomb and its effect on warfare was a major element of Xu Peigen's work in particular and *Xiandai Junshi* in general. Xu wrote in *Xiandai Junshi* during 1946, "Army weapons have already entered the atomic age, in the future victory or defeat will be determined by atomic bombs and the ability to produce atomic material in quantity."[55] In Xu's conception, atomic firepower would shape the battlefield, but forward thinking and planning, such as a shift to armored forces, which are both more mobile and sheltered from blast effects, would be a useful reform.

Many Chinese military intellectuals felt that the atomic bomb was both symbolic of profound shifts in warfare toward scientific methods of fighting and a potentially useful weapon if used on the battlefield. In 1947, a special issue of *Xiandai Junshi* focused exclusively on the role of atomic bombs in warfare, drawing from a wide range of foreign commentary and Chinese analysis of future atomic warfare.[56]

In addition to its battlefield use, Chinese officers worried about defending cities from an atomic bombing campaign. One 1947 article used American projections of an atomic bombing on Washington, D.C., with detonations centered on the Pentagon, Washington Naval Yard, and the Mall, to discuss a hypothetical atomic threat. At the time the article was published, the Soviet Union was still two years away from developing their own atomic bomb and had no viable delivery system. Moreover, at this time Mao Zedong was living in a cave in northwest China.[57]

The Chinese obsession with atomic bombs completely transcended any semblance of near-term military utility. For example, in 1947 *Xiandai Junshi* published two articles that detailed the American atomic bombs tests at Bikini Atoll (Operation Crossroads). Two articles offered a straightforward and insightful analysis of the testing, but failed to see the contradiction between the purpose of the American tests, to evaluate the effects of atomic bombs detonated underwater on naval ships, and any conceivable relevance to Chinese strategic or tactical conditions.[58]

The Chinese military's infatuation with technology and the most advanced military equipment approached the surreal. An article in early 1948 focused on defense procedures of major cities from cruise and ballistic missiles, based on London's experience when it was attacked from V-1 and V-2 rockets.[59] Another 1948 article stated matter-of-factly that "future warfare will be push button warfare, atomic warfare, we should not dwell on the military lessons of WWI but look at the recent lessons of WWII."[60]

Mobility

In addition to a strong affinity for the Unites States and belief in a military paradigm shift toward "scientific" warfare, *Xiandai Junshi* articles frequently discussed military history and reoccurring challenges for Chinese forces. A primary discursive thread running through the military history articles was the importance of mobility.

In mid-1946, a major article by Maj. Gen. Lu Fengge, head of the history department at the War College, analyzed the experiences of successive Chinese dynasties in defending the northern frontier, and what lessons could be drawn for the future. After examining over ten individual dynasties and their frontier policies, Lu argued that strategic and tactical mobility was crucial in securing border areas. Lu found that dynasties such as the Han and Tang had been more successful in defending themselves because they had a more highly developed cavalry force, which could engage invading groups on their own terms, while more defensive postures, such as those employed by the Song, only led to eventual defeat.[61] In a thinly veiled critique of the United Nations, Lu alluded to the Song dynasty's short-sighted diplomatic policy of using money, gifts or flattery (zhong wen qing shi) while neglecting the development of military power.[62]

Almost immediately after the Japanese surrender, Chinese officers began discussing future conflicts and future military requirements. Gen. You Fengchi argued that the lesson of World War II was the dominant role played by motorized and armored warfare. General You calculated that a force of forty regular infantry divisions, ten armored divisions, ten motorized divisions, and ten cavalry divisions would be sufficient to defend Chinese borders. This proposed military structure would have been forced to rely on external—that is, American—support for the majority of the tanks, trucks, and artillery equipment. The structure of the force also pointed to Manchuria as the most likely area of future conflict, and the Soviet Union as the most likely future antagonist.[63]

The most obvious and frequently discussed example of the effects of mobility on modern warfare was the German invasion of France in 1940, and the success of Blitzkrieg warfare to accomplish in six weeks what Germany could not achieve in four years during World War I. Xu Peigen wrote of these changes: "[A]s global communications and transportation rapidly develop the world is becoming a smaller and smaller place, we cannot cling to conservative habits but should embrace the new world. . . . For example, France won the last victory of WWI under the leadership of General Gamelin [commander of French forces in 1940], but they clung to old victories, ignoring new thinking and failing to evolve and adapt."[64] The negative example of the French collapse in the spring of 1940 was also used to suggest that officers should be careful that civilians would unwisely step into military affairs with firm opposition. Fu Chaojie, writing in 1947, argued that France had poor strategy pushed on it by a weak government, not a weak military. "In 1934 the French High Command came out with a new plan, *The Army of the Future*, which advocated establishing a mechanized force of 100,000 men, in order to better defend the country but this was voted down by the legislature."[65]

With the benefit of hindsight, the most glaring omission from *Xiandai Junshi* is the almost complete lack of discussion about the contemporary difficulties of containing the Chinese Communist movement or operations against the People's Liberation Army (PLA). In spite of over a dozen articles that deal with the role of the atomic bomb in future warfare, an entire special issue on the role of naval forces in history, or discussion of the opportunities presented by jet-propelled aircraft, there is only one article that deals with the CCP. In spite of the brevity of discussion, the sole article presents a highly nuanced and proactive approach to defeating the CCP through an integrated doctrine of counterinsurgency.

Published in the fall of 1948, *How to Eliminate Communist Bandits* (*Ruhe jiaojian gongfei*) is a brief, almost terse analysis of the core issues of dealing with an insurgency, and proscribes a short list of methods for dealing with the problem. The writer, Ye Du, did not publish other articles and was not a high-ranking official. The detailed descriptions of low-level concerns suggest that he had experience in northeast China in a military position.

Ye's primary argument regarding the civil conflict is that the CCP thrives in situations of disorder. In areas with a weak government, poor economic conditions, and a socially segmented population. the CCP will exploit opportunities to entrench itself. The behavior of the CCP is presented as opportunistic, with CCP efforts directed to areas of persistent weakness rather than a policy of direct confrontation. Based on this assessment, Ye believes that an integrated political, economic, and military response will be necessary to both eliminate the preconditions for CCP success and to destroy CCP organizations already in place.

The majority of Ye's recommendations for ending the CCP's growth were related to political and economic development. The most important political factor determining CCP success is the political climate of law and order. Ye contends, "We must recognize that the CCP thrives in areas with social disorder and poverty; they swim in this chaos like a fish in the sea."[66] Ye's proscription for dealing with political chaos was increasing the stability of social order by encouraging the formation of local groups and providing government assistance to community efforts. In a similar vein of thinking, Ye argues that unless the army is able to protect commerce and industry from attacks on transportation, economic development will stall, further fueling popular dissatisfaction.

Ye's proposals for the Chinese military are a radical oppositional view of the dominant military school of thought concerning the role the Chinese army should play in society, how it should be structured, and where is should place its mission priorities. In a brutal five-point critique of contemporary standards and procedures, Ye attacks the Chinese army as neglecting personnel at the expense of hi-tech new equipment. Points one and two both focus on the debilitative effect of poor financial support on officers and soldiers of the Army. Ye argues that the rapid inflation occurring in China during the late 1940s was having a large and adverse effect on soldiers' performance. Third, the Army was neglecting the issue of morale and had been unable to articulate a clear military-political vision of why it was fighting and what it was fighting for. Ye writes, "We must attach greater importance to political work and increase our intelligence efforts; at the present time our forces are highly centralized, with difficult living conditions and our soldiers are often homesick [low morale]; at the same time our understanding of the role of ideology in this conflict is lacking, and when we get into an enemy area or clear an enemy village our military-political efforts are disjointed and often ineffective."[67] Fourth, the major area of military involvement should be at the local level, working in villages, towns, and districts in a hybrid military/political role.

The most radical of Ye's points, number five, argues that the army should promote the development of local self-defense organizations, which often serve to fulfill valuable roles in organizing local youth and leadership, for mutual benefit. Ye writes, "All weapons in a district should be collected for the creation of local self-defense forces, relying on regular army units is not appropriate for small groups of bandits."[68] Ye argues that encouragement of local self-defense forces will increase security against CCP forces, encourage the identification of local residents, especially young men, with the government, and free up regular army units for offensive operations. This point is directly opposite to the highly centralized vision of a national army expounded in other articles, and in a country recovering from an era of local warlords was likely viewed skeptically by officers eager to make the army the sole military institution.

Although only a small fraction of ROC officers wrote for *Xiandai Junshi*, the ideas it generated were shared throughout the force. For example, in Xi'an, which had a military academy, the local military journal also included articles on the "atomic age."[69] In addition, the Xi'an journal highlighted the need to be "modern military men and global military men." The article bluntly states that to be global military men means "to stand with the first-rank powers, in every way to catch up with them," and to represent "our country."[70]

Chinese Officers at American Schools

In addition to military journals, Chinese officers also used foreign military education opportunities to develop new ideas about military structures and strategies. During the 1945–50 period, several dozen Chinese officers attended American military schools, such as the Armor School at Fort Knox, Kentucky, or the Command and General Staff College in Fort Leavenworth, Kansas. In these schools, Chinese officers were expected to produce, like their American classmates, written research papers on a topic of their choosing. Chinese exchange officers ranged from junior lieutenants to senior colonels, and although their English language abilities varied, their written work shows a high degree of understanding of global military affairs and military history. After returning home, Chinese officers continued to be involved with American schools, and even contributed to American military journals, illustrating the deep professional connections.[71]

The selection of topics and the proposed solutions to military problems exhibited in the school papers mirrors the thinking expressed in ROC military journals. The two dominant themes developed by the Chinese military exchange students were, first and foremost, a need for increased professional competence among Chinese military personnel, and secondly, increased centralization of military organization in order to promote specialization.[72] One student summarized the failure of Chinese logistics in the war against Japan: "[I]f we confine our comment purely to the logistical professional point of view, I would admit that our logistical effort was a failure, because it was inefficiently managed, loosely knitted, and uneconomically organized, and operated to meet our military requirements."[73]

In another similarity to military journal mentalities, Chinese officers presented the post-1946 reorganization of the Chinese government and army to be the most important defense reform since the fall of the Qing dynasty. Lt. Col. Huang Chan-Kuei wrote that regarding the Chinese defense structure,

> [t]he establishment of the Ministry of National Defense and consequently the unification of the armed forces is probably the major military reform of postwar China, . . . the establishment of the Ministry of National defense was based on four important policies:
>
> (a) That military affairs should be subjected to the control of politics, and the Ministry of National Defense should be under the jurisdiction of the Executive Yuan.
> (b) That the control of the armed forces should be returned to the nation as a whole. As soon as the constitutional government is

formed, the armed forces will no longer be considered as a Party instrument.
(c) That the command of the armed forces should be unified.
(d) That the new system should be able to meet the requirements both of peace and war time.⁷⁴

During the period from 1945 to 1949, Chinese military journals and professional writings show a clear preference for an organizational model based on a highly professional, technically focused, and organizationally insulated military. The interests of Chinese officers in atomic weapons, mobile warfare, and firepower appears radically at odds with the reality of an impoverished country riven by internal conflict. This contradiction between military ideals and Chinese reality highlights the insularity of Chinese military officers and their professional objectives, in spite of the real-world consequences.

Although *Xiandai Junshi* was a very elite journal and the number of Chinese officers who studied in the United States, while significant, never approached 10 percent of total officer strength, the ideas of firepower, mobile warfare, and technologically advanced warfare did trickle down into the army. In complete symmetry with *Xiandai Junshi*, the mainstream military newsmagazine, *Zhongguo junren zhou kan* (*Chinese Soldier Weekly*), lauded U.S. military and technological forces as the primary victor of the world war. In cold calculations of troop strength, analysis of firepower, and the important ability to logistically support expeditionary forces, the weekly magazine agreed with the *Xiandai Junshi* that a new era of technologically determined warfare had arrived.⁷⁵ A subsequent article makes the connection between technology and warfare even more explicit. It stated, "Science is unceasingly advancing, weapons are being refined every day, what worked in the past will not work in the present, it's not that we should change our strategies, it's a fact that we cannot change because warfare has already moved on."⁷⁶

Another similarity to *Xiandai Junshi* was the disproportionate emphasis Chinese officers placed on aircraft and atomic bombs, both weapon systems that were tremendously expensive and of dubious utility in the Chinese setting of 1945–49. A 1946 article in *Zhongguo Junren* (*Chinese Soldier*) describes in glowing terms the combination of American technological advances in radar, atomic bombs, and long-range aircraft, specifically the B-36, all of which enabled highly destructive, and accurate, intercontinental bombing.⁷⁷

During the 1945–49 period, the dominance of ideas of scientific warfare found a healthy environment to grow, in part due to the absence of a strong political officer system. The lack of political interference was a product of a complex civil-military discussion from 1945 to 1947 and the creation of a "national army" idea in China.

Political Officers in Retreat

By the end of the war with Japan in August 1945, the Political Department could take credit for training and placing over 20,000 political officers with the KMT army, thereby contributing to the defeat of Japan by improving the morale and cohesion of KMT forces. In reality, at the organizational level, the massive numbers of poorly trained political officers increasingly weakened the Political Department throughout the course of the war. It had also never been able to regain administrative control over political officers at the unit level, where many remained isolated by skeptical or hostile military commanders.

A key indicator of the poor level of training was the inability of the Political Department to create a centralized school for political officers, where training could be monitored, students taught the same material, and the faculty would systematically conduct evaluations. Instead, political officers trained at ten different programs attached to either civilian or military schools, with ad hoc "training detachments" conducting five-week courses whenever needs were particularly acute. Training was also conducted through correspondence courses.[78] The result of this chaotic system of piecemeal organization and shoddy training was a complete lack of organizational standards, shared norms or feeling of group identity.

In addition to training problems, during the 1937–45 period the content of KMT party and political work also became increasingly devoid of meaning and significance. The tentative United Front between the KMT and CCP meant that explicit demands for KMT unity were submerged beneath broader patriotic themes in propaganda and recruiting. Relocation of the primary political education schools from the cosmopolitan region around Nanjing to undeveloped interior provinces also destroyed the ability of the KMT to inculcate new leaders in high-quality education institutions, and hindered the teaching and training staff from developing new materials. The demands of conducting military operations also reduced the amount of time senior KMT leaders could devote to political education and training. The result of this degradation of the intellectual foundations of the KMT military's political structure was a steady erosion in the applicability and sophistication of political officer material.

Less than two years into the war, KMT journals devoted to the political indoctrination of military members had become intellectually barren. A typically inane article from 1939 reads, "The military's implementation of political training is in order to receive the [KMT] Party's training, receive Party ideas, and to allow every soldier to believe."⁷⁹ No mention is made as to what exactly to believe in. At no time does the article express what types of content are applicable to the wartime situation or how it might differ from concepts developed during the Nanjing decade. Rather than Sun Yat-senism or the tenets of Chiang's New Life Movement, wartime political discussion used the bland phrase "faith in belief" (xinyang zhuyi), without any development of exactly what soldiers should have faith or believe in.⁸⁰ Instead, a bland focus on the form of political training but a complete lack of function is evidenced. Political instruction still called for the forms of small-group discussion and formal teaching by political officers, but no material was given to political officers for use in lectures or classes. This situation continued throughout the war, with even the highest levels of the KMT lacking any clear understanding of what types of content and messages the Political Department should employ.⁸¹

The one concrete benefit to the political officer system to emerge from World War II was the creation of a dedicated supply system under American guidance. This complete system of acquisition and distribution eliminated the need for political officers to assist in the logistics of their units, which had been a major drain on their time and often created difficulties with local communities.⁸²

During the closing days of the war and into the postwar period, the Political Department came under increasing criticism from the Chinese public and American military advisers. In May 1945, Chiang Kai-shek attempted to assuage public feeling and prepare for a postwar "national army" by publicly calling for the removal of all KMT organizations from the military.⁸³ Besides an attempt to curry popular support, Chiang appears to have been genuinely concerned that political officers remained a distraction for military commanders, and cited the old Chinese saying, "Power unified is strong, power divided is weak" (Quan chuyu yi zhe qiang, chu yu er zhe ruo).⁸⁴

Army Nationalization

Between August 1945 and March 1946, a variety of political forces—including the aspirations of Chinese military officers, U.S. diplomatic pressure, and public opinion—worked in concert to pursue an agenda of military "nationalization" (jundui guojiahua). The effect of this six-month process was to create a public consensus around the creation of a Chinese army, conceptualized as a small elite force, separate from civilian administration, and oriented toward combat along China's northern border. The desire for an elite army was directly manifested in plans to cut the military strength of the Chinese army from over 4 million to 800,000. The desire for a professional, national military rather than hybrid party-army authority was highlighted in legalistic discussions over militia versus army responsibilities. Moreover, the negotiations clearly directed the Chinese army into an offensive force posture, with the majority of forces positioned along China's northern border with the Soviet Union.

At its most basic level, the Chinese military nationalization debate derived from two core political concepts. First, Chinese military forces need to be centrally organized, funded, and controlled by a civilian ministry of the national government. Second, military forces should operate only through a civilian chain of command that functioned within the Executive Yuan of the government, not within a political party structure. Affecting both of these core ideas was the more practical issue of military organization. By 1945, the organizational baggage of over twenty years of CCP-KMT conflict, United Front efforts, and wartime initiatives had left a trail of frequent departmental reorganizations, as well as the creation of new offices and myriad "coordination" groups. Many of these offices had overlapping fields of authority, conflicting missions, and mixed civilian/military functions. Albert Wedemeyer identified over sixty independent sections, reporting to the National Military Council, that had duplicated functions with unclear statutory authority.[85] A fundamental reshaping of the organizational chart of the Chinese military system became the only way to achieve the goal of centralization of authority and civilian control.

A major player in Chinese military reforms was the United States, specifically in the personal role of George Marshall. In November 1945, President Truman ordered General Marshall to China as his special representative to assist in the "unification of China by peaceful, democratic methods" and to limit the possibility that the United States or USSR would be drawn into an internal Chinese conflict.[86] While in China, Marshall developed a diplomatic strategy of mutual engagement between the CCP and KMT, which he hoped would develop into political competition within a government rather than military conflict between two party structures. A key component of this strategy was to comingle KMT and CCP forces under the control of the civilian leadership of the government Executive Yuan. Between December 1945 and March 1946, Marshall attempted to broker a framework of military reorganization and encourage Chinese leaders "to develop a nationalized, non-political armed force."[87]

Political leaders within China echoed Marshall's strategy of military reorganization around the ideas of "nationalization" of military force. In January 1946, a Political Consultative Conference (PCC) met with representatives from the KMT, the CCP, and many smaller Chinese political parties in attendance. Advocacy of military nationalization was a prominent component of many of the smaller political parties that operated in the shadow of the massive KMT and CCP organizations. Military nationalization was also a politically useful strategy for small parties because it was a "wedge issue," which denigrated military CCP-KMT methods. Also, because the two large parties would each likely veto their counterpart's appointment into the senior position in a Ministry of Defense, it was also possible for a minor party official to become a senior government minister as the compromise candidate. In January 1946, the Youth Party and the Democratic League cosponsored a statement calling for an end to internal conflict, the reduction of Chinese military forces, and the nationalization of all Party-controlled military forces into a national army organization.[88] On 10 January 1946, the PCC approved the formation of a military subcommittee to consist of representatives of the KMT, CCP, and the United States.[89]

To provide guidance to the military representatives, the PCC adopted a detailed resolution of principles. The first point was brutally direct: "The Army belongs to the state."[90] To achieve this goal, the PCC resolution outlined several more concrete steps that the military subcommittee would have to organize: first, the separation of party systems from military systems; second, the separation of civilian and military authority, with military officers expressly forbidden from holding office as a civil official in any capacity; and third, the desired end goal of a military drawdown to a force of fifty to sixty divisions.[91]

The PCC tasked a military subcommittee, to be composed of representatives of the two major parties, KMT and CCP, with General Marshall as chairman, to work out the details of a comprehensive military reform. The KMT representative, Gen. Zhang Zhizhong, was a well-respected military leader, but one who had spent more time behind a desk than in command positions. The CCP was represented by Zhou Enlai, technically also a general but with negligible military experience and training.

The guidance provided by the PCC was a useful starting point for discussions, but during the six weeks of intensive talks, three areas of concern were most salient and occupied the majority of the discussion. First, the size of the proposed national army, with troop strengths, the ratio of KMT to CCP personnel, and the timing of troop reductions needed to be worked out in detail. Second, the duties of the national army versus other branches of the national and local government needed to be firmly fixed and agreed upon. Marshall was extremely careful that neither side could "hide" military personnel under the title of paramilitary or police forces. Lastly, the three representatives needed to establish where the Chinese army would be deployed.

Reduction of the size of military forces had been one of the reoccurring goals of all foreign advisers to the Chinese military, especially the German and American contingents, and was outlined by the PCC as a core element of the reorganization. They hoped that a reduction in the number of Chinese military personnel would bring about numerous financial, political, and military benefits. Financial savings from cutting the government payroll of over 2 million personnel would allow the saved funding to be used on infrastructure development. Limiting the numbers of soldiers would also limit the amount of trouble they could cause, and would prevent a return to the 1920s era of numerous but decentralized military forces. Lastly, the commitment to a reduction in the number of military personnel rested on the belief that increased emphasis on training, the acquisition of new equipment such as trucks and tanks, and increased professional behavior by officers would create a smaller, but more effective, fighting force.

Even with small reductions in the strength of KMT and CCP forces after the Japanese surrender, the military strength of both sides was unsupportable in a peacetime environment. In January 1946, U.S. observers estimated that a total of 3.1 million military personnel remained in the KMT military, spread across more than 250 divisions. This was after the reduction of forty-nine divisions, containing 500,000 men, between August 1945 and January 1946.[92] CCP forces included over 1.2 million personnel, not including extensive CCP militia organizations.

The tentative goal set by the PCC called for a drawdown to a force of fifty to sixty divisions, with ten of these divisions under CCP control. From a baseline of over three hundred divisions, this was highly ambitious. American plans during World War II had foreseen a force of ninety Chinese divisions being eventually created, but American estimates after the war stated that sixty divisions, if properly trained and equipped, was the limit of China's economic and industrial capacity.[93]

As an incentive for the Chinese to reduce troop numbers, and as part of the continuation of American wartime supply and advisory efforts, a streamlined Chinese army was planned to be trained by Americans and would use American equipment. General Wedemeyer argued that a strong American commitment to developing Chinese military power would benefit China economically and politically as well as serve U.S. national interests in creating a long-term partnership in East Asia. Wedemeyer bluntly stated that this program would mean the training and equipping of Communist military forces on an equal basis as KMT forces if the training program was to be a viable program.[94]

The second major area of detailed staff work was the restriction of military personnel from contact with civilian administration or police functions. An easy agreement among the three representatives was the banning of military personnel from holding public office, in either the Legislative Yuan or government, while on active duty.[95] Much more complicated was the role of Chinese paramilitary forces. In addition to strictly military forces, China had developed a militia system, organized and led by local leaders, and a "Peace Preservation Corps" (bao an tuan), who were professional soldiers operating in a gendarmerie function. Throughout the discussions, General Zhang consistently attempted to downplay the importance of clearly defining the militia system and its relationship to the national army, but General Marshall, especially, slowly forced Zhang to define each militia organization, its responsibility, and its authority.

As early as 25 January, in one of his first meetings with General Marshall, Zhang Zhizhong argued that provincial control over militia forces was a Chinese custom that should be retained. Marshall skeptically believed that "militia" units could be used as a "local army" by both the KMT and CCP, in addition to local warlords.[96] In February, Zhou Enlai also expressed concern about the ambiguous status of "military police" and "railroad guards" in China.[97] Unlike the American system of small military police units attached to military commands, Chinese military police units operated mostly in urban areas, often far removed from the front lines, to enforce authority among military personnel. Officially, military police units reported to the central government and in times of emergency could be used by the central government to exert authority, but on a daily basis they were heavily involved in mundane policing, such as providing security at bus and train stations.[98] Marshall agreed with Zhou that the ambiguous nature of the military police and their pattern of involvement in civilian law and order needed clarification, and also their mission needed to be restricted.[99] The railroad guards were even more problematic, because they technically fell under the authority of the Ministry of Communications, but their large size—eighteen regiments with a total strength of over 75,000 men, and heavy weapons—made them a potent military force.[100]

On 16 February 1946, the panelists talked at length on the issue of military police and the Peace Preservation Corps. Both Zhou and Zhang accepted the need for prefecture and provincial administrations to be the sole authority for law and order, including large-scale disorders such as riots. Zhang and Zhou differed on the issue of military police, with Zhou maintaining that "in the future, the military police should have nothing to do with civil order and civil affairs."[101]

After direct questioning by Marshall and Zhou, Zhang agreed with the principal of limiting militia organizations, but no strict, clear framework was confirmed. The effect of Zhang's attempted obfuscation and the resulting discussion was to establish a clear public agreement in favor of a military devoted to combat action, but with an undefined and unclear system of provincial-level gendarmes handling domestic emergencies.

The greatest practical factor facing the military subcommittee was the basing of a streamlined and integrated national army. The PCC had not given any guidance as to the strategic threats facing China, but for KMT and CCP negotiators the location of military bases was a major area of uncertainty and distrust. Both the KMT and CCP sought to have their forces be preponderant in vital military regions of China, with their opposition scattered across the country. Moreover, the low level of strategic mobility among Chinese divisions (most were infantry that could move only ten miles a day) meant that a Chinese army needed to near likely trouble spots. The development of a viable "force posture," the structuring of the military organization to suit potential threats, is revealing of the strategic environment of 1946 and of Chinese military leaders' view of the world.

At the conclusion of World War II, the majority of KMT forces were deployed in south China, beginning a drive on the Chinese coast, while the CCP was primarily based in north China, scattered in dozens of base areas. The scramble to occupy Manchuria in 1945 resulted in a confused mixture of KMT-CCP control, with Soviet administration further complicating matter.

In late February 1946, Zhang, Zhou, and Marshall agreed to the division of China into five military regions: Northeast (encompassing the vital Manchurian area), Northwest, Central, North, and South China. In each area they fixed a number of divisions for both the KMT and CCP armies, with the CCP concentrated in their base area regions. The final plan allocated the overwhelming majority of Chinese forces to the northern border region, with six armies to the Northeast, five to the Northwest, and ten to North China. Central China was allocated eight armies, and South China, six.[102] In total, twenty-one out of thirty-five armies were planned to be garrisoned along China's northern border, in spite of severe logistical challenges in the relatively undeveloped region.

The final agreement worked out between Zhou, Zhang, and Marshall was an unambiguous expression of military nationalization. Completed on 25 February 1946, the military reorganization agreement stipulated that all command and control authority would be centralized in the executive branch through a National Military Council, with the president as its head.[103] Moreover, the purpose of the army was also specified as follows: "[T]he primary function of the Army shall be to defend the Republic in time of war. In time of peace the principal function of the Army shall be training."[104]

The plan for the drawdown of Chinese military forces outlined a time period of twelve months in which to reach a target of 108 divisions. Restrictions on the size of these divisions to less than 14,000 men each meant a total force strength of roughly 1.5 million at the conclusion of the program. Of the total of 108 divisions, it was stipulated that eighteen "shall be formed from Communist forces," which allowed for the reassignment of CCP officers as necessary but with enlisted forces left intact.[105] This meant approximately nine KMT divisions for each CCP division, a ratio the KMT felt would be sufficient to prevent the CCP becoming a credible military threat within the reformed army.[106] After the completion of the initial drawdown over a period of twelve months, a second phase of defense personnel cuts was planned, to reduce the composite army to a final strength of fifty Nationalist government divisions and ten Communist, with a total strength of 840,000 men.[107]

On the contentious issue of using military forces for law and order activities, the final agreement allowed military forces to "quell domestic disorders" only after the certification that local police and the provincial level Peace Preservation Corps was unable to cope with the situation. Usage of military forces following a governor's request would also require approval of the full State Council, encompassing several civilian ministers, rather than the approval of the smaller military council.[108]

Armament for the Peace Preservation Corps was to be restricted to light weapons: pistols, rifles, and light machine guns. Peace Preservation Corps units were to be funded, trained, and administered at the provincial level.[109] Coordination of high-level training for Peace Preservation Corps officers, standardization of equipment, and regular coordination with military units were left unclear, a reflection of China's diverse provincial administrations but also because of a lack of specificity reached by the three representatives.

Two days after the Military Subcommittee agreed on the reorganization directive, Zhou, Zhang, and Marshall agreed to designate the American Executive Headquarters in Beijing as the primary executor of the program.[110] The headquarters' staff, although it was an American organization, did include Chinese Nationalist and Communist personnel. Nevertheless, the designation of a foreign government entity as the primary agency to execute the military reforms revealed both the distrust between the KMT-CCP and the critical American role in the process.

Although the program for Chinese army nationalization and depoliticization quickly ran into difficulties after the outbreak of fresh fighting in Manchuria, the public statements of senior KMT and CCP personnel remained on record as the guiding principles. During the discussions, both Chiang Kai-shek and Mao Zedong were kept informed of the specifics being discussed and did not offer objections. By publicly lending their approval to the army nationalization program, even if it was a cynical political maneuver, senior Chinese leaders, particularly KMT leaders, gave further impetus to officers who sought a more professional military structure.

As the de facto ruling party of China, the KMT under Chiang Kai-shek sought to reassure the Chinese public that they supported the army nationalization program as part of a larger transition to democracy and civilian administration. In early 1946, Chiang stated, "The objective of this reorganized army is simple, to change from a militarily dysfunctional force into a powerful army, from an army seen as a shameful disgrace into [a] glorious beacon for the nation."[111] Publicly available KMT military publications were equally gushing in their praise of the new constitutionally structured military. The *Guofang Yuekan* (*National Defense Monthly*) hailed the creation of a civilian Ministry of National Defense as "the most important day in China's constitutional development in half a century."[112] Chiang's public speeches from mid-1946 highlight a continued desire to be personally involved, but did not include any overt mention of the KMT as a party in the new national army structure.[113]

Zhou Enlai emerged as the public face of the CCP in the army nationalization discussion, and made numerous public statements supporting the process of military integration and de-politicization. In a statement for Xinhua, the CCP news service, at the announcement of the final agreement on 25 February, Zhou was gushing in his praise, "We believe that this agreement will change our ways from eighteen years of armed conflict into a new era for China of peace, democracy, and unity."[114]

On an organizational level, the structural changes to China's military system were extensive. Between 1945 and 1947, over 75,000 personnel were cut from staff positions within the Ministry of National Defense, and all military functions were reorganized into six staff sections.[115] The reorganization program also implemented an American-style system of staff offices, arranged from G-1 to G-6, responsible for training activities. After the ROC constitution went into effect on 1 January 1947, the Ministry of National Defense, which began operating in June 1946, took on all authority stipulated by the PCC, including the appointment of a civilian minister.[116] Although the integration of KMT and CCP forces never took place, and the force reductions of Chinese military units never occurred, subsequent Chinese military and political leaders did have to work within the administrative structures and precedent established by the PCC and the military subcommittee. Moreover, the public debate and on-record agreement of senior political leaders, with the goals of a professional, nationalized military, provided normative support for reformers within the Chinese military

On a theoretical level, the effects of the army nationalization debate were far-reaching and reaffirmed Chinese military claims to exclusive professional jurisdiction over military affairs. Claims to legal jurisdictions by professions can occur in three areas: legislative, judicial, and administrative. Successful attempts to gain legislative support can result in laws prohibiting rival occupations from participating in certain fields of work, require qualifications that favor certain groups, or grant self-disciplining functions to professional groups. Judicial contestation involves both an articulation of a legal basis for a professional's claims to expertise, the organizational backing to pursue professional claims within the often lengthy and expensive judicial process, and a continued presence within the judicial sphere to pursue cases of non-compliance by competing occupations with legal prerogatives. Lastly, administrative contestation utilizes government procedures and codes, in both their drafting and enforcement phases, to gain professional advantage and a monopoly of occupational authority. In all three of these areas, the ROC constitution of 1946 affirmed the professional role of an apolitical, national military.

During the constitutional debate, the formerly KMT but now ROC army, had been essentially silent. Discussion of the changes occurred after the constitution became law on 25 December 1947, but military officers did not overtly disagree with the political changes. Military officers seemed pleased by the changes and, in several articles in military journals, felt confident that the organizational changes would be implemented quickly and efficiently. In an article in the army's weekly news magazine, a front-page column praised the constitutional changes as allowing for a truly "democratic army" for the first time. More specifically, the column argued that the key change would be that the military must now "obey the law" (shoufa), a subtle critique of the party-army concept of political supremacy.[117] Another front-page article argued that, under the terms of the new constitution, "the army must strive to be above politics and regions, not serve the interests of individuals, and not serve as a tool of political battles."[118]

Among the organizational changes during the transition from a National Military Council under KMT control to a civilian Ministry of National Defense

(MND) of the ROC was a reform of the Political Department system. On 30 May 1946, the Political Department was abolished and some of its political functions, but not party work functions, were assumed by the Information Bureau (xinwen ju) of the Ministry of Defense.[119] Officers assigned to the information bureau were highly restricted in their duties, with building up the morale of soldiers being most important, while surveillance and monitoring of military activities was not allowed.

The Information Department was headed by Deng Wenyi, a former private secretary of Chiang Kai-shek who had previous experience as a political officer, but Deng had few connections within the military.[120] During the brief existence of the information department no attempt was made to create a more centralized political education structure. The Information Department produced pamphlets, short films, and articles based on the model of the U.S. Office of War Information, but had little contact with ordinary soldiers.[121]

Although the Information Department allowed "political work," this type of work was defined as promoting nationalism rather than party loyalty. During the brief 1947–49 period, the Information Department was unable to develop an intellectually coherent or meaningful ideology. Working materials from the period use a variety of terms: vocation (tianzhi), spirit (jingshen), and national responsibility (guojia de zeren), but none of the terms were defined or resonated with the political education material.[122]

After the relocation of KMT forces to Taiwan an extensive review studied all aspects of KMT policies and organizational practices to determine the reason for the failure to limit the CCP. KMT studies of the Political Department during the 1928–49 period highlighted a wide variety of poor organizational strategies and anemic implementation. One of the primary critiques concerned the steady erosion of the prerogatives of the political officer compared to military commanders. KMT analysts believed that due to the failure to create an independent, proactive political officer system, policies that should have ideally been a combined effort between the ROC civilian government, KMT party apparatus, and the military became almost exclusively military operations.[123] The lack of a Political Department with centralized authority and aggressive leadership was identified a key aspect of this de facto militarization.

Thus, after the retreat of KMT forces to Taiwan in 1949, senior KMT leaders, especially Chiang Kai-shek and his son Ching-kuo, became steadfast in their opposition to a professional, apolitical military and sought to subvert the ROC military structure under KMT political control.

5

Refining the Army Profession, 1950–1953

After the withdrawal of ROC military forces to Taiwan in 1948 and 1949, significant changes in personnel composition, equipment, and mission requirements were necessitated by the changing strategic environment, but the core ideals and structures established in the 1947 ROC constitution remained intact. Between 1950 and 1953, the ROC military became a highly focused military organization with a clear mission, opposing a Communist invasion, a streamlined military structure built around well-trained and fully equipped infantry divisions, and a reliable, long-term security relationship with the United States. Underneath these surface considerations the core elements of the ROC military, especially its key doctrinal, intellectual, and educational concepts, remained essentially unchanged from the professional model developed from 1942 to 1949.

Training Centers and the Central Military Academy

One of the key differences between the pre-1949 and post-1949 ROC military was the amount of time devoted to training activities and exercises. Training in the pre-1949 period had been restricted due to a lack of funds, as well as geographic and transportation difficulties, which made moving military units difficult and led to a focus on current operations at the expense of preparing for future activities. After 1949, the ROC military became highly focused on conducting high-intensity military training exercises, which were used to introduce key concepts to soldiers and served as a method of evaluation for officers.

Training in Taiwan was often highly specialized around skills such as night fighting, parachute training, and close air support. Training was spread throughout the island, with American advisers attached to all training staffs, ensuring that instruction was uniform across all units. Large-scale exercises were led at least once a year and were observed by military staff officers and American advisers. Both training and exercises were conducted at very high intensity, with live-fire exercises and close interservice coordination, such as beach landings or air support, creating stressful situations and realistic evaluations.[1]

Gen. Sun Li-jen's successful establishment of a comprehensive military training system on Taiwan during the 1947–49 period proved invaluable to the ROC military as it sought to regain its footing. Rather than reform the Central Military Academy (Zhongguo lujun junguan xuexiao), which had been located in Nanjing, the ROC Ministry of Defense assigned staff and students to the officer training facilities Sun had developed at Fengshan. Although the name of the school was transferred to emphasize continuity, the reliance on Sun's appointed instructors and training schedules meant there was little real crossover between the schools.[2] This de facto organizational takeover of the core elements of the ROC military training system by schools established by Sun represented a clear opportunity for Sun to spread his beliefs and ideas throughout the military.

The new Central Military Academy (CMA) at Fengshan quickly became a key node in the rejuvenation of the ROC military, training officers for all three services. Beginning with an initial class of 950 students in October 1950, the school provided yearly classes of roughly one thousand students with an integrated, two-year training program prior to commissioning as officers.[3] During the 1950–55 period, distinguished guests such as President Chiang Kai-shek, American ambassador Karl Rankin, U.S. Military Assistance Advisory Group (MAAG) officials, and senior American military officers frequently visited the school to inspect the cadets and speak on a wide range of issues.[4] The visits were also interpreted as clear expressions of political support for Sun's training program, increasing his prestige and influence within the ROC military as an institution.[5]

The content of the training at the CMA was a balance of military science courses on weapons, tactics, and military history, combined with courses in writing skills, basic science, and engineering, as well as Chinese culture. Political education encompassed roughly 15 percent of coursework and was conducted by political officers, but during the early period from 1950 to 1953, political instruction was focused on moral training, such as the cadet honor code, rather than KMT propaganda.[6] Physical fitness was highly emphasized, and Sun Li-jen in particular appears to have encouraged the creation of a large system of physical training instruction and intramural sports leagues among cadets.

Military Journals

In comparison to military education and training, which improved remarkably after 1950, military journals show little change in their subject matter or tone. In addition to journals published by military schools, Taiwan in the early 1950s had a robust commercial press, with popular military magazines such as *Junshi zazhi* featuring defense commentary alongside ads for GMC trucks.[7] Small military publishing houses also continued to brush aside the defeat in China in favor of technical analysis. In 1950, one of the first short studies was an examination of the role of nuclear weapons and how conventional forces must adapt and change.[8]

The primary journals of the ROC Army continued to show an emphasis on highly technical military skills such as armored attacks, combined arms operation, and air-ground coordination. Many of the journal articles of the period also presented military analysis of areas such as Xinjiang and Mongolia, locations far removed from the military realities of the ROC in Taiwan. The tone expressed by the journals revealed that the ROC military retained a strong affinity for the organizational structures and tactical thinking it had developed during the 1940s and viewed its status in Taiwan as temporary. This "army in exile" mentality appears to have only been brought to an end in 1955, when intellectual discussion finally became more focused on defensive operations and the Taiwan region exclusively.

As in the 1945–49 period, a large percentage of Chinese military journals focused on U.S.-related military topics. Technical developments, American organizational techniques, and combat experiences in Korea were all prominently featured. Analysis of American methods often focused on the organizational structure of the U.S. Army, particularly the staff officer system, which Chinese officers felt was an effective way to provide a wide range of capabilities without infringing on the power and authority of the commander.[9] Another topic of frequent study was the American officer education system, which included both public and private military schools, as well as military officer training at civilian schools, such as the Reserve Officers Training Corps (ROTC) program.[10] This interest in a massive officer training program appears excessive considering the context of a small island whose military contained a disproportionately high number of officers (up to 20 percent in some units), but this type of program would have been applicable after a return to power in China.

The development of armored forces and offensive doctrines also seems excessive for an infantry force based on defensive tactics, but this similarly highlights aspirations for a return to China and large-scale warfare. In a lengthy article in 1952, it was argued that the combat experience of World War II validated the reliance on "fluidity of force" (huodongxing) and that the development of atomic weapons had only accelerated this change away from infantry forces. The article concluded that the ROC military must enter the era of "roadless tactics" based on tanks and armored cars.[11]

Another area of seeming incongruence between the strategic situation of the ROC military in Taiwan and the topicality of research was the high degree of interest in German operations on the eastern front during World War II. Throughout the early 1950s, Chinese officers were fascinated by the tactical methods, equipment, and experiences that German officers developed while fighting the Soviet forces. As in the analysis of the American staff system, Chinese analysts argued that in a fluid tactical environment, a military commander needed to have unhindered command and control over his forces with no interference from external authorities, such as political leaders.[12] A key element of the German system was the use of mission-type orders (Auftragstaktik, renwu xing de mingling), which gave a commander an objective and a deadline but left all other functions to his discretion.

In 1950, only months after relocating to Taiwan, *National Defense Magazine* (*Guofang yekan*) resumed publication. With articles by Chiang Kai-shek and other senior KMT-affiliated generals, it presented analysis of military affairs that emphasized government policy rather than professional skills.[13] Throughout the 1950–55 period, military intellectuals within the ROC military continued to promote policies, weapons acquisitions, and training programs remarkably similar to those of the 1945–49 period. Within the journals, ROC officers argued for a simplified organizational structure with a clearly defined military staff system, the development of a mission-type order system, and increased specialization of technical branches such as armored forces. These affinities exhibit a clear preference for a military isolated from political interference or civilian oversight, as well as a strong preference for offensive military action. Throughout the articles, the role of the commander as the sole focus of power and authority within military units is presented as both a military necessity, to enable decisive action, and a moral requirement, because it links power and responsibility.

Structures and Equipment

The basic structure of the ROC military, in terms of organizational system, chain of command, and branch networks, remained in place after the transition to Taiwan in 1949. During the early 1950s American military aid enabled the full equipping and funding of many of the army branches, especially armor, which had been hindered by a lack of equipment or funding. By the end of 1952, all three services had reestablished separate command and general staff schools, officer academies, and one or more specialized courses, such as anti-air raid or communications school, for junior officers.[14]

One new element of the Ministry of National Defense was the creation of the Mainland Operations Division to conduct guerilla operations inside the People's Republic of China (PRC). During the early 1950s this organization operated from small islands controlled by the ROC, and carried out several dozen raids, reconnaissance operations, and infiltration of areas of Fujian province.[15] United States CIA officers supported these operations because they had some intelligence value, but they were not central to either the ROC or MAAG military programs.

American aid solved the biggest contradiction in ROC military doctrine and reality, a gap between the desire to pursue mechanized warfare and the economic means to support the logistics required, through direct transfer of equipment at no cost. American military transfers also resolved the problem of ad hoc acquisition of weapons. Speaking in 1953 on the new weapons, Sun Li-jen noted favorably that in contrast to 1949, when the ROC military used over ten kinds of basic military rifles, the army now had a standard rifle in use for all troops.[16] The effect of these weapons transfers was to improve not only the combat potential of ROC forces but also the morale of its troops. In 1952 Sun remarked, "Our present defense capability, compared to where we were two years ago, is beyond our dreams."[17]

Taiwan's constrained economic base placed stress on military budgets throughout the early 1950s and led to real cuts in military strength. In 1950, the ROC military consisted of thirty-nine divisions. Many of these formations suffered under an abundance of officers in staff positions but a shortage of junior enlisted personnel. By July 1952, the ROC military had been streamlined into a force of twenty-four divisions, arranged in eight armies falling into two army groups.[18] This was accomplished by assigning over 24,000 officers, who were either too old or poorly trained for the demands of modern warfare, into "officer combat groups" (junguan zhandou tuan), where they received full pay but lacked any real military authority.[19]

During the 1950–53 period, the branch of the ROC Army that benefitted the most from American aid and the program of creating a technology-intensive force was the ROC armored forces. Between 1950 and 1953, the ROC Army took possession of dozens of American M5 Stuart, M4 Sherman, and M24 Chaffee tanks, as well as hundreds of trucks, half-tracks, and armored cars.[20] The armored force also benefited from personal connections because Chiang Wei-kuo, the adopted son of Chiang Kai-shek, was the commander from March 1950 through May 1953.[21]

Sun Li-jen: Commander in Chief

Sun's ability to influence the ROC military identity benefitted tremendously from the increasing numbers of schools, personnel, and equipment under his command jurisdiction. Rather than Taiwan being a dead-end post and his responsibility being confined to basic training of short-term draftees, Sun now had authority over the entire ROC army school system. The first officer school to be reestablished in Taiwan was the Central Military Academy, which reopened in Fengshan, on Taiwan's southern coast, in August 1950. This was closely followed by the infantry officer school in February 1951, the artillery officer school in March 1951 and the armor officer school in January 1952. A command and general staff school for senior officers was established in the summer of 1951, and with the opening of specialized engineer and communications schools in 1952 the ROC army school system was completely reestablished.[22]

Political leaders such as Chiang Kai-shek saw the development of a de facto independent training system by Sun as dangerous. The high numbers of personnel who had previous experience with Sun, the comprehensive nature of the training, and Sun's reputation for independence were all regarded with suspicion. More directly, Sun's development of military training programs for women and youth represented a system of military penetration of key social groups, which KMT political leaders needed to keep within their own political bases.[23]

The period from August 1950 through April 1954 was the time of Sun's greatest influence in shaping the internal culture and intellectual framework of the ROC Army. Like many Chinese commanders, Sun used frequent speeches and lectures to increase the morale and esprit de corps of his troops. The collected public speeches of Sun are a rare resource to study the development of ROC officers and their conceptions of professional responsibility, mission, and shared culture.

Sun's intellectual concepts illustrate the interplay between Chinese and Western military concepts during the early twentieth century. The ideas expressed by Sun during the crucial 1947–54 period drew from his experiences studying in the United States, wartime exploits, political views, and his interest in Chinese history. At their most basic, Sun's ideas revolve around four key concepts: nation, people, profession, and honor. Sun frequently used these four concepts during his public speeches to describe his aspirations for the Chinese army and to instruct his audiences on their role in the army's development.

Nation (guojia)

Of the four concepts that Sun regularly alluded to, "nation" was the least used and most vague. Throughout Sun's speeches, lectures and writings, he almost never uses the word "party," Kuomintang, or uses party positions to describe the political leadership of China. Instead he used the term "nation." But Sun left out any specifics on what a nation encompasses. Sun spoke of the nation as a governing body that ruled by the consent of the governed, but did not include a discussion of any specific government institutions or organizations. The deliberate ambiguity in Sun's use of "nation" appears motivated both by a desire to avoid messy political ideology and by a lack of interest on Sun's part in political forms and civilian governance.

The one aspect of the relationship between the army and the nation that Sun frequently and articulately promoted was the idea of a clear military obedience to civilian authority. Sun states that the primary objective of the army is to protect the nation from external threats and enemies. Sun's notion of objective civilian control was in stark contrast to official KMT ideology, which held that the army was primarily under the direction of the Nationalist Party. Sun firmly rejected the KMT idea of party rather than national control. Thus, in public speeches Sun was sharply critical of this ideology, "Our Army officers belong to the nation, the Army as a whole belongs to the nation, it is not a private army."[24]

People (minzu)

Like his concept of nation, Sun developed his notion of the "people" of China as both a partner of the army and as an object needing protection. The theme of civilian-military cooperation ran throughout Sun's public statements and highlighted his strong belief that the army must pursue tasks that are valuable and legitimate in the eyes of the Chinese people. The second theme Sun developed was that the army must serve as the protector of the people. Although most of Sun's public comments occurred during a period of civil war, the prospective enemy Sun alludes to was rarely the Communists but vaguely defined foreign forces. In Sun's speeches on this theme, there is a clear tension between a desire to protect the people and a caution about military involvement in a messy civil war, which might jeopardize civilian support.

A major element of Sun's desire to create a more cooperative and respectful relationship between civilians and the military was to exorcise the past notions of warlord or Japanese army authoritarian rule. Sun sought to create a sharp break with the negative connotations of the military in China, and to place the

KMT army in a less politicized role. Speaking to military officers, Sun noted, "Today we can tell our fellow citizens, don't be afraid of our homeland's army, our military is your sword, its stands up for you, all of the military's actions are according to your thoughts and needs. Protecting the nation and people is the army's sacred mission; everyone in the army wants to help the common people, love the common people, and never again harass or bother the common people."[25]

Sun's concepts of honor and profession were closely linked to his notion of the people, in that the army would receive honor from the people if, and only if, it maintained its professional discipline and military bearing. During his period of command in northeast China, Sun castigated several units for poor behavior and the resulting breakdown in trust between local populations and the KMT army. Sun lambasted the officers of the 3rd Division for letting the men behave worse than the Japanese: "When we [the KMT army] got to Haicheng there were big problems, our hard-won reputation for honor and glory was ruined by some bad elements who lost their conscience. . . . People told me that when the Japanese were here there were many things that were oppressive and unfair but at least their troops had discipline. . . . If we as an army maintain our discipline, cherish our honor and dignity, the people will respect us."[26]

Profession (tianzhi)

The concept of profession, and the military as a profession, was the most complicated of the four terms Sun repeatedly emphasized. Sun used two distinct intellectual strands to highlight the military as a profession: technical competence in their chosen field and the need for concepts of self-policing and internal organizational control.

Sun's notion of technical competence for all military personnel led him to emphasis rigorous training, especially intensive weapons training and physical fitness, as a hallmark of the military profession. Throughout Sun's numerous commands, long periods of time were devoted to the training of soldiers, first at the individual level and later in progressively larger units and formations. Embedded within Sun's focus on training was a strong desire to accentuate the differences between a modern army, with the highly technical requirements of its personnel, and poorly trained warlord soldiers, motivated by money or personal loyalty. The term Sun used to define this idea was "skilled," or "well-practiced abilities" (shu lian). This term encompasses not just the ability to conduct specific functions but also a sense of craftsmanship and a clear sense of defined abilities that are different than other occupations and professions.

The poor performance of KMT forces during the Chinese civil war from 1945 to 1949 was particularly galling to Sun, because it meant that organizational changes to develop a mechanized, combined arms force would be wasted due to poor performance of basic skills. In 1948 Sun identified basic military skills as the most pressing army issue:

> Today our army's biggest weakness, from the top to the bottom, is that in military techniques and tactics we lack the necessary skills, even if we are shooting from only 200 meters we can't kill the enemy, with these kinds of skills how can we win? . . . If skills aren't up to the necessary level, you might have great weapons, great equipment, all sorts of great things but they will have no utility. Being a modern military soldier means being able to use all kinds of weapons to achieve victory.[27]

Sun's use of the term "zizhi"—self-control or being in command of oneself—highlights the notion of the military as an autonomous, self-contained organization. Sun frequently used the concept of zizhi when describing his time at VMI in the 1920s, and the formative effect it had on his conception of a military that utilized peer pressure, behavioral norms, and internal disciplinary functions to inculcate good behavior. VMI utilized senior classmen as the primary instructors of all basic military training such as marching, shooting, and field exercises. Staff restricted their instruction to technical and academic subjects with little interaction, between staff and cadets outside of the classroom. VMI's system was also famous, sometimes notorious, for extreme hazing of new students and extremely harsh disciplinary measures implemented by cadet officers. Another example of VMI's self-discipline concept was the honor code that stipulated expulsion for any cadet caught lying or cheating, and that fellow cadets who did not report incidents would be similarly expelled. Sun felt that this style of mutual responsibility and mutual observation was a vital part of military education. In late 1944 he spoke to members of the Chinese Army in India that, like VMI, "I think that no matter what kind of school, all should cultivate the sense of duty, a sense of shame, a desire for public responsibility, to not just rely on managers for supervision; this is true autonomy."[28]

Honor (rongyu)

The concept of honor was how Sun sought to link profession, nation, and people together into an integrated whole. In Sun's intellectual framework, the military gained honor by serving the people and fulfilling their need for defense. The military also gained honor from the nation by being focused on its distinctive mission and not interfering in civilian affairs. Lastly, the military gained honor by remaining true to its internal values and professional competency. Sun's frequent references to honor, dignity, self-respect within the military, and respect shown to the military by the Chinese citizenry, are pervasive and highlight a deep-rooted sense of insecurity. Like many other KMT officers of his generation, the formative experiences of Sun's youth, when large, undisciplined warlord military forces became an object of social scorn and derision, remained salient features of Sun's thinking and a prominent negative example.

Sun frequently spoke of the concept of honor as a term that applied not to an individual but to the army as a discrete body and institution:

> An individual has his own honor, which functions like a second life apart from his body; an organization also has its own honor that functions in exactly the same manner. No matter if it is an individual or an organization, both must value their honor as equal in importance to their very existence. . . . Our untarnished honor is something we have earned by spilling blood and the sacrifice of many of our comrades' lives; it is something that we have struggled to earn and it has not been an easy task.[29]

Sun's notion of honor as the connective tissue linking together the military's role, the Chinese nation, and the Chinese people was possible, and was evident during the brief "honeymoon" period after the victory against the Japanese. Speaking in 1946, Sun noted the when the army had returned to Beijing and Tianjin in 1945, relations with the civilian population had been respectful and cooperative. He noted:

> If we needed a house to stay in, people of their own volition volunteered a place for us to stay; if we needed to do something people helped us . . . this was because our great reputation had preceded us and influenced the people; so that even though our army had not been to this place before, the people believed we were their heroes. The military's model was to be the protector of the nation's people, this was why the people adored and respected us.[30]

Conspicuously missing from his four ideals were the notions of ideology (zhuyi), and leaders (lingxiu), both of which were cardinal virtues of the KMT.[31] While for the moment, Sun was unopposed when speaking to his soldiers and fellow officers, after 1953, the gap between KMT ideals and Sun's ideals would become starkly apparent.

The United States in Taiwan, 1950-1953: Influence through Education

After the collapse of the ROC military during 1948 and 1949, the United States faced the unenviable choice of either supporting a government that appeared to have little competence in economic, political or military affairs, or acquiescing to a Communist-dominated China. Multiple domestic constituencies that sought conflicting goals in East Asia also buffeted the formation of American policy toward the ROC on Taiwan. Strong elements within the Republican Party, led by Senator William F. Knowland of California, advocated strong support for the ROC and emphasized the need for a strong anti-Communist ally on Taiwan, both for immediate American security interests and, if possible, as an example of reform and development for East Asia.[32] Elements of the American military, particularly the Joint Chiefs of Staff (JCS), also sought to aid ROC forces on Taiwan, through large-scale transfers of equipment, training, and logistical support. Although not advocating military action in support of the ROC, the JCS argued that American support for the ROC could distract Chinese Communists from the ongoing conflict in Indochina.[33]

The Truman administration and the State Department strongly opposed continued support for the ROC and argued, that based on intelligence estimates, ROC forces on Taiwan could not defend themselves without direct U.S. military support, which was not in the interests of the United States. Accordingly, in January 1950, President Truman suspended military aid to the ROC allocated under the China Aid Act of 1948.[34]

With the ending of official American support for the ROC forces on Taiwan, several private American sources offered military advice and equipment. In February 1950, retired Adm. Charles M. Cooke arrived in Taiwan as an accredited correspondent of the International News Service with an official side business in selling fertilizer. Unofficially, over the next six months, Cooke arranged the transfer of millions of dollars' worth of military equipment, including large amounts of aircraft spare parts, artillery shells, and armored cars, from the United States and Japan.[35] Cooke also offered personal military advice to Chiang Kai-shek, achieving some policy changes to ROC military strategy, most notably the abandonment of several vulnerable islands off the Chinese coast that were indefensible and difficult to supply.[36]

Only after the North Korean invasion of South Korea on 24 June 1950 did official American policy shift to support for the ROC government on Taiwan. On 27 June 1950, Truman ordered the U.S. 7th Fleet to prevent any attack on Taiwan and prevent ROC attacks on China.[37] On 28 July, the State Department announced the dispatch of a representative to Taipei as a chargé d'affaires with responsibilities for maintaining diplomatic contacts, which had lapsed since the U.S. Embassy had closed in China.[38] More significantly, on 31 July, Gen. Douglas MacArthur visited Taipei to hold meetings and conduct joint planning with Chiang Kai-shek and other senior ROC leaders, to meet any possible attack on Taiwan. MacArthur also dispatched his deputy chief of staff, Maj. Gen. Alonzo P. Fox, to Taipei on 4 August to serve as permanent military liaison with the ROC government.[39]

While in Taipei, General Fox and a small staff of Americans worked with ROC military officers to prepare a comprehensive report on the necessity of American military assistance, and the potential for a successful defense of Taiwan. Complicating the work of the Fox Survey Group were the statements of General MacArthur, who in November and December recommended that ROC forces deploy to Korea.[40] The Fox Group report identified the ROC ground forces as the most "important deterrent" of a Communist invasion of Taiwan, although their actual fighting ability was hurt by logistical problems.[41] American evaluators felt that the ROC military training and morale was good, but a lack of small arms and sufficient ammunition made realistic exercises difficult.[42] The Fox Survey Group recommended a large military aid, package estimated to be over $158 million dollars in value, to raise the immediate combat effectiveness of ROC forces, with additional follow-on funding bringing the total over $200 million.[43] By March 1951, after the Survey Group report wound through the Washington bureaucracy, the total cost estimate for military aid had risen to $300 million.

The State Department initially argued against such a large advisory and aid package, favoring a "light footprint" approach of less than two hundred officers in any advisory mission. Furthermore, the State Department argued that all military efforts in Taiwan should fall under the authority of the American ambassador in Taipei.[44] In light of the massive quantity of equipment, specialized military skills required, and difficult military situation in the Far East during early 1951, the State Department program to take control of the mission was rejected. Instead, to assist in the distribution, usage, and training of the ROC Army as it integrated the massive American aid program, a large, explicitly military, assistance group was formed in April 1951. Modeled after the Joint U.S. Military Assistance Group that had operated in China from 1947 to 1949, the group, named Formosa MAAG (Military Assistance Advisory Group) was under the command of Maj. Gen. William Chase. Initial strength for the group was set at 116 officers and men, but with the expectation that future expansion would bring the final strength up to 400–500 advisers.[45]

Formosa MAAG operated under a set of assumptions and guidelines developed by multiple government agencies during the winter of 1950. First, the objective of the MAAG was not to create an ROC military capable of offensive action. This was in accordance with the president's 27 June 1950 statement.[46] Second, assuming the support of the U.S. 7th Fleet, ROC forces should include a ground force component of thirty-one divisions, a Navy of roughly twenty ships, and an Air Force fielding four fighter groups and one light bomber squadron.[47] Last, American support would focus on areas of funding, equipment, and transportation where the ROC was deficient in supporting itself.[48]

Although the State Department concurred with the establishment of a MAAG on Taiwan, it continued to argue strongly that MAAG operations should fall under the control of the ambassador in Taipei, Karl Rankin, rather than Commander in Chief, Far East (CINCFE), Douglas MacArthur.[49] The State Department even went so far as to notify the ROC ambassador that the Formosa MAAG was under the direction of the American ambassador in Taipei, without consulting with the Department of Defense or executive administration.[50] While the State Department ultimately lost the jurisdictional battle, with the Commander in Chief, Far East being designated as the primary supervisory authority over the MAAG group, in reality Formosa MAAG was largely independent. Unlike the JUSMAG effort in China from 1947 to 1949, where Americans had operated from a headquarters separate from the Chinese, MAAG on Taiwan established offices in the same building as the ROC Ministry of Defense, with staff sections directly attached to their ROC counterparts.[51] For the duration of the 1951–55 period, the most important relationship for MAAG was not with the U.S. Embassy or U.S. military but with the officers of the ROC military with whom they worked with on a daily basis.

Gen. William Chase and Complicated Chains of Command

The assignment of a senior American general to the command of the MAAG force on Taiwan was potentially tricky, because many American officers with experience in China were associated with the discredited Stilwell program of American military training for Chinese forces during World War II. Moreover, many of officers who had served under Stillwell and Wedemeyer had been relatively old.

Many retired after the war or had been assigned to the China-Burma-India (CBI) theater against their wishes, and had no particular affinity for China and no wish to return. Command of a MAAG unit was also as much a political assignment as a military one, with the cultivation of good relations with the host country being a primary, and often difficult, task of the American commander.

In early 1951, Gen. William Chase was chief of staff to the Third Army, which handled military affairs in the southeast United States, and was likely destined for a succession of quiet administrative positions followed by retirement. Unlike the overwhelming majority of American senior officers during this period, Chase had not gone to West Point but had instead entered the Army through the National Guard. Chase had enlisted in the Rhode Island National Guard while attending Brown University, and had entered active duty as a private when several National Guard units deployed to the Mexican border raids during the Mexican Revolution.[52] Chase rose in rank as the Army expanded during World War I, reaching the rank of captain in 1918. He was one of the few provisional officers given a regular Army commission after the war. During the interwar years Chase was assigned to a variety of academic positions as a student at Army command schools, an instructor in training units, and with ROTC detachments at civilian schools.[53] Chase's affinity for schools and education continued after his retirement when he became a professor at the University of Houston.

During World War II, Chase was assigned to the Pacific theater, commanding the 1st Cavalry Division in the Admiralty Islands and the 38th Infantry Division in the Philippines. Chase served in the American occupation forces in Japan from 1945 to 1949, and became associated in Army circles with General MacArthur, who had been his direct superior from 1943 to 1949. The connection to General MacArthur made Chase's appointment as MAAG commander understandable, in that it would aid coordination with the East Asian region. The political firestorm resulting from the relief of General MacArthur by President Truman in April 1951, however, made association with MacArthur a source of concern for many in Washington. Only through the personal support of Gen. George Marshall was Chase confirmed, and he arrived in Taipei on 1 May 1951.[54]

The MAAG officers' initial impression of the ROC military was not good. Chase noted the most common equipment as "grass sandals, palm leaf hats, very brief shorts, and old [World] War I Springfield rifles."[55] In spite of this less-than-promising beginning, the sheer number of available troops offered strategic potential: "Here was a strategic reserve capable of being moved ashore on the mainland of China or almost anywhere else in the Orient."[56]

An implicit assumption of United States planning, which the Fox report had seemingly confirmed, was that the core ROC military was not in need of systematic reform but merely needed increased material support. In this context, the role of chief of MAAG was often as a facilitator of supplies and promoter of education, rather than a director of hands-on training. The mission statement given to General Chase specified that his primary task was "advising the military staff of the Chinese National Government on the initiation and development of requests for aid."⁵⁷ This would have given the Chinese armed forces the primary responsibility of producing assessments of their abilities, requirements, and necessary equipment, with MAAG refining, and then delivering requests to Washington.

General Chase, however, perceived his job slightly differently than as a facilitator of Chinese requests. He stated, "Our job . . . is to get them the hardware they need—what I say they need, not what they think they need—and then teach them how to use it and take care of it. It doesn't do radar any good, you know, to set it up in a rice paddy."⁵⁸

While not explicitly stated in the MAAG mission, one of the primary tasks of General Chase and MAAG was working with American political leaders, the source of all appropriations and military aid, and encouraging their commitment to the MAAG effort. In just one month, November 1953, General Chase welcomed numerous American delegations, including Vice President Richard Nixon, two senators, one congressman, the chief of Naval Operations, as well as the owner of the *Chicago Tribune* newspaper.⁵⁹ General Chase was the most senior American official in Taiwan during 1951–53, because a chargé d'affaires rather than a fully accredited ambassador headed the U.S. Embassy in Taipei. This meant that Chase was compelled to represent the Unites States government at numerous ROC ceremonial functions as a demonstration of American political support for the ROC.⁶⁰

During his time on Taiwan, General Chase does not seem to have been particularly interested in Chinese culture or history. When asked if he had learned any Chinese during his time with MAAG he replied, "Oh, yes. I now speak fluent Chinese. Shih Shih nee. Okay. Coca Cola. With that I can get by anywhere in Formosa."⁶¹

Refining the ROC Army

The military reform programs developed by MAAG shifted from an initial focus on defensive operations during the 1951 and 1952 period into a program designed to develop offensive capabilities during 1953 and 1954. Within the broader system emplaced by MAAG were three main areas of emphasis. First, the immediate problem for MAAG was downsizing the ROC Army from a top-heavy force of forty to fifty understrength divisions into a smaller but more combat-effective force. Second, extensive training and education was required to allow ROC forces to fully utilize more sophisticated American equipment and to conduct military operations with increased unity of air/sea/land forces. Third, MAAG was consciously aware that extensive military aid programs eventually diminish, so the ROC needed to increase the sustainability of its manpower and equipment by encouraging the development of local sources of supply.

Throughout the early years of MAAG on Taiwan, Americans benefitted from the support of a group of ROC officers who shared their aspirations for the ROC Army. Sun Li-jen's excellent English skills and reputation as a competent commander in the Burma campaign under Stilwell endeared him to American MAAG officers.[62] Sun had no strong political ties to the KMT, and like many younger and professional officers, Sun stood to gain in power and influence from American plans to increase the combat effectiveness of the ROC Army.

An additional problem faced by MAAG officers on arrival in May 1951 was the chaotic organization of the ROC military. The poorly planned retreat to Taiwan in 1949 had resulted in bits and pieces of forty to fifty divisions being present on Taiwan, but with none at full strength in terms of personnel or equipment.[63] Moreover, ROC military forces suffered from a surplus of officers and poorly trained, often illiterate junior soldiers, but with very few NCOs and competent junior officers to provide tactical leadership. Tactically, the priority task of American advisers was "changing a Chinese Nationalists' concept of defense from a pattern of static defense to a pattern of mobile defense."[64]

After 1951, with the U.S. Seventh Fleet continuing to limit either PRC or ROC military attacks in the Taiwan Strait, and the increasing effectiveness of ROC Army units, the rationale for American development of the ROC Army was often referred to not as a strategic necessity but a "strategic bargain."[65] General Chase frequently used the idea of a "strategic bargain" when advocating greater aid for the ROC. Chase noted that for $300 per year, the United States could pay for all expenses for a ROC soldier, while an American soldier was estimated to cost $5,000 per year to supply and train. Although ROC forces were less effective than American units, the massive gap in the cost of fielding military forces, particularly in an area like East Asia, made further aid a good financial as well as a military investment.[66]

Early in the MAAG program, plans shifted a large portion of the American assistance effort toward developing a comprehensive, American-type military school system. General Chase fully supported a heavy emphasis on officer education rather than low-level training: "[T]he more professionally qualified their senior officers are, the more chance of success they have."[67] Drawing on General Chase's affinity for formal schooling, and building from the framework of ROC military schools developed in 1947–49, a large percentage of American MAAG personnel served at ROC military schools.

Prior to 1949, the ROC Army had operated eighteen military schools, most patterned on American organizational structures and using variations of American course material. With MAAG assistance, the number of schools more than doubled, eventually including thirty-eight separate institutions offering nearly four hundred courses.[68] The crown jewels in this pedagogical network were the senior officer colleges: the National War College, Armed Forces Staff College, and the Command and General Staff College, all established in 1952. Below these graduate-level schools was a large network of officer training programs, with branch schools for armor, infantry, air defense, and so forth, providing the main locations for officer exposure to sophisticated equipment and tactics. MAAG's interest in ROC military schools even extended to assigning a U.S. Army bandmaster to establish an ROC military band school.[69] Supplementing these schools was an extensive program of overseas study, with thousands of ROC military personnel, the majority of whom were officers, attending civilian and military schools in the United States.[70]

MAAG officers assigned to ROC military schools tried to remain in the background, if possible, and let qualified ROC personnel conduct direct training. American advisers focused their efforts on "training the trainers," and tried to allow Chinese instructors to be seen as independent, a technique that was believed to be important for morale and in keeping with concerns that MAAG personnel not be seen as a separate chain of command within the ROC military.[71] The assignment of large numbers of MAAG officers to widely dispersed military schools, many of which were in the southern part of the island, also had a political purpose in removing American officers from political intrigues in Taipei and avoiding a concentration of American personnel in the capital, which might give the appearance it was an "occupied" town.[72]

In addition to the personal involvement of American advisers at ROC military schools, MAAG undertook a large-scale program to translate American military manuals into Chinese. During the 1950s hundreds of training manuals, pamphlets, and guides were produced, on a wide range of subjects. These translated materials covered not only technical subjects, such as how to fix engines or plot artillery trajectories, but also cultural patterns, such as how to convey authority in a briefing, or appropriate body language for officers.[73]

At the end of his four years in Taiwan, General Chase regarded American success in developing the ROC school system as his most important accomplishment. He noted that, "Increased numbers of well qualified instructors, in many cases trained in the United States, is [a] major contribution to the improved stature of these schools. In turn the graduates of these schools have improved training and planning in units."[74] General Chase also referred to MAAG success within the ROC military education system when briefing Congress: "We have been very successful with the schools. The schools have been modeled after our own service schools, Army, Navy, and Air Force, and we find that the Chinese accept our tactical doctrines and our principles of staff procedure almost entirely—not completely, but almost entirely."[75] The similarity in U.S. and ROC schools that Chase lauded had become so apparent that many American officers assigned to MAAG referred to locations as "Little Fort Benning" or "Little Fort Belvoir" instead of the ROC infantry or engineer school respectively.[76]

One example of this process of pedagogical influence was the artillery school, established in Tainan, July 1952. The school exclusively used American equipment such as the 75-mm and 105-mm howitzer, with all training techniques borrowed from American methods. The artillery school course gave commissioned officers a three-month program of instruction that was able to graduate over two hundred officers per course. Twenty American artillery officers were assigned to the school, tasked with assisting the Chinese instructors. The latter were led by Maj. Gen. Wang Kuan-chow, a graduate of École Militaire (St. Cyr) in France and five Chinese officers who had graduated from the U.S. Army artillery course at Fort Sill.[77]

The U.S. MAAG on Taiwan also coordinated extensive visits to the United States by senior ROC officers. This program exposed dozens of senior ROC generals to U.S. training institutions such as West Point, the Army War College, and technical schools such as the Armor training center at Fort. Knox.[78] Many of these trips lasted over one month and had the unintentional effect of giving more day-to-day authority on Taiwan to the lower-ranking ROC officers. Gen. Chou Chih-jou, chief of the General Staff, was particularly targeted for these official visits, and during the 1950s he spent a solid month touring the United States every two years with a large delegation, leaving administrative control with younger officers.

Direct advisory efforts were more challenging for American personnel because of the large number of variables during daily operations, which made planning more difficult than in a school environment. Throughout the MAAG mission the cardinal rule for advisers was that "no United States officer or enlisted man in the advisory group has any command authority over any member of the Chinese armed forces."[79]

The last substantive military reform that changed the inherent structure of the ROC military was the introduction of a military draft on Taiwan in 1955. Unlike Japan, the United States, or all the European nations, China had never had a functioning military draft system, even during the 1937–45 Sino-Japanese War. On paper, the KMT had established a Ministry of Conscription in November 1944, but American pressures to downsize the Chinese Army and political disputes over the status of the army in the 1945–49 period meant that conscription was never implemented.[80]

In part, this was also due to large numbers of Chinese men available for military service who could be either bribed, threatened, or entreated to enlist in the Chinese army. Although the Chinese Army under the KMT (pre-1947) and the ROC Army in China (1947–49) had been able to rely on these loose, informal methods to gain sufficient recruits, the small population on Taiwan, roughly 10 million in 1950, meant that skimming a large pool of potential recruits was no longer a viable policy.

A more enduring reason for Chinese military units not creating a military draft system were concerns about loyalty and a lack of administrative capacity. The Chinese state, going back to the dynastic period, has been authoritarian in method, with little opportunity for civilian participation in government. With a lack of political participation to manage grievances, there was potential danger in arming large numbers of civilians and giving them military training and organizational structures. At best, Chinese leaders had strong doubts as to the loyalty of military forces under them, and at worst, such as during the 1911 Revolution, military units formed the core of political rebellions against authority. Moreover, the Chinese state often lacked the administrative and managerial abilities to induct large numbers of men on an annual or biannual basis and to provide them with training, equipment, and sustenance. In August 1954, the first draft law in the ROC was established, making men aged eighteen to forty-five obligated to serve two years in the Army or three years in the Navy or Air Force.[81]

In Taiwan, the necessity of a military draft became increasingly apparent during the mid-1950s, as the soldiers who had occupied Taiwan following their defeat in China aged. As early as December 1951, records show that over 20 percent of soldiers in the ROC Army were over thirty-five years of age and 10 percent were over forty.⁸² By 1955 the average age of many ROC units was sufficiently high (the average age of enlisted men was twenty-nine while officers averaged thirty-two years of age) that it attracted concern from MAAG personnel worried about the combat effectiveness of older soldiers, especially in physically demanding positions such as the infantry.⁸³ Moreover, because officers had been a disproportionate share of the evacuees who moved to Taiwan in 1948–49, the ratio of officer to enlisted man was highly skewed, with only three soldiers for every officer in 1951.⁸⁴ MAAG officers hoped to cut 80,000 ineffective soldiers from the ROC Armed Forces, and add 70,000 young, healthy draftees.⁸⁵ In April 1955, ROC military leaders finally responded to MAAG appeals and began the first of a series of phased cutbacks of older personnel, and their replacement with native Formosan young men.⁸⁶

During the initial phase of MAAG Formosa, from 1950 to 1953, the MAAG office was responsible for the defense of Taiwan in addition to the advising and equipping of ROC forces. This task was problematic because the U.S. chain of command in East Asia was divided between the Commander in Chief, Far East (CINCFE), a post held by General MacArthur until his relief in 1951, and the commander of the Pacific Fleet, Adm. Arthur Radford. In the event of a Chinese invasion of Taiwan, the main air and naval operations, which would take place in the Taiwan Strait, would be under the command of Admiral Radford, with only military operations on the main island of Taiwan being under the authority of General Chase.⁸⁷ Moreover, several CIA organizations operated from the offshore islands, and acted in partnership with elements of the ROC military and intelligence services to conduct raids and reconnaissance within China.⁸⁸

As part of President Eisenhower's strategy of ending the Korean War, the U.S-imposed "neutralization" of the Taiwan Strait by the Seventh Fleet was lifted, allowing for the possibility of ROC military operations against China.⁸⁹ This decision further complicated the role of MAAG, and its mandate to assist with the supply and coordination of ROC military activities now had to integrate offensive actions into its plans. Although MAAG was assured that it would have advance notice of ROC operations against China prior to any "significant" raids, the meaning of the word "significant" was sufficiently broad to allow virtually unchecked ROC initiatives with no limiting factors.⁹⁰

Eisenhower's decision further modified the MAAG planning objectives—which had shifted from purely defensive in 1950–52, to being able to conduct small-scale offensive operations (battalion-sized attacks) in 1953—into an expectation that by the end of 1954 a force of 25,000 men would deploy to the Korean Front.⁹¹ The first report on the situation on Formosa, prepared by the Eisenhower administration's

National Security Council, outlined three primary objectives. First, ROC forces needed the capability to conduct raids into mainland China to gather intelligence and disrupt People's Liberation Army (PLA) operations. Second, the ROC military needed to present "an increasing threat to the mainland," presumably to tie down large numbers of PLA troops. Third, ROC forces needed to be capable of functioning as part of a larger free-world military network in East Asia.[92]

The policy decisions made in Washington, to shift from a defensive to an offensive military posture on Taiwan, resulted in a tremendous boom in the size and importance of MAAG Formosa. In the spring of 1953, MAAG personnel strength had reached its assigned level of nearly nine hundred men, which was sufficient to staff all major ROC training units, have advisers at the regimental level and above, and exercise oversight on military aid. Offensive operations required a far larger American MAAG presence, especially in the advisory capacity, resulting in a jump in MAAG requirements to over 2,500 personnel.[93] In addition, the difficulty of coordinating ROC military operations with American military units, such as the Seventh Fleet, placed a premium on reliable communications, necessitating the assignment of a full U.S. Army Signal Battalion of seven hundred personnel to Taiwan in 1954. The addition of the Signal Battalion not only raised total MAAG strength to 3,240 men, almost four times the total strength of 1952, but also was the first assignment of regular American military forces to Taiwan.[94]

The changing mission requirement entailed slight changes to the organizational structure of MAAG. The MAAG established General Staff sections to work with the ROC Ministry of National Defense and Pacific Fleet Headquarters in Pearl Harbor. U.S. advisers were also deployed to Jinmen (Quemoy) Island, where there was a much greater chance of them being involved in combat.[95]

Sensing the mood in Washington, ROC leaders seized the policy initiative and circulated a grandiose plan for further military development that would have made the ROC Army one of the largest and best equipped in the world. The "Kai Plan," proposed in December 1953, entailed a massive expansion in American military aid to bring the ROC Army to a total force of forty-one divisions, later reduced to twenty-seven (from twenty-one in 1952), including three armored divisions.[96] The navy would be augmented by six destroyers and ten destroyer escorts, in addition to a wide range of amphibious landing craft added to the ROC fleet. The ROC Air Force was slotted to receive over one hundred new jet aircraft, including the F-86 fighter and the B-29 strategic bomber.[97] The overall manpower requirements for these new forces would have raised the number of men in the total ROC military forces to over 629,000, from a population of less than 10 million.[98]

The Kai Plan was not met with enthusiasm by MAAG. General Chase noted trenchantly, "[M]uch of the plan is completely infeasible of execution and that nearly every aspect requires a vast augmentation in the level of U.S. support, as well as a material modification in U.S. strategic policy."[99] Although Ambassador Rankin noted that many elements of the Kai Plan were "grandiose," he thought it was a conceivable structure and argued that the utilitarian logic of the low cost of supporting ROC soldiers compared to American soldiers made further expansion of ROC forces consistent with U.S. policy.[100] MAAG's successful argument against the Kai Plan marked the first limit on the growth of ROC military forces, as well as an emphasis on defensive rather than offensive military operations, in spite of political rhetoric from ROC and U.S. leaders.

By the end of 1953, ROC-U.S. relations had finally achieved the potential of intense military and government partnership first discussed in 1942. The ROC military had utilized American support and advice to create a highly effective and professional force, under the leadership of officers who were military professionals rather than party appointees. From the perspective of MAAG and Sun Li-jen, the partnership had developed a solid organizational foundation for an enduring military relationship. The main problem in this "Golden Age" of U.S.-ROC partnership was the animosity of senior ROC political leaders, most notably Chiang Kai-shek and Chiang Ching-kuo, toward accepting the limited role for political and party control over the armed forces. During the 1950–53 period, the overwhelming necessity of defending a weak ROC on Taiwan led to the acquiescence of the KMT to a professional military. However, the desire to return the ROC armed forces to a de facto party-army status, and eliminate competing sources of intellectual and organizational authority on Taiwan, remained constant, and from 1953 to 1955 the KMT was ready to go on the offensive.

6

Restoring the Party to Dominance, 1953–1955

By mid-1952 and into 1953, as the scale of American military assistance increased, the ROC armed forces were dramatically reshaped, and as officers began to graduate from fully developed specialty schools, the future of the ROC military seemed certain. After decades of struggling with limited budgets, poor equipment, and politicized administration, military officers could now conduct training using the most sophisticated tactics, supported by modern equipment. While this process of military reform and foreign engagement had transformed the ROC military, the KMT had sought to rebuild its control over the military and develop a new network of political officers.

The training and role of political officers in the post-1950 period, especially after 1953, differed remarkably from the 1928–37 period or the war era. First, there was a much higher degree of institutionalization. With the establishment of the political warfare school at Fuxinggang outside of Taipei, political officers received intensive education and indoctrination for the first time since the Whampoa period (1924–26). This resulted in a much more cohesive and capable political officer cohort. Second, senior leadership (most notably Chiang Ching-kuo) took a direct role in military affairs and in designing political officer training, each leader personally identifying himself with the collective identity of the political officers, and providing organizational support for the political officer takeover of what had been previously military tasks. Last, political officers after 1950 began a program of comprehensive party functions and political activity that included all military personnel and a wide variety of civilian groups such as the China Youth Corps (CYC, Zhongguo qingnian qiuguo tuan). This was a much larger scope of activity than had previously been allowed. By 1953, these reforms were bearing fruit, and the political department began a sustained challenge to the professional identity of military officers. In spite of continued American opposition to political officers in military units, the increasing strength of Chiang Ching-kuo's organization led to a change in American policy in 1954, which recognized the principle of political oversight. Following this policy shift, Sun Li-jen became increasingly isolated and was eventually purged from his military position and sentenced to house arrest in 1955.

The defeat of ROC forces in 1948 and 1949, followed by the withdrawal to Taiwan, began a process of massive strengthening of the role and authority of political officers. During the 1950–55 period, political officers again became an integral part of the ROC military, with broad authority over military operations and personnel management. Beginning in late 1949, senior KMT leaders made revitalizing political control over the military a priority, and as early as February 1950, they were working on new policies to recreate a strict party-army concept of civil-military relations.[1]

The rebuilding of the KMT on Taiwan in the form of the creation of a viable party structure provided one institutional pillar of the post-1950 political structure on Taiwan, with a capable ROC military being the other pillar. Without a dynamic KMT organization to which the political officers could connect their efforts within the ROC military, their efforts would have been fruitless. The revitalized KMT, under the day-to-day leadership of Chiang Ching-kuo, used the political officer system as part of a larger strategy of organizational penetration of all areas of the ROC government and Taiwanese society.

From the very beginning, a key aspect of rebuilding the KMT and the ROC military on Taiwan was the harnessing of the substantial American military support that flowed to Taiwan after June 1950. Rather than refute American practices and simple reestablish traditional KMT structures, Chiang Ching-kuo was clever to embrace some American-inspired reforms, stall on many, but outright reject only a few. Peter Heinlein asserts that the "military establishment which evolved on Taiwan was the product of an artful Chinese manipulation of organizational form foisted on them by American advisors."[2]

The expansion in the size and scope of political officer authority in post-1950 Taiwan was closely linked to the political guidance of Chiang Kai-shek's son, Chiang Ching-kuo (Jiang Jingguo). The appointment of Chiang Ching-kuo as head of the Political Department of the Ministry of National Defense served a variety of political purposes for Chiang Kai-shek, for the KMT, and most importantly in the fulfillment of Chiang Ching-kuo's personal ambitions. Chiang Ching-kuo became head of the KMT organization in Taiwan in January 1949 and began a program of party revitalization and centralization. On 5 August 1950, Chiang Kai-shek, as party chairman, formed the Central Reform Commission (CRC), which was composed of sixteen trusted subordinates, including his son, Chiang Ching-kuo. The CRC began a comprehensive program of broadening the party's reach in Taiwanese society, by increasing membership and by strengthening discipline among party members through increased meetings and personal surveillance.[3]

As part of the CRC's efforts, the KMT established many new organizations, particularly in the fields of security, and Chiang Ching-kuo commonly occupied either the head position or a key role in multiple organizations. In 1949 he became head of the Political Activities Committee, responsible for policing KMT members' behavior. In 1950, in addition to his role on the CRC, he became the head of the Anti-Communist Youth Corps (CYC). Within the military itself, Chiang Ching-kuo was head of the Political Department during the formative years of 1950–54.[4] Chiang Ching-kuo also became the head of the Central Party School, which made his support crucial for anyone wishing to advance to the senior ranks of the KMT.[5]

These concurrent posts allowed Ching-kuo to link policies and initiatives in both party and military organizations. These appointments were also due to Chiang Kai-shek's fear that military officers would coopt political officers without a high-level "patron" for political officers to call on. In an interview with American MAAG chief General Chase, Chiang Kai-shek noted that in the past,

> [in China] the political workers in the army were appointed by the local commander, hence they had no loyalty to the government but only to the commander, he said. On Taiwan he was determined to remedy this situation. . . . To ensure loyalty and remove any fear the political worker might have of reporting disloyalty even in high-ranking officers, he had appointed his own son (Chiang Ching-kuo) head of this organization so that its officers might know they would be in no danger if they reported information derogatory to some strong commander.[6]

The most direct method of increasing political control was the execution of several high-ranking ROC officers in early 1950 on charges of corruption. The subsequent exposure of dozens of Communist conspiracies, some real but many likely fabricated for political purposes, was a regular occurrence over the next four years.[7] A more effective long-term solution to KMT control was the rapid expansion of KMT membership from 50,000 in 1950 to nearly 300,000 by 1952.[8] Special attention was given to recruit potential leaders in Taiwan and coopt them into the KMT. The increasingly dense network of KMT members after 1952 made organization of an effective opposition difficult without alerting the KMT. The crossover affiliation between military-political-civilian members meant that opposition to the KMT within the army could also have repercussions after a return to civilian life.

In April 1950, a successor department to the Information Bureau was established as the renamed Political Work Department (it was later changed to the General Political Warfare Department in 1963), and given an expanded mission.[9] Six major areas of work, detailed in the *National Revolutionary Army's Guidelines of Political Work* (*Guojun zhengzhi gongzuo gangling*) established the principle concerns of the KMT. Of the six areas, four were most relevant to the role of political officers within the military:

1. The political warfare officer in each unit was to be equated to the chief of staff. He would have a staff that would be parallel to the military staff.
2. An inspection system was to be established to monitor military administration (particularly financial and personnel accounts), technical development (the military must get what it pays for), and combat capability (from a discipline perspective in time of war).
3. Security (protecting documents) and counterintelligence (preventing penetration of the military by spies) systems were to be strengthened.
4. Party work within the military was to be restored.[10]

The key idea expressed in the *Guidelines of Political Work* was the diminution of a military commander's authority. These guidelines provided political officers with formal authority to maintain a distinctive identity within the military, regardless of the commander's wishes. More specifically, the guidelines required political officers to review the age, school performance, personal habits, and political beliefs of all officers, and to retain detailed files for examination by other departments.[11] Political officers were instructed to review all military orders, administrative procedures, and matters of military discipline. In addition, political officers were instructed to develop an investigation system to maintain control over unit activities, such as supply inventories, treatment of equipment, and unit funds.[12] Although the mandate of political officers to conduct such intensive scrutiny of all military affairs was in many ways an understandable and effective way to limit corruption, the practical effect was to give the political officer oversight and de facto veto authority over all military matters.

Less newsworthy but more substantial was the steadily increasing number of highly trained and ideologically reliable political officers within the ROC military, and the creation of an extensive KMT organization within the military. On a purely quantitative scale, the level of investment in personnel and training was massive. By 1957, there were over 17,000 political officers in the ROC Armed Forces, out of a total personnel strength of only 600,000 men, a ratio of thirty men for every one political officer.[13] In contrast, during the Sino-Japanese War, the most favorable ratio of political officers to men had been over 150 to one. Moreover, in 1957, of the total of 17,000 officers, approximately 86 percent had attended a complete course at the Fuxinggang Staff College, a much more thorough and consistent training than political officers had previously received.[14]

Party Work and Political Work in the ROC Army

Within the ROC military, the role of the political officer was frequently more mundane than sinister. The main tasks of the political officer, both in party work and political work, was most often a paperwork-laden exercise in filing and research. Organizational reforms of the Chinese Army had eliminated the need of political officers to serve as de facto logistics suppliers, but another important change post-1950 was the capacity of the ROC government in Taiwan to staff local government offices and direct policy to a sufficient extent to limit the need for the direct involvement of political officers in local politics. For the first time since the formation of the party-army system in 1924, the ROC military could operate in an area that had a fully staffed, well trained, and sufficiently competent civil service. In addition, because the ROC military in Taiwan was essentially defensive and based in unchanging garrisons, there was no need for redeployments, which meant relocating families and dependents, another major task of political officers. Political work had continued in the ROC army under the Information Bureau from 1946 to 1950, and remained essentially unchanged after 1950. Illiteracy remained a lingering problem, with over 50 percent illiteracy among soldiers from 1950 to 1955. The introduction of new conscripts who were better educated, the retirement of many of the older soldiers, and a literacy campaign within the military raised literacy rates to over 90 percent for the first time in 1955.[15] Once the literacy rate had been improved, political work could include a wide variety of instruction on current events, Chinese history, and "character guidance" readings.[16]

Political work also included a wide variety of troop welfare activities expanded with the assistance of American aid, such as a U.S.-style post-exchange (PX) system and job placement for retired or wounded personnel. Due to the severe gender imbalance among the refugees who had moved to Taiwan in 1949–50, the possibility of finding a spouse for most of the soldiers was extremely low. During the 1950s and 1960s the Political Department ran a network of military brothels, so-called "tea houses," that were even located in frontline locations such as Jinmen Island, and employed over one thousand hostesses.[17]

Party work in the post-1950 ROC military benefited from the official creation of a separate chain of command for political officers.[18] This reversion to the 1924–27 model of political officer power meant that political officers were now under the direct command of their superior political officers, not the commander in the unit in which they were assigned. Political officers at the company level on up now directed their attention to the commander of the Political Department.

Empowered by the new chain of command, the political officer in Taiwan had three primary ways to influence military commanders and modify orders. First, because political officers had to ensure "compliance" of military personnel to government and party policies, they were allowed at all meetings and briefings, giving political officers not only a seat at the table but access to all planning decisions.[19] Second, political officers were entitled to see official orders and could disagree with the commander's interpretation of the orders or plan of action.[20] Lastly, political officers down to the company level were able to have several assistants, greatly easing their administrative burden and allowing for their staff to function as a mirror of the military staff.[21]

The significant way the political officer could exert power within the ROC military on Taiwan was through the political evaluation system, where he was required to write reports on all officers and many of the soldiers.[22] Dossiers on all members of the unit were kept by the political officer on every member of the unit, but these were not regularly submitted to higher headquarters except when a soldier was preparing to leave the military, was under review for promotion, or had been selected for a specialized training course.[23] Highly unfavorable reports could lead to an officer's removal from command and impact his career progression.[24] The political evaluation system gave political officers a de facto veto over officer promotion. Because they were submitted through the separate Political Department chain of command, officers had no right to see or review their records, creating a sense of ambiguity that could be utilized by political officers.

The enhanced role of the political officer and particularly the intrusive nature of the political evaluation system was not well liked by ROC military officers, who felt it infringed on their authority. A general officer interviewed in 1966 referred to "the good old days" before 1949 when there had been no "looking over his shoulder on business the Political Department did not understand."²⁵ Another observer noted that in spite of the military principle of unified command authority, "the political officer no doubt has the final say on all matters."²⁶ American officers had an ingrained distrust of political officers and concurred with their ROC counterparts that that divided command was an "inherent weakness" in any political officer system.²⁷

While the political officer did represent a threat to the military officer's personal authority he also threatened the underlying principles of military behavior. American observer W. W. Whitson noted, "In the philosophical realm, the commissar's faith in the efficacy of nonviolent techniques inevitably clashed with the military professional's faith in firepower . . . nonviolent techniques would appear naïve and ridiculous, if not threatening and insulting to a line officer."²⁸ Especially in frontline positions like Jinmen (Quemoy) Island, the role of political officers in diverting training time to propaganda activities, such as launching balloons filled with toilet paper to drift into China, must have seemed a ludicrous, if not dangerous, diversion from military activities.

Fuxinggang College

The central core around which Chiang Ching-kuo, who was appointed director of the reformed Political Department of the ROC military on 1 April 1950, sought to institutionalize KMT control of the ROC military was the political officer cadre school at the Fuxinggang College, located in the suburbs of Taipei.²⁹ Over the course of several decades, Fuxinggang graduates would become entrenched in every area of the ROC government and military, and the personal connections between students and Chiang Ching-kuo earned Fuxinggang the reputation as Chiang Ching-kuo's "private Whampoa Academy."³⁰ Unlike the short-term training programs of the 1928–46 period that were designed to give political officers only two or three weeks of training, the Fuxinggang program included a minimum of eighteen months of full-time instruction. The rigid curriculum, strenuous training, and the attempt by Chiang Ching-kuo to create a distinct political officer identity, which was a distinct hybrid military and party identity, resulted in the creation of a homogenous social norm among the graduates. After their placement within the KMT military, the highly trained Fuxinggang graduates utilized the strengthened statutory power of their political officer positions to undermine the ROC military authority from within the military organization.

The Fuxinggang College was formally opened on 1 July 1951 as part of an effort to consolidate and centralize political training. After the transfer of KMT and ROC government institutions to Taiwan, the Political Work Department had operated three separate facilities: in Danshui, Taipei, and Zuoyang. In addition, each military area within Taiwan operated its own one-month refresher courses at six locations throughout the island.[31] These schools were all closed after Fuxinggang was opened, and all political officer training, from initial training to advanced research, was done at the one Fuxinggang campus.

The first commandant of the school was the mild-mannered Air Force general Hu Weike, who was a graduate of Sandhurst, but real authority rested in the school director of student affairs, Col. Wang Sheng, who was responsible for the curriculum development. Wang was seen as Chiang Ching-kuo's right-hand man and he quickly rose to become the school's dean in 1953 and commandant in 1955.[32] Col. Wang Sheng, who had risen through the KMT ranks in the intelligence field and had worked with Chiang Ching-kuo in China, imagined Fuxinggang as the incubator of a new KMT elite on Taiwan.

Under the day-to-day supervision of Wang, the Fuxinggang campus quickly expanded the course length of the first two classes to a full twenty-four-month period by 1953, and by the end of the 1950s Fuxinggang offered a four-year college program and a graduate school with MA and PhD programs.[33] Later in the 1950s, as the political officer position in the military became fully staffed, Fuxinggang broadened its curriculum to include programs in journalism, music, fine arts, and theatrical music, to train political officers assigned to cultural positions within the armed forces.[34]

The course curriculum at Fuxinggang was prepared in an incredibly detailed and methodical manner. The majority of instruction, 80 percent, consisted of political training in theoretical topics such as Sun Yat-senism (san min zhuyi) and the threat of Communism, as well as practical issues such as how to conduct effective political lectures. Only 10 percent of instruction covered military-related topics, mostly training in basic military skills such as rifle marksmanship and close-order drill.[35] Each instruction period was logged on an hour-to-hour chart for each class, with continual changes to course curriculum due to changing world events or new techniques.

After graduation, Fuxinggang graduates were assigned to all branches of the KMT military. The majority of the first class, 361 out of 994, went into ground force units, but large numbers, 198 and 197, went into the Air Force and Navy respectively.[36] Although in his later years Wang Sheng denied a close connection between political officers and the internal security apparatus in Taiwan, forty graduates of the first class were assigned to positions in the Military Police and Taiwan Defense Command organizations.[37]

While the main purpose of the Fuxinggang School was to train political officers for assignment to the ROC military, Fuxinggang graduates were also trained to conduct basic military training at civilian schools. The main vehicle for this was the China Youth Corps (CYC, zhongguo qingnian qiuguo tuan), a military training program under the jurisdiction of the Ministry of National Defense. The CYC had languished due to a lack of resources or attention by senior leaders, but once reestablished in 1952 under the command of Chiang Ching-kuo, the CYC became an organizational mechanism to expand the role of the Political Department into civilian schools and Taiwanese society at large.[38] Between 1952 and 1960 over six hundred Fuxinggang graduates were assigned to civilian schools, and they were credited with training and indoctrinating over 100,000 students during this eight-year period.[39] In speeches, Chiang Ching-kuo stated that "military education and the education of society should be done together . . . with officers at every elementary school, middle school, and high school."[40]

Chiang Ching-kuo and Civil-Military Relations

A prominent feature of Fuxinggang's educational pattern was frequent visits and interaction with senior government and KMT leaders. At every graduation ceremony of the first five classes, Chiang Kai-shek was the keynote speaker. Although Chiang Kai-shek had prestige and symbolic importance, his military concepts had not changed significantly since the 1920s, and his moral concepts of the role of military officers were neither interesting nor distinctive. Chiang Ching-kuo was a frequent visitor to the campus, and in the first full month of classes he delivered speeches and lectures to Fuxinggang students at least once a week.[41] In his speeches, Chiang sometimes referred to Fuxinggang as a "spiritual bastion" not only of the military but of Taiwan, or in his words "Free China," as a whole.[42] The ideas and norms that Chiang Ching-kuo developed at Fuxinggang differed substantially from the propaganda and educational programs used by the KMT and ROC government. In all his speeches, Chiang Ching-kuo attempted to develop the idea that political officers were a select elite, possessing both the right of authority by virtue of their ideals and the responsibility to manage the affairs of the military and society.

The cultivation of a sense of esprit de corps, organizational mission, and tight loyalty to each other was not a unique concept adopted by Chiang Ching-kuo, but the unlimited scope of authority he developed was a new development in KMT history. Fuxinggang graduates were told repeatedly that there were no fixed boundaries to their concerns, and that although their primary field of work would be within the military they had a role to play as creators and guardians of a broader social structure. This broad mandate was in sharp contrast to ideas of military autonomy and insularity developed by Gen. Sun Li-jen. The ideational struggle between these two systems of belief emerged as the primary organizational challenge of the 1950–55 period.

Chiang Ching-kuo developed a coherent ideology at Fuxinggang built around five key values: ideology (zhuyi), leadership (lingxiu), country (guojia), duty (zeren), and honor (rongyu).[43] Country, duty, and honor were commonly used by military organizations and schools around the world, most notably West Point, but the frameworks of ideology and leadership were added by the KMT. While Chiang Ching-kuo would use many of the same words as military officers to describe his goals, the implications were far different.

During the period of Soviet support for the KMT in the 1920s and 1930s, Chiang Ching-kuo had been sent to study in Moscow, along with dozens of other Chinese from the KMT and CCP. From 1925 to 1937, Chiang studied and worked in the USSR during a period of intense political conflict between Josef Stalin and Leon Trotsky. He was also present during the early "show trials," organized by Stalin to purge the Soviet Communist Party of political enemies. Chiang Ching-kuo's emphasis on creating a tightly controlled and closely monitored political organization, responsible to a single leader, never reached the extremes of the Stalinist model, but his system was clearly different from both Chiang Kai-shek's or Sun Li-jen's systems. Chiang Ching-kuo's use of what historian Chen Hung-hsien has called "Soviet political-military models" gave KMT efforts to create a party-army in the 1950s a much more structured and tightly controlled system than had existed in the 1920s.[44]

In addition to Soviet models, the ideological training at Fuxinggang drew from a wide assortment of KMT theory developed by Sun Yat-sen and later acolytes, but Chiang Ching-kuo simplified the ideas and increased the intellectual prerogatives of party leaders. Chiang Ching-kuo cynically noted in 1951 that ideology was a simple formula, "one part thought, one part belief, and one part power."[45] Chiang Ching-kuo retained the notion of the KMT as a "vanguard" party, that had a right to define political policy without elections, but he did not outline any goals or objectives to justify this usurpation of Chinese political rights. Moreover, none of his speeches maintain that the period of "tutelage," defined by Sun Yat-sen as a temporary period, could ever be ended. In Chiang's conception, political power was self-legitimizing, because the unity and success of groups in achieving power made them best qualified and most entitled to it.

While the political and military situation after 1949, with the KMT restricted to a relatively small environment and challenged by a dominant CCP in China, was certainly difficult, Chiang attempted to highlight rather than downplay unique aspects of the challenge. Throughout his speeches and lectures, Chiang emphasized that the current situation was "special" in terms of difficulty and importance. The terms "new day" and "modern era" were frequently used to draw a sharp distinction between the pre-1949 and post-1949 KMT and ROC. Chiang's denigration of the pre-1949 ROC did not extend to one element: Chiang Kai-shek was held to be a great leader, retaining the wisdom of Sun Yat-sen's vision with a lifetime of experience. Walking this mental tightrope of criticizing the past structure of KMT efforts without undermining the KMT's claim to ideological authority was a difficult task at Fuxinggang, but Chiang Ching-kuo was able to develop criticism without attacking the underlying core beliefs of party rule. Chiang noted in early 1950, "Our country is a poor country, with little money or weapons, but for the people's existence we must continue to oppose the CCP and USSR. This war is a revolutionary war. Our military is a revolutionary army. It cannot base itself around material things."[46]

Chiang Ching-kuo was a harsh critic of military officers, most prominently Sun Li-jen, who sought to base the ROC military structure, mission, and norms on global military patterns. In 1954 Chiang lambasted this idea at a Fuxinggang graduation ceremony:

> In our society we have a highly inaccurate and wrong-headed idea circulating, which is that some people think a military should be just a military. What does this mean? It means they want a military to be like a machine . . . thinking that what will work in China is what works in the rest of the world. Moreover, some people think that no matter where, a military organization should use similar organizations and training. They think that a military model can be used anywhere in the world. . . . [I believe] every country's military, in the areas of spirit and thought has the unique character of their country, every country's military will have a different military character.[47]

Chiang's critique of "foreign models" came at a time when officers within the ROC military and the American advisory group were pushing for organizational changes designed to increase the level of ROC military professionalism. The unsubtle denigration of the military as a distinct institution working on global norms was a key aspect of Chiang's effort to stress the discontinuity of Taiwan's situation, rendering outside ideas irrelevant.

Chiang Ching-kuo was unambiguous in his belief that the role of the individual, except for the leader, was characterized by service to others rather than personal interest. In Chiang's speeches he makes the clear point that in the Political Department the idea of the power of the individual will not be tolerated. He argued, "Today's tasks are collective tasks, and today's battles are fought by organizations against other organizations."[48] Drawing on KMT experiences with warlords during the 1920s and 1930s, Chiang was skeptical of private interests. He noted in an early speech at Fuxinggang, "Our first task is to completely abolish the conception of private interest at this school . . . to our country, to its leaders, and to the school we must have absolute loyalty and obedience."[49]

Chiang Ching-kuo felt that the total defeat of the KMT in the 1945–49 civil war had been due in large part to the failure to control military operations with systematic oversight. On this point he was strongly supported by Chiang Kai-shek, who argued that without a "system," which to him meant a system of political control over the military, defeat in the long term was inevitable. He lectured that during the civil war, "our military commanders had total freedom in the northeast [Manchuria] and what happened? In the north, south, northwest, and southwest our commanders all had freedom from authority, but it became only their freedom to lose it all. Now in Taiwan some military people want the same kind of freedom, they oppose the new personnel system."[50]

To achieve a sound military system Chiang argued for four main points that Fuxinggang graduates would need to master. First, political officers needed not only to understand the main points of the ideology in a literal sense but to be able to understand the larger purpose and mission of the KMT. This meant that Fuxinggang graduates would need to be educated to work with ideas rather than simply receive training. Second, the military needed to understand that its efforts were part of a unified government effort toward "common objectives" set by political leaders. Third, the military needed a "system" that could integrate policies with strategy. Finally, military forces needed to have tight discipline in the organizational sense.[51] In each of these areas, Fuxinggang graduates were a focal point: integrating ideology, focusing the mission, creating a system, and maintaining the organizational structure.

The abjection of the individual to the needs of the organization was lauded as selfless and efficient. In 1950 Chiang noted, "An organization's greatest achievement is to unify and cultivate cadres."[52] To achieve organizational unity, Chiang argued that discipline needed to be extremely strict, with constant supervision of members by senior leaders.

Sun Li-jen and the Political Department

Although Sun's prominence as the primary partner for the massive American military aid program increased his influence and power, it also made him a target for KMT officials worried about threats to their social and political control. Frequent news reports that placed Sun side by side with senior American officers, such as during the 1953 visit of Gen. Mark Clark, commander of United Nations Forces Korea, portrayed him as a dynamic and vigorous military leader.[53]

The greatest threat to Sun's conception of an apolitical, professional officer corps was not the PLA but the political officer system developed by Chiang Ching-kuo during the early 1950s on Taiwan. The political officer system in Taiwan was a regeneration of the political cadre position that had first been developed at the Whampoa Academy during the 1920s. In Taiwan though, it became a much more powerful and coherent element within the Army. By 1957 there were over 17,000 political officers in the military, one for every thirty-five personnel, with powers over military justice, promotions, and assignments.[54]

The political officer framework developed at Whampoa in 1923 and 1924 had been the product of two objectives: to ensure the loyalty of the KMT Army and to enable the Army to operate effectively in the weakly governed and fragmented Chinese political arena. The first objective was accomplished through political officers indoctrinating officers and men in KMT ideology, evaluation systems that linked promotion to achievement of party objectives, and direct involvement of political officers in the military discipline system. The second objective entailed that the political officer would serve as a liaison between civilians and the military, an educator to teach KMT ideology to the public, and a political organizer acting to build coalitions within the army around KMT policies. Both of these roles waned during the 1930s and 1940s due to external events that limited the necessity of political officer functions. The KMT-CCP split in 1927 and the KMT's successful development of central government administration meant that the role of political officers in interacting with the public could be fulfilled by government departments. The increasing emphasis on specialized military skills during the 1930s and the military necessities of the Sino-Japanese War also functioned to push political officers into the background of the KMT army.

By the late 1940s, the continuing atrophy of the political officer role, internal desires for professional autonomy arising from within the KMT army, and American opposition to a "political commissar" system led to the abolishment of the political officer system in 1946. A residual office of war information remained within the KMT army organization, but it functioned much like its American counterpart, and was geared toward improving the morale of soldiers and distributing propaganda to enemy units.

Following the collapse of the KMT army in 1948–49 and the retreat of the KMT government to Taiwan, Chiang Kai-shek outlined a series of comprehensive reforms designed to unify the party, increase political control over the military, and eliminate his political opponents. In a speech to KMT members on 1 March 1950, Chiang claimed that one of the primary causes of the military collapse was a lack of spirit and loyalty among KMT units, and that the KMT had failed to maintain a system of overt control over military operations.[55] On 1 April, new guidelines for the establishment of a political work system within the military were announced and Chiang Kai-shek's son, Chiang Ching-kuo, was given authority to develop a system of political instruction and political supervision within the armed forces.[56]

Sun was able to successfully limit the authority of political officers to areas outside of combat operations, which preserved the authority of commanders to conduct operations without oversight. Although blocked from combat roles, political officers gained the power to evaluate military officers for political fitness, giving themselves a veto over promotions and dominance over military disciplinary functions. Moreover, within three years of the reestablishment of political officers, roughly one-third of the armed forces—210,000 out of 600,000—and almost all of the officers had officially joined the KMT, creating a unified party structure within the military.[57]

U.S. Military Opposition to Political Officers

The tension between Sun's professional officer corps and the party-army notion advocated by Chiang Ching-kuo was frequently noted by observers. American MAAG reports and State Department messages frequently noted the difficulty of reconciling the two systems of values. In April 1954, a MAAG officer translated large portions of a Chiang Kai-shek speech attacking certain "senior officers" (i.e., Sun Li-jen), for not displaying proper respect for the political officer system. Chiang argued that "some of the senior officers are still unwilling to accept and observe the system of political work in our armed forces. They even abuse it before foreigners. . . . If you have anything to complain [about] or protest, you can always tell your direct boss or a military conference. Why must you secretly approach foreign advisers for this?"[58]

There had been friction surrounding the role of "political officers" within Chinese units dating back to American efforts to improve the performance of

Chinese Army units during World War II. Technically, these officers had become "information officers" after the adoption of the 1947 Constitution of the Republic of China that made the military, which had previously been under the control of the KMT, a department under the authority of the Ministry of National Defense. American officers had been uncomfortable with political officers since the beginning of the Sino-American partnership in 1941, and felt that political officers were a form of political interference in military operations and a potentially dangerous division of command authority. Chinese political leaders argued in turn that Americans "did not sufficiently understand" the need for ideological conformity and political surveillance within the ROC Army.[59]

In one of the first meetings between General Chase and Chiang Kai-shek, political officers emerged as an area of disagreement. In General Chase's initial survey of ROC military units, conducted immediately after he arrived on Taiwan, he noted that, "There is, throughout the Armed Forces, a highly objectionable system of Political Commissars, that acts to penalize initiative and undermine the authority of commanders of all echelons."[60] Chase's use of the term "political commissars," rather than Chiang's and the U.S. State Department's favored usage of "political officers," is reflective of underlying negative associations of a Soviet-style system of political monitoring of the armed forces. Chiang Kai-shek disagreed with Chase's desire to eliminate the political positions, and stated that he would approve all MAAG recommendations "[w]ith the exception of the parts dealing with political workers and the Combined Services, which are features particularly demanded by the circumstances of the day."[61] Chiang's reasoning was that, after the disastrous experience in the Chinese civil war when senior commanders and sometimes even whole units had switched sides, there was little alternative to the system, in spite of American objections.[62] Unwilling to take sides in the dispute, the State Department hedged its position:

> The question of political commissars, however, lies close to the heart of the gap which separates American and Chinese thinking. ... Unquestionably the Chinese Government must have a means of coping with subversion and espionage among both the Armed Forces and the civil population. There must also be appropriate provision for indoctrination and morale building among the troops in particular. However, informed Americans and many if not most Chinese military officers consider the present methods used in both fields to be seriously deficient ... it seems likely that more harm than good is being accomplished as regards the effectiveness of the military establishment.[63]

Undeterred by Chiang's intransigence or State Department insensitivity, General Chase continued to attack the political department, and as his military schools became operational he identified specific areas where political interference was hindering military training. In a memorandum to Chiang Kai-shek on 28 December 1953, General Chase stated that political officers were directly interfering with the training of the expanded armored force, which was being developed into one of the most capable units of the ROC Army. Chase argued that "[p]olitical channels outside command channels destroy the commander's prerogatives," and that "the attitude of political officers to U.S. advisors leaves much to be desired," increasing tensions and hindering training. Chase specifically identified political instruction as a severe hindrance because it was often scheduled in the evenings, when troops needed to rest, and it often ran over time, into scheduled military activities. Political officers' use of school equipment, such as printing facilities and classrooms, both of which were vitally important for newly established schools, also hindered the military portion of the instruction.[64]

In addition to American military objections to the political officer system, Chinese officers, including Gen. Sun Li-jen, commanding general of the ROC Army, felt that the system represented "an almost insurmountable barrier to the achievement of good military discipline, high morale, and effective combat potential."[65] MAAG reported that concerns about the political officer system were shared by larger numbers of officers down to the platoon level, and that many well-qualified junior officers were expressing their concerns and frustrations to American advisers.[66]

In contrast to American military concerns about the erosion of commanders' authority, American government officials were skeptical of the political officer system because it was perceived to be part of a broader secret police system, responsible not to the government of the ROC but to the KMT and the Chiang family. A State Department cable bluntly stated, "The political commissar system, at present, is the creature of General Chiang Ching-kuo, the Generalissimo's son and Director of the Political Department of the Ministry of National Defense. Formosa does not have a unitary secret police system; it comprises the political commissars in the army, Chiang Ching-kuo agents other than the commissars, the Peace Preservation Corps of General Peng Meng-chi, the agents of the Ministry of Interior, the Generalissimo's own bodyguards, etc., etc."[67]

General Chase and officers within MAAG understood the limitations of their authority, and did not attempt an administrative reordering of the Chinese military to include eliminating the political officer position. Instead, they tried to ignore political officers as much as possible and to limit their role within the daily activities of military units. Acquiescence was the accepted policy, "as long as it does not consume too much time, and as long as it does not introduce a separate chain of command within the military organizations."[68]

Rather than cooperate with the political officers, MAAG sought to limit the role of political officers and gradually isolate them within the military organization. American officers resisted assigning an adviser to the Political Department and eventually assigned a token officer from the several hundred on Taiwan to serve as a liaison.[69] MAAG also devoted no resources to assisting the Political Department, in spite of the large amount of American funding available. Within military units, American MAAG officers encouraged regular Chinese military officers to fill most of the functions that political officers were assigned to, such as promoting morale through sporting activities, presenting lectures, or helping soldiers with personal concerns such as moving their families after reassignments.[70]

MAAG and Department of Defense (DoD) efforts to limit the role of political officers continued into 1954. In February 1954, under prolonged pressure from General Chase, Chiang Kai-shek formed a combined Sino-American study committee to investigate allegations that the Political Department of the ROC military was "increasingly interfering with the authority of the Chinese Army Commanders."[71] MAAG, with the support of the DoD, also continued to refuse to send American officers to act as liaisons and advisers in the Political Department, a position that the State Department did not support.[72] Under State Department pressure, MAAG-Formosa assigned only one American officer at a time to "observe" the Political Department of the ROC military.[73]

Throughout the 1951–54 period, the State Department continually argued for a closer relationship between MAAG and political officers. In February 1954, the U.S. ambassador in Taipei, Karl Rankin, wrote to the secretary of the Office of Chinese affairs, Walter McConaughy, to describe the lack of coordination between MAAG and Chiang Ching-kuo's political officer administration as "one of the most serious gaps in our effort on Formosa."[74] Rankin further argued that the constant "sniping at political commissars and police state methods" by MAAG officers was counterproductive and simplistic. By the end of 1954, the steadily increasing power and pervasive influence of the Political Department of the ROC Ministry of National Defense had reached a point where even the CIA noted it. A National Intelligence Estimate from September 1954 states:

> The [ROC] army's effectiveness is impaired by a failure of the highest command echelons to delegate authority and by a political officer

system which interferes with command functions but has not resulted in infusing a great amount of political zeal in the army. . . . The MAAG's task in this respect is difficult, however, for these proposed changes impinge upon certain of President Chiang's most strongly held desires: to maintain a tight grip on the army command, not to delegate authority, and to maintain a political officer system outside of the normal chain of command charged with the duties of political indoctrination, surveillance, and enforcing loyalty to himself.[75]

During late 1954, MAAG also lost its main partner within the ROC Army, because Gen. Sun Li-jen was removed from his command position and given the empty title of military adviser to Chiang Kai-shek. During his period of leadership from 1950–54, Sun had supported MAAG in opposing the political officers' inclusion in the ROC military. By 1954, Chiang's Political Department had also strengthened its position within the ROC military by installing over 10,000 political officers, trained at a newly founded Political Department academy, in all units of the ROC military.[76]

As a result of continued intransigence by senior Chinese leaders, especially Chiang Kai-shek and his son Chiang Ching-kuo, the loss of MAAG's main Chinese ally, Sun Li-jen, and MAAG desperation, American military policy changed from isolation of political officers to an attempt to moderate their influence through education. In the words of General Chase, "We could not whip it, so we joined it."[77] This change was signaled by the assignment of American military officers to Political Department schools, and the inauguration of new courses designed to teach political officers military affairs in order to better integrate their efforts.[78] The MAAG belief was that the overall combat effectiveness of the ROC military would be improved through a "change from its former policy of opposing the Political Department to one of trying to work with the Political Department and in the process bend it to the MAAG will."[79]

The "Sun Li-jen Incident" and the Decline of the ROC-MAAG Partnership

By the spring of 1955, Sun's position within the army was increasingly vulnerable. In June 1954, Sun had been reassigned from his position as commander in chief of the army to duty as the personal chief of the Military Staff in the Office of the President.[80] This move removed him from any direct command of troops and relocated him to the capital, Taipei. American advisers noticed that the reassignment had not been viewed positively by Sun: "[Sun] Does not like his assignment as Senior Military Aide to the President. An active soldier, he does not like a desk job."[81] Although the new position provided Sun with more political access, he had never been close to Chiang Kai-shek and had few supporters within the KMT. In place of Sun as commander in chief of the ROC Armed Forces, Chiang appointed a party loyalist, Huang Jie, who had served under Chiang for twenty-five years and had graduated from the first class of the Whampoa Academy. The signing of the Sino-American Mutual Defense Treaty (Zhongmei gongtong fangyu tiaoyue) in December 1954 also hurt Sun, because it entailed clear treaty obligations on the part of the United States to defend Taiwan, making the effectiveness of KMT military units less crucial. The treaty also stipulated that no military forces in Taiwan would invade China, a goal that Sun and many younger officers had been planning and training for since 1949.

With decreasing military utility and few political allies, Sun was an inviting target for Chiang Ching-kuo's faction to subvert through political accusations. In June 1955, two officers at the Army Infantry School, Guo Tingliang and Chiang Yunchin, were accused of engaging in armed rebellion. Chiang Kai-shek later informed the U.S. Embassy that the officers had been planning a mass protest during a military review on 6 June to demand the removal of army general Peng Mengji, who was seen as a stooge of Chiang Ching-kuo, and the return of Sun Li-jen to command of the army.[82] American intelligence felt that, although Chiang's reported fear of mass protest was dubious, there were increasing signs of division within the army. CIA reports detail that young military officers were coming under harassment due to the political officer system, and were being constrained from taking offensive action toward China. The report stated that both factors were leading young officers to a "dead-end future on Formosa."[83]

Sun Li-jen had served with Guo since 1942, and Guo had followed Sun throughout his career as a subordinate commander and staff officer. With Guo charged with subversion and suspicion of being a Communist agent, the implication was that Sun was either an accomplice to Guo's activities or incompetent in his supervision. On 3 August, Sun Li-jen resigned as chief military advisor to the president, and accepted responsibility for inadequately supervising Guo while serving as his commander. Chiang Kai-shek accepted Sun's resignation but ordered a special party investigative committee to examine Guo and Sun's relationship. The special committee was chaired by Vice President and Premier Chen Cheng, and concluded that since Guo Tingliang and others had confessed to plotting a coup, Sun Li-jen had therefore obviously been negligent in his supervisory duties. On 8 October, Chiang issued an order that, rather than the death penalty, Sun would be "granted special permission for reformation with no additional punishment and should be under the constant observation from the Ministry of National Defense for improvement."[84]

While the KMT conducted its own investigation, the Control Yuan of the ROC government also launched an investigation under the guidance of Harvard-trained lawyer Tao Baichuan. Tao's investigation diverged sharply from the KMT investigation committee in both its methods and conclusions. Tao found that Guo Tingliang and the others had demonstrated no indication of inciting a military rebellion and had only confessed to their involvement under torture. This evaluation led them to conclude that, because there was no wrongdoing, Sun could not be found guilty of being an accomplice or negligent. The tremendous gap between the KMT and government investigatory findings led to the Tao Investigation Committee report being classified as a state secret, until it was finally released in 1988.[85] Sun was kept under house arrest in Taichung, until 20 March 1988.[86]

Foreign evaluation of the "Sun Li-jen Incident" found it to be a blatantly political puppet show by Chiang Ching-kuo. The CIA felt the entire affair was a dangerous distraction, because "[t]his callous throat-cutting serves as example to the army, which could dangerously weaken Chiang regime, [which is] dependent on continued loyalty of troops."[87] The CIA placed the blame for Sun's downfall squarely on Chiang Ching-kuo: "Downfall of Sun appears mainly work of Chiang Ching-kuo, arch-conservative leader on Formosa . . . will be interpreted as victory for young Chiang, and thus will depress morale of westernized Chinese still on Formosa."[88] The *Washington Post* cited the former governor of Taiwan, K. C. Wu, who argued that Sun was purged because "he is too popular and has too democratic views," both of which are a threat to the Chiang family.[89]

Military officers in Taiwan were shocked by the persecution of a war hero and military leader. In oral history collections of former ROC officers, the feeling of shock and subtle fear of political power was a nearly constant observation of military officers.[90] Many of Sun's closest aides, several of whom were now senior commanders and generals, had served with Sun for nearly fifteen years, but were forbidden to have further contact with him after the house arrest.

The transparently political Sun Li-jen incident was only one, albeit the most important one, of a series of developments that slowly redefined and restricted the ROC-MAAG relationship in 1955. By 1955, the large American presence on Taiwan was firmly established, with military advisers under MAAG, economic aid coordinated by the State Department and strong American political support for the ROC from the Eisenhower administration. During 1955 the Sino-American partnership shifted from a relationship seeking to develop the ROC Army and into a period geared toward preserving the status quo. The result was a diminishment in the importance of the MAAG effort.

The most direct diminishment of the MAAG mission in 1955 was the signing of the Sino-American Mutual Defense Treaty, which came into effect on 3 March 1955. The treaty stipulated that the United States had a formal obligation to defend Taiwan from attack. This stipulation removed much of the urgency from the ROC's military efforts, because it could rely on American military power, including nuclear weapons, to defend its territory. With increased military security, Chiang Ching-kuo was able to move against the ROC's most effective military officer, Sun Li-jen.

The Mutual Defense Treaty between the United States and the ROC was the culmination of a steadily increasing network of political, economic, and military cooperation during the early 1950s. Signed in Washington on 2 December 1954 and entering effect on 3 March 1955 the treaty stipulated that armed attack against the territory of either party would result in common action. Although this mutual defense treaty was only one of the many international agreements proposed by the Eisenhower administration, the treaty expressly restricted American action to defend the island of Taiwan and the Pescadores.[91] Any action against the ROC on the islands of Jinmen and Matsu was de facto not covered by the mutual defense conditions. This position was modified in January 1955 by the "Formosa Resolution" of the U.S. Congress, which authorized the president to employ armed forces on Taiwan, the Pescadores, and "related positions and territories of that area."[92] Although the congressional resolution removed any ambiguity about areas under protection, both the treaty and resolution explicitly restricted American action to defensive operations, making any attacks on the Chinese coast by ROC forces outside treaty responsibilities.

The Sino-American Mutual Defense Treaty also clarified the command and control arrangements on Taiwan through the creation of an official United States Taiwan Defense Command (USTDC), mandated to coordinate military operations in the event of war. The USTDC assumed this task on 11 November 1955 from the MAAG liaison office, and operated from a military base in Taipei separate from MAAG facilities.[93] The USTDC's commander was designed as a naval position, in contrast to the chief of MAAG, which was an Army position. The USTDC command position also designated the senior American military officer on Taiwan with a rank of vice admiral (three stars), rather than the major general (two stars) assigned as MAAG chief. The superior rank of the USTDC head meant that he represented the senior United States military presence in the ROC.

Lastly, in June 1955 General Chase retired from U.S. Army active duty and was replaced by Maj. Gen. George Smythe.[94] During his four years as chief of the MAAG mission, General Chase had worked closely with senior U.S. and ROC officials to initiate the MAAG program and undertake a wide range of political, military, and training duties. After the retirement of General Chase, successive MAAG commanders did not radically alter the organization of MAAG, and they had a much-reduced role in political issues. For the remaining years of MAAG Formosa, the commanding officer would serve a shorter term, less than two years, followed by retirement.

Although the organization of MAAG would continue to exist until the transfer of U.S. diplomatic recognition from the ROC to the PRC in 1979, the continued development of the ROC forces and the economic growth of Taiwan made U.S. advising and assistance increasingly unnecessary. MAAG personnel strength steadily dropped, from a peak of over two thousand staff members in 1955 to less than three hundred remaining after 1968. U.S. military aid to Taiwan ended in 1968, with a total amount of $2.4 billion transferred between 1949 and 1968 (roughly $16 billion dollars in 2012 USD value).[95]

During the 1950–55 period, Chiang Ching-kuo and the KMT were able to reintroduce political officers into the ROC military and intellectually challenge the concept of a professional military advocated by Sun Li-jen and MAAG advisers. By leveraging connections to other KMT organizations, the Political Department was able to steadily insert itself into military procedures, limiting the authority of commanders. The end of this de facto "hostile takeover" of the ROC military, through the arrest of Sun Li-jen, marked the end of the period of military professionalism within the ROC military and the beginning of over thirty years of KMT control of the ROC military.

Conclusion

The arrest and sentencing of Gen. Sun Li-jen was the capstone event of a larger process of steadily increasing political control by the KMT over the ROC military. The power of the Political Department to monitor and coerce ROC military officers rested on a solid bureaucratic foundation that remained relatively unchanged until the mid-1980s. The period from 1955 until 1987 saw steadily increasing involvement by the ROC military in Taiwan's society, with military personnel assigned to roles as policemen, teachers, and intelligence officers. U.S. support of the ROC military continued, albeit at a reduced rate, as the ROC military and Taiwan's economy became capable of supporting their own defense establishment. Only after the shocks from the U.S. decision to recognize the PRC in 1979, the end of martial law in 1987, and the death of Chiang Ching-kuo in 1988, did a renewed push for a professional and apolitical ROC military gain momentum.

After 1955, the ROC military became a core support for KMT authoritarian rule, and Chiang Ching-kuo was instrumental in pushing the ROC military into closer relationships with KMT party organizations and domestic security roles such as police work. In 1957 the military became a key member of the National Security Council (Guojia anquan huiyi), which had been newly formed to support the "temporary provisions" of martial law and to function as a centralized advisory body for the ROC president. Military officers also began to be assigned to the National Security Bureau (NSB, Zhonghua minguo guojia anquan ju), which was the official ROC government agency responsible for coordinating intelligence operations. Unlike the U.S. Central Intelligence Agency (CIA), the ROC NSB was responsible for both external intelligence operations and domestic security. In both of these new organizations, military officers formed a large part, often a majority, of the personnel.[1]

In 1958 a further revision of the national security architecture dramatically reshaped the role of the military in Taiwanese society through the creation of the Taiwan Garrison Command (TGC, Taiwan jingbei zong siling bu). The Taiwan Garrison Command combined several smaller military and civil defense functions into one unit under the command of a three-star general. The TGC had primary responsibility for enforcing martial law, which included surveillance of communications (mail and telephones), suspected political dissidents, and censorship of media. According to the provisions of martial law, TGC police units superseded all civilian police and could indefinitely detain suspects, or conduct trials in military courts. Volunteers from the ROC officer corps mainly staffed the TGC leadership, but border patrol troops often included large numbers of drafted army personnel.[2] TGC had a broad range of authority because, under the provisions of ROC martial law, civilian personnel were subject to a military trial if suspected of sedition, espionage, theft or black-market activities. In 1976 these provisions were expanded to include a wide range of "normal" crimes such as robbery, kidnapping, and burglary.[3] The ROC military officers were now directly responsible for enforcing a wide range of restrictions on civil liberties and rights, none of which required specialized training as professional military officers.

The use of military personnel for political coercion and law enforcement involved the ROC Armed Forces in a wide range of human rights abuses. At military detention centers, such as the infamous Green Island prison twenty miles off the east coast of Taiwan, torture of suspected Communists or Taiwanese activists was common. The TGC worked closely with the NSB, an intelligence organization led by three-star army general Cheng Jiemin that quickly gained a reputation as "Taiwan's KGB." TGC agents were especially notorious for "agent provocateur" assignments that involved infiltrating opposition groups, funding anti-KMT publications and, once the material was printed, arresting the writers. These agent provocateur assignments make it difficult to ascertain what political opposition to the KMT was real and what was contrived by the TGC.

U.S. assessments of the increasing military involvement in domestic security missions were negative and highly critical. The tendency of ROC military personnel, inexperienced with police and domestic intelligence work, to use what the Americans called the "saturation method" of intense focus on potential threats, was inefficient and heavy-handed.[4] U.S. analysts were also worried that the use of military forces in internal security functions lessened public support for the military and government in general.[5] The poorly established administrative boundaries of the overlapping military and domestic security functions could result in "clumsy, and heavy-handed, even brutal," treatment by military forces, compared to more traditional police and judicial systems.[6]

Redefining the role of the military away from national defense and a professional identity had a negative impact on Taiwan's perception of officers and soldiers. A 1959 reader letter to the journal *Free China* (*Ziyou zhonghua*) was titled, "Why the Military Should Consider Themselves Dogs."[7] Articles published in foreign publications, such as former Taiwan governor K. C. Wu's 1954 article "Your Money is Building a Police State in Taiwan," drew attention to the increasing use of military forces to control society.[8]

As ROC military officers became more completely controlled by the KMT and integrated into nonpolitical roles, the intellectual and professional debate in military journals and ideas faded away. Rather than engage with core elements of military affairs, which required open-ended discussion of politics, history, and social affairs, the post-1955 crackdown led to the rise of "management" studies in the ROC military. ROC military publications and translations of foreign books from the late 1950s onwards featured prominent commentary on "administration" (xingzheng), "management (guanli) and the pursuit of "efficiency" (xiaolu).[9] Other terms borrowed from business schools, including "decision-making" (juece), began appearing in military publications.[10] The overall effect of this shift to improving the productivity (shengchanlu) of military officers was to allow officers to retain some technical skills, but neuter their intellectual development. The format of military publications also shifted, with wide-ranging essays and research papers replaced by narrowly focused handbooks and heavily structured checklists of procedures for military officers to follow.[11]

The U.S. Partnership

The demotion and house arrest of Sun Li-jen had removed the most natural ally and competent military professional on Taiwan for American advisers, but the overall MAAG program was insulated from political turmoil. The MAAG emphasis on creating a durable structure of military education and training had given prominence to long-term professional development, and the removal of dozens of ROC military officers did not create immediate problems for American mutual security programs.

U.S. military aid continued to arrive on Taiwan in the late 1950s, and the Taiwan Straits Crisis of 1958 accelerated the growth of ROC Air Force and Navy units, making the ROC military a more balanced force. During the 1958 Crisis, ROC Air Force units began using the state-of-the-art Sidewinder heat-seeking missile and that, combined with excellent training and well-developed skills, helped ROC pilots achieve a staggering 14:1 kill ratio against PRC MiGs. When Military Assistance Program (MAP) grants ended in 1964, the ROC armed forces were well supplied with fully modern equipment, such as M-48 main battle tanks, C-119 transport aircraft, and over a dozen naval frigates and destroyers.[12]

The Kennedy administration continued to place a large importance on Taiwan as a deterrent force and balancer against the PRC. The Johnson administration's decision to end direct military aid to Taiwan in 1964 was motivated by a desire to redirect military aid funding, mostly to South Vietnam, and emphasize foreign military sales rather than grants. The end of military aid to Taiwan was also a subtle message from the United States to the PRC that ROC military capabilities were limited to defensive capabilities.[13] Despite the end of military assistance, the generous sales terms, with payment often deferred and favorable loans arranged by the U.S. government, ensured that new military equipment continued to improve ROC capabilities.

Throughout the 1950s and 1960s, the United States acted to restrain military activity by the ROC Armed Forces against the PRC. The most severe test of this policy was in the early 1960s when Mao Zedong's Great Leap Forward led to the deaths of over 30 million people, weakening the PRC. In late 1960, Chiang Kai-shek argued that "recovering the mainland" had reached a key moment and offensive action was possible, but firm U.S. efforts by both the Eisenhower and Kennedy administrations deterred unilateral ROC actions.[14]

Long-term U.S. plans during the 1960s called for continued assistance as the ROC military transitioned into a smaller force focused on deterrence.[15] The U.S. decision to transfer diplomatic recognition of "China" from the ROC to the PRC in 1978, leading to the official end of the defense relationship on 1 January 1980, adversely affected the size and scale of U.S. weapons transfers but did not end them completely. During the Reagan administration (1981–89), military sales to Taiwan averaged $367.73 million per year.[16]

U.S. congressional anger toward the poor conduct of the Carter administration in the transfer of diplomatic recognition (the news was conveyed to the ROC in a late-night telephone call) led to the passage of the Taiwan Relations Act (TRA) in late 1979. The TRA states that it is U.S. policy to consider nonpeaceful means to influence Taiwan's status as "a threat" to the peace and security of the Western Pacific and a "grave concern" to the United States. The act mandated that the United States Department of Defense was legally obligated "to provide Taiwan with arms of a defensive character" through foreign military sales, and "to maintain the capacity of the United States to resist any resort to force or other forms of coercion" regarding Taiwan. These assertions, while not clearly legally binding like the mutual defense treaty, gave firm diplomatic and military assurances of the U.S. commitment to Taiwan's future.

Section three of the TRA states unequivocally that "the United States will make available to Taiwan such defense articles and defense services in such quantity as may be necessary to enable Taiwan to maintain a sufficient self-defense capability."[17] The TRA also reestablished a U.S. diplomatic presence on Taiwan, in the form of the American Institute in Taiwan, where "unofficial" State Department and U.S. defense officials could work, in addition to handling more mundane tasks like visa processing.

Although the TRA restored a wide spectrum of the government-to-government relationship, its passage could not influence the strategic rapprochement between the United States and the People's Republic of China during the 1980s. The election of Ronald Reagan, who had visited Taiwan several times and was a strong supporter of the ROC, was followed by an integrated global effort against the Soviet Union. The United States needed PRC support for anti-Soviet operations in Afghanistan, and during the early 1980s ties between Washington and Beijing rapidly increased in importance. In this strategic context, the U.S.-PRC Joint Communiqué, signed on 17 August 1982, stated that at, the behest of the PRC, the United States agreed to set limits on arms sales to Taiwan. A quickly drafted "Six Assurances" memo sent to Taiwan assured the ROC that the United States did not intend to phase out arms sales entirely, would not consult with Beijing on ROC purchases, and intended to maintain a military balance in the Taiwan Straits.

Despite U.S. assurances, the practical issues of arms sales presented difficulties for Taiwan. During the 1980s, ROC officials would present an annual weapons request in January or February, and the United States would take sixty to ninety days to declare which items were approved and which were not allowed that year.[18] This awkward approval process not only took time but was biased against small, "hand-over" items that could be delivered before the end of the year. Beginning in 1982, the ROC repeatedly requested the F-16 fighter to replace its aging fleet of F-5 and F-104 Starfighters, both of 1950s design, but was annually denied a sales contract. In response to American hesitation to sell F-16s, Taiwan began the development of the Indigenous Defense Fighter (IDF), as a joint project between multiple foreign companies and the military-operated Aerospace Industrial Development Corporation (AIDC).

Only after thirty years and a radically changed social and political environment in Taiwan were political opposition forces and reformers within the KMT able to challenge the party-army relationship. Between 1986 and 2002, a systematic pattern of reforms was able to eliminate the formal basis of KMT control over the military. This top-down approach was remarkably successful in establishing a new civil-military consensus, with little opposition from the KMT or elements within the military. Although the return of the ROC military to civilian control, and evaluation based on professional norms, rather than party loyalty, may appear to be a return to the values and role of the army in the 1945–55 period, the ROC military mission had changed radically. The ROC military during the 1945–50 period had perceived itself as the military of a world power, and the army of 1950–55 was a professional army in exile; the ROC military after 2002 was a professional army, but its mission was now focused solely on defending Taiwan.

Although the return of the ROC military to full civilian control became noticeable as a political trend in the 1990s, the position of the military in Taiwan's society had been declining since the 1970s. Until 1972, an active-duty military officer was customarily assigned to serve as the governor of Taiwan, and military membership constituted 30 percent of the KMT's Central Standing Committee, but beginning in the 1970s a new generation of well-educated Taiwanese began to move into the civilian government, party, and military systems.[19] After the death of Chiang Kai-shek in 1975, his son Chiang Ching-kuo assumed the ROC presidency in 1978 and began the process of increasing the authority of native Taiwanese KMT and civil officials. This process of "Taiwanification" of the ROC was especially important in the rise of Lee Deng-hui as mayor of Taipei in 1978 and later as governor of Taiwan Province in 1981.[20] By 1988, 16 percent of general officers and 33 percent of all officers, including a majority at the lower ranks of lieutenants and captains, were native-born Taiwanese.[21] The process of ethnic Taiwanification of the ROC military continued in the 1990s and 2000s, aided by political support from presidents Lee Deng-hui and Chen Shui-bian, to select and promote native Taiwanese officers.[22]

As in the 1940s and 1950s, international factors played a role in catalyzing change and organizational reform during the 1970s and 1980s. On 8 September 1971, the ROC lost its diplomatic representation in the United Nations, which shook the confidence of ROC leaders that they could "wait out" the PRC. The death of Chiang Kai-shek on 5 April 1975 led to his son, Chiang Ching-kuo, succeeding him as the de facto leader of the ROC, eventually assuming the presidency in 1978. The notification by the U.S. government that it would sever diplomatic relations with the ROC on 1 January 1980 was further shock to ROC leaders and highlighted the increasing political isolation of the ROC. During this period of uncertainty, in 1979 and 1980, a series of domestic political protests—the Taichung,

Kaohsiung, and Chungtai Hotel incidents—were violently suppressed by the Taiwan Garrison Command.[23] Trials of the protestors in military courts resulted in heavy sentences, including life imprisonment for the leader, Shih Ming-teh.

Faced with a growing domestic opposition and international criticism, the KMT regime began a series of limited steps toward removing the ROC military from intelligence and law enforcement functions. Gen. Wang Sheng, who had helped Chiang Ching-kuo establish the political officer system in the ROC military during the 1950s, led conservative KMT elements within the ROC military. In September 1983, Chiang Ching-kuo had reassigned Wang Sheng, his long-time political ally and former head of the Political Department, to be Taiwan's ambassador to Paraguay.[24] Wang Sheng was a possible successor to Chiang Ching-kuo, but by the mid-1980s Wang was viewed as a political reactionary and overly identified with the military within the KMT.[25] In a 1986 interview, Chiang Ching-kuo stated that after his death "there would be no military rule whatever," which hindered the ability of military officers to seize power in the future and retain legitimacy within the party.[26]

A further blow to the KMT's control of the ROC military was the political fallout from the killing of the Taiwanese professor and American citizen Henry Liu in California. Details of Henry Liu's intelligence role is unclear, and some have described Henry Liu as a "triple-agent" working for the ROC, PRC, and the United States, but his killing was perceived as a "rogue act" in violation of international norms. After the U.S. Federal Bureau of Investigation (FBI) revealed evidence directly implicating ROC military and intelligence organizations, the director of the ROC Intelligence Bureau of the Ministry of National Defense, Gen. Wang Hsi-ling, was given a life sentence for complicity in the murder.[27]

Driven by increasing political weakness and the international context, President Chiang Ching-kuo allowed the formation of an official non-KMT political party, the Democratic Progressive Party (DPP, Minjindang), in September 1986. On 15 October 1986 the ROC government announced that martial law, which had been in effect since 1949, would be lifted the following year, and that the Taiwan Garrison Command would relinquish its security and judicial functions to civilian police and courts.

The announcement that martial law would end in 1987 required a major realignment of the ROC military functions. Since the ROC was protected by American security guarantees during the 1950s, 1960s, and 1970s, and secure from a militarily weak PRC during the 1980s, the domestic security function had increasingly dominated senior KMT officers' time and attention. While the majority of the ROC military had continued to operate during the 1955–87 period along the guidelines established by Sun Li-jen and General Chase, many higher-ranking officers had become linked to conservative KMT politicians and intelligence departments.

In 1986 and 1987, the ROC military began the slow and difficult transition to focus its role on military operations and warfighting, but progress was hindered by the intellectual limitations of the 1955–87 emphasis on political control. The military school system established by General Chase remained in place but, safe behind American nuclear and naval protection and pushed into time-consuming domestic police activities, the ROC military had not innovated its doctrine or force structure. KMT control of the ROC military had stunted the intellectual development of its officers, and during the 1950s through the 1980s only a foolish military officer would have risked his career by presenting an independent critique of Taiwan's civil-military relations or security policy. The clear challenge for the ROC military in an increasingly liberal and open Taiwan would be to redefine its identity and place in society.

An early challenge to reform was the continued role of senior military leaders who had risen due to their connections to the KMT. After Chiang Ching-kuo's death in January 1988, Lee Deng-hui assumed the presidency for two years, before winning it outright in the 1990 election. Lee appointed a prominent army general and political conservative, Hau Pei-tsun, as premier, a move some observers felt was a step back from democratization and civilian control of the military. While in office, Hau's political inexperience and lack of civilian support made it easy for Lee Deng-hui to isolate him, and after a poor showing by the KMT in the 1992 elections, Hau resigned.[28] The elimination of Hau as a political force represented the end of any attempt by strongly pro-KMT "mainlanders" within the military to intervene in politics.

As president, Lee Deng-hui used his official rhetoric to promote army nationalization. Speaking on Jinmen Island, a Cold War outpost, Lee remarked that, rather than think of the military as separate branches (army, navy, air force) controlled by the KMT, officers should understand that "military unity and army nationalization were the common people's consistent beliefs and he hoped that military officers would be pragmatic" in changing their behavior.[29]

Through Lee's efforts and social pressure, personal attempts by pro-KMT officers like Hau to become directly involved in politics were contained, but the bureaucratic and organizational framework developed during the 1950s proved more difficult to reform. Reforming the military institutions was aided, however, by the growth of the opposition parties, especially the Democratic Progressive

Party, in the Legislative Yuan. President Lee Deng-hui was able to make some administrative changes through a presidential order, and the Taiwan Garrison Command was disbanded in August 1992. In October 1993, the Legislative Yuan continued this effort, and passed laws that prohibited the establishment of political party organizations in schools and in the military.[30]

Restoring legislative power over the ROC military, which was part of the original concept of the 1947 ROC Constitution, required significant legal and constitutional maneuvering. In 1992, the Temporary Provisions of the 1947 Constitution, which had been the formal authority of the extra-legal activities during the "Period of National Mobilization for the Suppression of Rebellion" that had been in continuous force since 1948, were revised to limit the ROC president's direct command authority over the armed forces. The National Security Council shifted from the office of the ROC president to become part of the Executive Yuan, improving transparency and limiting its powers. Furthermore, a revision of the Organic Law of the National Security Council (Guojia anquan huiyi zuzhifa) modified the statutory language away from a concept of direct control by a single political leader and toward a more institutionalized command authority.[31]

The most important and concrete reform of the ROC military occurred in January 2000, with the passage of a new National Defense Law (Guofang fa) and Defense Ministry Organization Law (Guofangbu zuzhifa).[32] The National Defense Law mandated that the national defense chain of command include the Ministry of National Defense, the Executive Yuan, and the National Security Council, in which the president of the ROC was the dominant authority. The National Defense Law also stipulated that the minister of defense must be a civilian, and that military orders from the president must pass through the defense minister before reaching military commanders.[33] The Defense Ministry Organization Law eliminated the statutory power of the General Staff Headquarters, which had been the dominant military staff organization, responsible for all military operations and answering only to the ROC president.[34] The two national defense laws (guofang erfa) gave the civilian leadership at the Ministry of National Defense the statutory authority and, with increased numbers of trained civilian staff, the expertise to develop budgets and spending priorities without military dominance of the process.[35] The combined effect of this reduction in the bureaucratic power of the military was to further restrict the military role to operational and tactical concerns, with the majority of coordination with outside government agencies handled by civilians.

During the long transition to a civilian-led ROC military, the Political Department and political officers decreased in importance and power. By the 1980s the role of political officers to undertake political work had been reduced by the rising education levels of army recruits, the well-developed economy in Taiwan, and a stable political system. These factors made many of the soldiers' welfare activities, which had been so crucial in the 1950–55 period, irrelevant. The de facto exiling of the main KMT leader associated with the Political Department, Gen. Wang Sheng, also led to a decrease in the influence of the Political Department. In late 1984, the Political Department lost its official power to review military orders, a key element of the political officers' "monitoring" function.[36] Moreover, in April 1988, Premier Yu Kuo-hwa, proclaimed that party leadership of the military was officially ended. His statement came after an official order to end party work in the military on 1 January 1988.[37]

The organizational changes resulting from the two national defense laws of 2000 further restricted the Political Department to activity directed toward foreign countries, rather than an internal role. After 1988, although the political officers were forbidden to promote a political party's ideology, "opposing Taiwan independence" (fan tai du), which had clear implications of attacking the DPP, continued for many years. The anti-independence education program was allowed because technically it was in keeping with the ROC's claim to authority over all of China. By the 2000s, though, this program was also eliminated.[38] In 2012 the Political Warfare Bureau website lists its internal military functions only as "psychological counseling, psychological warfare training, military news handling, and cultivation of soldiers' spirits and combat abilities."[39]

In a complete inversion of the key principle of absolute loyalty to the KMT, on which Fuxinggang College had been built, in 2002 President Chen Shui-bian, spoke at the school and, while not openly challenging the continued need for morale support in the military, Chen stated in a thinly veiled criticism that Fuxinggang needed to change with the times and adjust their methods to a different contemporary situation.[40] In addition to political criticism from elected officials, political officers were increasingly open to attack by media outlets when they were perceived as politicizing their role. In December 2006, a political officer was publicly named in a prominent newspaper and attacked for being part of a "Stalinist throwback" organization after he was photographed participating in a political protest.[41]

The ROC Military in Contemporary Taiwan

The ROC military in Taiwan undertook a radical transformation after the depoliticization of the force, and because of changing demographics and missions. The changes in civil-military relations within the ROC military, during the 1986–2010 period, were reflected in a significantly revised force structure that favored the key elements of a more technically competent, long-term volunteer force, an increasingly prominent role for air and naval forces in military planning, and a shift to purely defensive military strategies.

The passage of the two national defense laws in 2002 was accompanied by a shift in the internal policies of the ROC military, to devote increasing percentages of the defense budget and an increasingly prominent role in military operations to air and naval forces. The elimination of the dual command structure and the integration of planning and training for the three services under a unified command had been explicitly cited as a key goal of the new legislation by defense minister Tang Fei in 2000.[42]

The steady decrease in the prominence of military affairs within the ROC government budget, measured in terms of total and percentage allocations, and reduction in the size of ROC military forces during the 1990s and 2000s, decreased the political and social importance of the military. In July 1997, a downsizing program, Streamlining and Consolidation (Jing Shih), was implemented, with the goal of reducing total personnel numbers below 400,000 by 2003, before reaching a target of roughly 340,000 by 2006 and 290,000 by 2012.[43] Most of the personnel cuts were made to the army, which by 2012 was reduced to 130,000 personnel, roughly a quarter of its peak post-1950 size. Most of the cuts were made by gradually decreasing the reliance on conscripted manpower. This was accomplished by shifting to a short period of military training to create a reserve force, rather than expecting lengthy active-duty service in the ROC military, resulting in a smaller active-duty force.[44]

The drop in total personnel within the military enabled a large percentage of the increasingly austere military budget to be used for the purchase of advanced equipment, especially aircraft and naval vessels. During the 1990s, Taiwan purchased over 16 billion dollars' worth of equipment from the United States and spent an additional several billion dollars on French and German fighter jets and naval vessels, as well as funding indigenous development of jet fighters and naval patrol ships.[45] The comprehensive increase in the firepower and technical orientation of the ROC forces, combined with the increasingly selective personnel system, was a return to the idea of an elite ROC military imagined during the post–World War II period, but without the same great power aspirations.

Despite the end of formal ties in 1979, the influence of the United States on the ROC military education system remained strong, with military-to-military exchanges supported by large numbers of Taiwanese students studying at private

American schools before entering the ROC military at both the enlisted or officer level. The most direct education connection is the enrollment of three Taiwanese students at any one time at each U.S. academy: West Point, Annapolis, and Colorado Springs. One student per year is also sent to two state-level military schools: Virginia Military Institute and the Citadel in South Carolina. Norwich University in Vermont accepts two per year.[46] At the graduate level, Taiwanese officers can attend a wide variety of U.S. military schools, including the Army War College, National Defense University, and Navy Staff College, at the discretion of the ROC Ministry of National Defense.[47]

The United States continues to serve as the primary security model for Taiwan, with ROC government reforms, such as the creation of a National Security Council system, explicitly designed to be similar to U.S. mechanisms. At the organizational level, the United States remains deeply involved in ROC discussions over strategy, training, and force structure. Talks between U.S. and ROC military leaders over these "software" issues is conducted at several venues: annual Monterey Talks at the Defense Language Institute in California, the annual U.S.-Taiwan Defense Industry Conference held in the United States, and consultations at the East-West Center in Hawaii.[48] These meetings are designed to increase the level of coordination between U.S.-ROC military staffs, and to provide a venue to develop personal connections through academic exchanges provided for military officers at research centers in the United States and Taiwan.

The renewed focus of the ROC military on high-tech air and naval warfare has meant significantly increased purchases of American military equipment since 1990. Notable purchases include: 150 F-16 fighters in 1992, ET-2 airborne early warning aircraft in 1993, Chinook helicopters in 1998, P3C maritime patrol aircraft in 2007, and Apache helicopters in 2008. In addition, substantial investments were made during the 2000s to harden ROC military sites and protect against PRC missile forces through the purchase of the Patriot missile defense system and early warning radars.[49] Similar to the post-1950 rebuilding of the ROC military, the United States has constrained weapons transfers to "defensive" systems that are unable to significantly threaten the status quo in East Asia or allow the possibility of attacking China.

It has been a challenge to recreate the intellectual discussion and debate within the officer corps that was a vital part of the 1942–55 period. Civilian political leaders instigated the major changes to the ROC military identity, role, and structure during the democratization era (1986–2000). Military officers, except in a few cases such as Wang Sheng and Hau Pei-tsun, were largely isolated from broader discussion of civil-military development. ROC officers as a group remained largely passive during the 1990s as the new structure of the ROC military was debated. The increasing pressures of a rising Chinese military power, especially the period surrounding the 1995 and 1996 Chinese missile tests, focused military attention on real-world issues rather than major reforms. Particularly after the implementation of the two National Defense Laws in 2003, officers supported the new civilian-dominated, functionally specific military structure. In polling data collected from 2004 to 2007, the overwhelming majority of military officers understood and approved of the new military structure. When asked if they understood the significance and importance of the term "army nationalization" (jundui guojiahua), 92 percent of surveyed officers answered that they understood the concept. When asked if they agreed with the two national defense laws and the concept of "army nationalization," 69 percent approved of the policies.[50]

A review of recent ROC military journals shows an increasing focus on highly specialized, technical issues rather than politicized appeals to "take back the mainland," but refined and sophisticated analysis of civil-military or professional norms is poorly developed. Military schools continue to produce journals such as *Guofang zazhi* (*National Defense Magazine*), *Fuxinggang Xuebao* (*Fuxinggang Journal*), and so forth, and new research centers focused on international relations have emerged. Despite a large quantity of material produced, the overall quality is low, with military officers clearly being hesitant to test the intellectual boundaries of this new civil-military environment.

The core historical argument presented in this work is that Chinese military officers within the KMT military were able to create a depoliticized military institution, develop foreign partnerships, and define a distinct military officer identity to create a true "national" army for the first time in Chinese history during the years 1942–55.

This work has traced the development of KMT/ROC military forces from 1942 to 1955, and analyzed the process by which armed forces constructed their identity and mission. This process was driven by the internal motivations of military officers to create a professional role that emphasized technical skills and insulated bureaucratic structures. These ideas, expressed most articulately by Gen. Sun Li-jen, were able to achieve many of the status objectives of military officers. The process by which Chinese military officers selectively adopted ideas that supported their professional claims to jurisdiction over the management of violence strongly supports the conception of normative isomorphism, whereby change is driven by desires for status and respect.

Throughout the 1942–55 period, Chinese officers found that, by adopting American military norms and conceptions, they could reshape their position within the KMT system, and later the ROC government. Throughout this process, the Unites States played a key role in introducing concepts and providing support to military officers but was never able to decisively shape the KMT/ROC military. The power of ideas—be they ideas of professional competence articulated by Sun Li-jen or political loyalty developed by Chiang Ching-kuo—and the ability to mobilize supporters of these ideas, mattered far more than foreign advice or equipment.

During the 1942–55 period, the power and influence of ideas of military professionalism fluctuated in inverse relationship to the power and influence of political officers. The power and influence of the political officer within the KMT military also varied widely from a high point in the 1926–28 period, through a long decline from 1928 to 1946, formal abolition of the political officer role from 1946 to 1950, and a resurgent political officer system created in Taiwan after 1953. With American support and political inattention from senior KMT leaders, military officers were able to move the KMT/ROC Army towards a technocratic and apolitical vision but could never fully eliminate the party-army idea. While the professionalization program was successful for brief periods, military officers were not able to defend their professional identity from a concerted effort by political leaders to reestablish KMT dominance.

Although the efforts of KMT/ROC military officers were unsuccessful in the short term, in the long term the driving forces of normative isomorphism, a desire for status, and professional identity have outlasted political domination in Taiwan, and perhaps eventually they will also do so in China.

Notes

Introduction

1. William McNeill, *The Pursuit of Power: Technology, Armed Force and Society Since* A.D. *1000* (Chicago: University of Chicago Press, 1984).
2. John Lynn, "The Evolution of Army Style in the Modern West, 800–2000," *International History Review* 18, no. 3 (August 1996): 509.
3. Terry Terriff and Theo Farrell, eds., *The Sources of Military Change: Culture, Politics, Technology* (Boulder, Colo.: Lynne Rienner Publishers, 2002).
4. See Max Boot, *War Made New: Technology, Warfare and the Course of History, 1500 to Today* (New York: Gotham Press, 2006); Frederick Kagan, *Finding the Target: The Transformation of American Military Policy* (New York: Encounter Books, 2006); Victor Davis Hansen, *Carnage and Culture: Landmark Battles in the Rise of Western Power* (New York: Doubleday, 2001); John Lynn, *Battle: A History of Combat and Culture* (New York: Basic Books, 2003).
5. See Mary B. Rankin, "The Origins of a Chinese Public Sphere," *Etudes Chinoises* 9, no. 2 (Autumn 1990): 147–75; William T. Rowe, "The Public Sphere in Modern China," *Modern China,* 16, no. 3 (July 1990), 309–29; Phil Huang, "Public Sphere"/"Civil Society" in China? The Third Realm between State and Society," *Modern China* 19, no. 2 (April 1993): 216–40; Prasenjit Duara, *Rescuing History from the Nation* (Chicago: University of Chicago Press, 1995).
6. Madeline Zelin, *The Merchants of Zigong: Industrial Entrepreneurship in Early Modern China* (New York: Columbia University Press, 2006); Frederic Wakeman, *Policing Shanghai, 1927–1937* (Berkeley: University of California Press, 1996); David Strand, *Rickshaw Beijing: City People and Politics in the 1920s* (Berkeley: University of California Press, Berkeley, 1993); Bryan Martin, *The Shanghai Green Gang: Politics and Organized Crime, 1919–1937* (Berkeley: University of California Press, 1996); Donna Brunero, *Britain's Imperial Cornerstone in China: The Chinese Maritime Customs Service, 1854–1949*

(London: Routledge Press, 2006); Julia Strauss, *Strong Institutions in Weak Polities: State Building in Republic China, 1927–1940* (Oxford: Oxford University Press, 1998).
7. Peter Wilson, "Defining Military Culture," *Journal of Military History* 72 (January 2008): 12.
8. Howard Greenwald, *Organizations: Management without Control* (Los Angeles: Sage Publications, 2008), 192.
9. Strauss, *Strong Institutions*, 2.
10. Peter Hall and Rosemary Taylor, "Political Science and the Three New Institutionalisms," *MPIFG Scientific Advisory Board* (June 1996), 8.
11. Ibid., 16.
12. Paul DiMaggio and Walter Powell, "The Iron Cage Revisited: Institutional Isomorphism and Collective Rationality in Organizational Fields," *American Sociological Review* 48, no. 2 (April 1983): 150.
13. Ibid., 152.
14. Ibid.
15. Xiaoqun Xu, *Chinese Professionals and the Republican State: The Rise of Professional Associations in Shanghai, 1912–1937* (Cambridge, UK: Cambridge University Press, 2001).
16. Greenwald, *Organizations*, 339.
17. Strauss, *Strong Institutions*, 10; A. J. Dray-Novey, "The Twilight of the Beijing Gendarmerie, 1920–1924," *Modern China* 33, no. 3 (July, 2007): 349–76.
18. Andrew Abbott, *The System of Professions: An Essay on the Division of Expert Labor* (Chicago: University of Chicago Press, 2007).
19. Ibid., 60.
20. Katherine E. McCoy, "Organizational Frames for Professional Claims: Private Military Corporations and the Rise of the Military Paraprofessional," *Social Problems* 59, no. 3 (August 2012): 333, 337.
21. Rana Mitter, *Forgotten Ally: China's World War II, 1937–1945* (Boston: Houghton Mifflin, 2013); Keith Schoppa, *In a Sea of Bitterness: Refugees during the Sino-Japanese War* (Cambridge, Mass.: Harvard University Press, 2011); Parks Coble, *China's War Reporters: The Legacy of Resistance against Japan* (Cambridge, Mass.: Harvard University Press, 2015); Micah Muscalino, *The Ecology of War in China: Henan Province, the Yellow River, and Beyond, 1938–1950* (Cambridge, UK: Cambridge University Press, 2016); Diana Lary and Stephen MacKinnon, *Scars of War: The Impact of Warfare on Modern China* (Vancouver: University of British Columbia Press, 2001); Hsi-cheng Chi, *Nationalist China at War: Military Defeats and Political Collapse, 1937–1945* (Ann Arbor: University of Michigan Press, 1982); Jui-Te Chang, "National Army Officers during the Sino-Japanese War, 1937–1945," *Modern Asian Studies* 30, no. 4 (October 1996): 1033–56; Marvin Williamsen, "The Military Dimension, 1937–1941," chapter 6 in *China's Bitter Victory: The War with Japan, 1937–1945*, edited by James Hsiung and

Steven Levine (New York: M. E. Sharpe Co, 1992); Frank Dorn, *The Sino-Japanese War, 1937–1941: From Marco Polo Bridge to Pearl Harbor* (New York: Macmillan, 1977).

22. Barbara Tuchman, *Stilwell and the American Experience in China, 1911–1945* (New York: Macmillan, 1911); William Grieve, *The American Military Mission to China, 1941–1942: Lend-Lease Logistics, Politics, and the Tangles of Wartime Cooperation* (Jefferson, N.C.: McFarland, 2014).; Hsi-cheng Chi, *The Much-Troubled Alliance: U.S.-China Military Cooperation during the Pacific War, 1941–1945* (Hackensack, N.J.: World Scientific, 2015).

23. Hans van de Ven, "Stilwell in the Stocks: The Chinese Nationalists and the Allied Powers in the Second World War," *Asian Affairs* 34, no. 3 (2003): 243–59.

24. Yuan Shouqian and Huang Jie, *Huangpu Jianjun* [Whampoa Army Training] (Taipei: Jiang zongton dui zhongguo yu shijie zhi gongxian congbian bianzhi hui, 1971).

25. Peter Worthing, "The Road through Whampoa: The Early Career of He Yingqin," *Journal of Military History* 69, no. 4 (October 2005): 953–85; F. F. Liu, *A Military History of Modern China, 1924–1949* (Princeton, N.J.: Princeton University Press, 1956); Richard E. Gillespie, "Whampoa and the Nanking Decade (1924–1936)" (PhD diss., American University, 1971); Richard Landis, "Training and Indoctrination at the Whampoa Academy," in *China in the 1920s: Nationalism and Revolution*, edited by F. Gilbert Chan and Thomas Etzold (New York: New Viewpoints Press, 1996); Martin C. Wilbur and Julie Lien-ying How, *Missionaries of Revolution: Soviet Advisors and Nationalist China, 1920–1927* (Cambridge, Mass.: Harvard University Press, 1989); Alexander Ivanovich Cherepanov, *As Military Adviser in China* (Taipei: Office of the Military Historian, 1970).

26. Hsiao-shih Cheng, *Party-Military Relations in the PRC and Taiwan: Paradoxes of Control* (Boulder, Colo.: Westview Press, 1990); David Shambaugh, "The Soldier and the State in China: The Political Work System in the People's Liberation Army," *China Quarterly* 127 (September 1991): 527–68; Jonathan Adelman, "The Formative Influence of the Civil Wars: Societal Roles of the Soviet and Chinese Armies," *Armed Forces and Society* 5 (1978): 93–116; Chien-jen Chiang, ed., *Kuo-chun cheng-kung shih-kao* [A History of Political Work in the National Army] (Taipei: Office of Military History, 1960); Joseph J. Heinlein Jr., "Political Warfare: The Chinese Nationalist Model" (PhD diss., The American University, 1974).

Chapter 1. The Development of the Chinese Army, 1850-1927

1. Bruce Elleman, *Modern Chinese Warfare, 1795–1989* (London: Routledge Press, 2001), 5; Mark Elliott, *The Manchu Way: The Eight Banners and Ethnic Identity in Late Imperial China* (Stanford, Calif.: Stanford University Press, 2001), 369.

2. Pamela Crossley, *Orphan Warriors: Three Manchu Generations and the End of the Qing World* (Princeton, N.J.: Princeton University Press, 1991), 13.

3. Francis Younghusband, *British Military Report; Coast Defense of China, The Construction of Chinese Railways, etc.* (Simla, India: Government Central Branch, 1887), 3.

4. Emory Upton, *The Armies of Asia and Europe* (Portsmouth, N.H.: Griffin and Company, 1878). 20.
5. Ibid.
6. Younghusband, *British Military Report*, 37.
7. Philip Kuhn, *Rebellion and Its Enemies in Late Imperial China: Militarization and Social Structure, 1796–1864* (Boston: Harvard University Press, 1970), Introduction.
8. Upton, *The Armies of Asia and Europe*, 18.
9. Evelyn Rawski, *The Last Emperors: A Social History of Qing Imperial Institutions* (Berkeley: University of California Press, 1998), 43–46.
10. Upton, *The Armies of Asia and Europe*, 22.
11. Crossley, *Orphan Warriors*, 176–80.
12. Jonathan D. Spence, *God's Chinese Son: The Taiping Heavenly Kingdom of Hong Xiuquan* (New York: Norton, 1996), 173–91.
13. Kuhn, *Rebellion and Its Enemies in Late Imperial China*, 7.
14. Zhang Pengyuan, "Qingmo minchu Hunan de junshi biange" [Military changes in Hunan at the end of Qing beginning of the Republic], *Bulletin of the Institute of Modern History* (Academia Sinica) 11 (July 1982): 101–3.
15. Richard Smith, "The Reform of Military Education in Late Ch'ing China, 1842–1895," *Journal of the Royal Asiatic Society, Hong Kong Branch* 18 (1978): 15–38.
16. Elleman, *Modern Chinese Warfare, 1795–1989*, 54–55.
17. Stanley Spector, *Li Hung-Chang and the Huai Army: A Study in Nineteenth-Century Chinese Regionalism* (Seattle: University of Washington Press, 1964), 152–65.
18. Richard Smith, "The Reform of Military Education in Late Ch'ing China, 1842–1895," 23.
19. Mark Bell, *China: Being a Military Report on the Northeastern Portions of the Provinces of Chih-Li and Shan-Tung; Nanking and Its Approaches; Canton and Its Approaches; etc.*, Vols. I and II (Simla: Government Central Branch Press, 1884), 46.
20. Upton, *The Armies of Asia and Europe*, 28–29.
21. Younghusband, *British Military Report*, 5.
22. Allen Fung, "Testing the Self-Strengthening: The Chinese Army in the Sino-Japanese War of 1894–1895," *Modern Asian Studies* 30, no. 4 (October 1996): 1007–31.
23. Powell, *The Rise of Chinese Military Power, 1895–1912*, 76.
24. F. F. Liu, "The Nationalist Army of China: An Administrative Study of the Period 1924–1946" (PhD diss., Princeton University, 1951), 10.
25. Powell, *The Rise of Chinese Military Power, 1895–1912*, 77.
26. *Notes on China*, U.S. War Department (Washington, D.C.: Adjutant General's Office, August 1900), 62.
27. Bell, *China: Being a Military Report*, 57.
28. Edward Dreyer, *China at War, 1901–1949* (New York: Longman Press, 1995), 20; Steven Mackinnon, "The Peiyang Army, Yuan Shik-k'ai, and the Origins of Modern Chinese Warlordism," *Journal of Asian Studies* 32:3 (May 1973), 405–23.

29. Thomas L. Kennedy, "The Peiyang Arsenal and the Evolution of Warlord Logistics, 1895–1911," *Bulletin of the Institute of Modern History* (Academia Sinica) 10 (July 1981): 425–28.
30. Dreyer, *China at War, 1901–1949*, 17.
31. Zheng Zhiting and Qiushan Zhang, *Baoding lujun xuetang ji junguan xue xiao shi lue* [A History of the Baoding Military Academy and Army School] (Beijing: Renmin chubanshe, 2005), 103–11; Zhu Bingyi and Yang Xuefang, *Lujun daxue yan geshi* [Army University Curriculum Development] (Taipei: Sanjun daxue, 1990), 5–8.
32. Powell, *The Rise of Chinese Military Power, 1895–1912*, 299.
33. Chang Rui-de, "Nationalist Chinese Officers during the Sino-Japanese War, 1937–1945," *Modern Asian Studies* 30, no. 4 (October 1996): 1034–35.
34. Anita O'Brian, in *Perspectives on a Changing China*, edited by William T. Rowe and Joshua Fogel (Boulder, Colo.: Westview Press, 1979), 163.
35. Montague Bell and H. G. W. Woodhead, *The China Yearbook, 1916* (London: Routledge and Sons, 1916), 297.
36. Odoric Wou, *Militarism in China: The Career of Wu P'ei-Fu, 1916–1939* (Dawson: Australian National University Press, 1977), 16.
37. Richard Smith, "The Reform of Military Education in Late Ch'ing China, 1842–1895," 22.
38. John Wands Sacca, "Like Strangers in a Foreign Land: Chinese Officers Prepared at American Military Colleges, 1904–1937," *Journal of Military History* 70 (July 2006), 708.
39. Edmund Fung, *The Military Dimension of the Chinese Revolution: The New Army and Its Role in the Revolution of 1911* (Vancouver: University of British Columbia Press, 1980), 99.
40. Hans van de Ven, "The Military in the Republic," *China Quarterly*, no. 150 (June 1997): 356.
41. Ibid., 357.
42. O'Brian, *Military Academies in China, 1885–1915*, 163.
43. Edmund Fung, "Military Subversion in the Chinese Revolution of 1911," *Modern Asian Studies* 9, no. 1 (1975), 103–23.
44. "Junguo xueshe jianzhang" [Military Study Group Leader], *Junhua* 1 (1911): iii.
45. Samuel Huntington, *The Soldier and the State: The Theory and Politics of Civil-Military Relations* (Cambridge, Mass.: Harvard University Press, 1957), 10.
46. *Dongya Bao*, "Zhongguo junzhi gaige" [China Military Reforms] 7 (1898); *Shiwu Bao*, "Lun zhongguo junzheng" [A Discussion of Chinese Military Administration] 50 (1897): 13–14; *Da Tong Bao*, "Zhongguo junquan jizhong zhi yiban" [Chinese Military Power Collected Works] 14, no. 10 (1910); *Dongfang Zazhi*, "Zhongguo junren jiaoyu zhi xianxiang" [China's Military Education and Appearance] 10 (1904): 220–24.;
47. Lu Yan, *Re-Understanding Japan: Chinese Perspectives, 1895–1945* (Honolulu: University of Hawaii Press, 2004), 26.

48. *Junxue jikan* [Military Studies Quarterly] (Shanghai: Shangwu yinshu guan, 1908).
49. Su Keli, "Ershi shiji de junshi geming-yi ri'ezhanzheng (1904–1905) weili" [Twentieth-century Military Revolution and the Russo-Japanese War], *Zhonghua junshi xuehui huikan* (April 2005): 23–50; Meng Guohan, *Minguo shiqi de lujun da xue* [The Military Academy in the Republican Period] (Jiangsu: Di er lishi dong an guan, 1994), 4.
50. Mackinnon, "The Pei-yang Army, Yuan Shih-k'ai, and the Origins of Modern Chinese Warlordism," 405–23.
51. Xi Jingheyan (Hosoi, Kazuhiko), "Nanjing guomin zhengfu shiqi de lujun daxue" [Nanjing Government Period Central Military Academy], *Wuhan kexue daxue bao* 13, no. 2 (April 2011): 219–20.
52. [Comments], *Junhua* 1 (1911): 22.
53. *Beiyang bingshi zazhi*, 1910.
54. *Nanyang jushi zazhi* (Nanjing: bingshi zazhi shi bianji, 1906–1911).
55. "Xuanshi wenti," *Junhua* 1–3 (1911): iv.
56. "Junshi diaocha," *Junhua* 3 (1911): 79–86.
57. Ibid., 86.
58. He Deng, "Zhongguo da jieji bianzhi zhi yanjiu," *Junhua* 2 (1911): 14–17.
59. Yi Wu, "Tongji yu junshi zhi guanxi," *Junhua* 1 (1911): 22–25.
60. Editors, "Kongzhong zhandou zhi jianglai" [The Future of Military Aviation], *Junhua* 1 (1911): 14–16.
61. He Deng (trans.), "Zhanbai hou zhi eguo jinzhuang," *Junhua* 3 (1911): 41–49.
62. "Riben luhai jun xitong," *Junhua* 3 (1911): 87–89.
63. Powell, *The Rise of Chinese Military Power, 1895–1912*, 272–80; Dreyer, *China at War, 1901–1949*, 26–28.
64. Dreyer, *China at War, 1901–1949*, 26.
65. Relevant works include: Joseph Esherick, *Reform and Revolution in China: The 1911 Revolution in Hunan and Hubei* (Berkeley: University of California Press, 1976); Edward McCord, *The Power of the Gun: The Emergence of Modern Chinese Warlordism* (Berkeley: University of California Press, 1993); Donald Sutton, *Provincial Militarism and the Chinese Republic: The Yunnan Army, 1905–1925* (Ann Arbor: University of Michigan Press, 1980); Fung, *The Military Dimension of the Chinese Revolution*.
66. Relevant works include: Diana Lary, *Warlord Soldiers: Chinese Common Soldiers, 1911–1937* (Cambridge, UK: Cambridge University Press, 1985); Hans van de Ven, "Public Finance and the Rise of Warlordism," *Modern Asian Studies* 30, no. 4 (October 1996): 829–68.
67. O'Brian, *Perspectives on a Changing China*, 165.
68. Ibid., 176.
69. *Yunnan junshi zazhi* [Yunnan Military Magazine] (Kunming: Yunnan junshi zazhi she, 1922–24).

70. Zheng Xueyu, "Wo guo dui wai junshi jichu jiaoyu zhi jiaoliu (1904–2005)" [Our country's military education in foreign nations], *Zhonghua junshi xuehui huikan* (October 1996), 159–68; Sacca, "Like Strangers in a Foreign Land," 706.
71. Jean Jaures, Liu Wendao, and Liao Shishao, *Xin Junlun* [New Military Law] (Shanghai: Shangwu yinshu guan, 1924); Friedrich Von Bernardi and Gao Lao, *Zhanzheng zhexue* [Military Thought] (Shanghai: Shangwu xinwu guan, 1924).
72. Cord Eberspacher, "To Arm China: Sino-German Relations in the Military Sphere Prior to the First World War," *Berliner China-Hefte/Chinese History and Society* 33 (2008): 54–74.
73. Gavan McCormack, *Chang Tso-lin in Northeast China, 1911–1928* (Stanford, Calif.: Stanford University Press, 1977), 126–28; Phillip Jowett, *Chinese Warlord Armies* (London: Osprey Publishing, 2010), 16.
74. Julie Lian-Ying How, *Soviet Advisors with the Kuominchun, 1925–1926: A Documentary Survey* (Armonk, N.Y.: M. E. Sharpe, 1986).
75. Chien Tuan-sheng, *The Government and Politics of China, 1912–1949* (Stanford, Calif.: Stanford University Press, 1970), 83–91.
76. Zhang Yufa, "Erci geming: Guomindang yu Yuan Shikai de junshi duikang (1912–1914)" [The Second Revolution: Military Confrontation of the Kuomintang and Yuan Shikai], *Zhongyang yanjiuyuan jindai shi yanjiusuo jikan*, no. 15 (1986): 270–75; Fu Zhengyuan, *Autocratic Conditions and Chinese Politics* (Cambridge, UK: Cambridge University Press, 1993), 153–54.
77. Sun Yat-sen, *Zhongshan quanshu* [The Complete Works of Dr. Sun Yat-sen], cited in Liu, *A Military History of Modern China, 1924–1949*, 3.
78. Marie-Claire Bergere, *Sun Yat-sen* (Stanford, Calif.: Stanford University Press, 1998), 280–81.
79. Ibid., 265–81.
80. Liu Zhi, *Huangpu junxiao yu guomin geming jun* [Whampoa Academy and the National Revolutionary Army] (Nanjing: Duli chubanshe, 1947), 7.
81. Gillespie, "Whampoa and the Nanking Decade, 1924–1936," 33.
82. Yuan and Huang, *Huangpu Jianjun*, 57.
83. Jianhua Chen, ed., *Huangpu junxiao yanjiu* [Whampoa Academy Research] (Guangzhou: Zhongshan daxue chubanshe, 2007), 224–26; Richard Landis, "Institutional Trends at the Whampoa Military School" (PhD diss., University of Washington, 1969), 15–16.
84. Gillespie, "Whampoa and the Nanking Decade, 1924–1936," 38.
85. Liu, *A Military History of Modern China, 1924–1949*, 14–15.
86. A. I. Cherepanov, *As Military Adviser in China* (Moscow: Progress Publishers, 1982), 36.
87. Gillespie, "Whampoa and the Nanking Decade, 1924–1936," 106.
88. Liu Zhi, *Huangpu junxiao yu guomin geming jun* [Whampoa Academy and the National Revolutionary Army] (Nanjing: Duli chubanshe, 1947), 14.

89. Gillespie, "Whampoa and the Nanking Decade, 1924–1936," 111–12.
90. Ibid., 114–15.
91. Cherepanov, *As Military Adviser in China*, 87.
92. Ian Germani, "Terror in the Army: Representatives on Mission and Military Discipline in the Armies of the French Revolution," *Journal of Military History* 75 (July 2011): 733–68; Brian Taylor, *Politics and the Russian Army: Civil-Military Relations, 1689–2000* (Cambridge, UK: Cambridge University Press, 2003), 138–46.
93. Monte Bullard, *The Soldier and the Citizen: The Role of the Military in Taiwan's Development* (London: M. E. Sharpe, 1997), 70–71: Cheng, *Party-Military Relations*, 38.
94. Cheng, *Party-Military Relations*, 39.
95. Liu, *Huangpu junxiao yu guomin geming jun*, 24.
96. Goufangbu zong zhengzhi bu, *Guojun zhenggong shigao* [A History of National Army Political Work] (Taipei: Guojun zhenggong shibian, 1960), 258–62; Shaokun Feng, *Guo junzheng zhan shi* [National Military Political Warfare History] (Taipei: Zhengzhi zuozhan xuexiao bianying, 1972), 48–50.
97. Cheng, *Party-Military Relations*, 20.
98. Ibid., 21.
99. Shaokun, *Guo junzheng zhan shi*, 37, 217.
100. Ibid., 38–40.
101. Ibid., 70–72.
102. Goufangbu zong zhengzhi bu, *Guojun zhenggong shigao*, 258–62; Jiang Pei, "Zhongguo guomindang zaoqi jundui zhenggong zhidu de yanbian: 1924–1928" [The Political Work System of the KMT in Its Early Period], *Anhui shixue* 4 (2008): 59.
103. Liu, *A Military History of Modern China, 1924–1949*, 14.
104. Landis, "Institutional Trends at the Whampoa Military School: 1924–1926," 134.
105. Liu, *A Military History of Modern China, 1924–1949*, 13.
106. Cherepanov, *As Military Adviser in China*, 32–40.
107. Landis, "Institutional Trends at the Whampoa Military School: 1924–1926" 75–76.
108. Chen Jian Hua, ed., *Huangpu junxiao yanjiu* [Memories of the Whampoa Academy] (Guangzhou: Zhongshan daxue chubanshe, 2007), 77–81.
109. Elleman, *Modern Chinese Warfare, 1795–1989*, 169–71.
110. Shen Keqin, *Sun Liren zhuan* [Sun Liren Biography] (Taipei: xuesheng shuju youxiangongsi, 2005), 1.
111. Ibid., 13.
112. Ibid., 15.
113. Mo Shaoke, "Sun Liren: beiqing jiangjun de shishi" [Sun Liren: An Epic Military Tragedy], *Renmin Wenzhai*, June 2011, 46.
114. Shen Jingyong, *Zhongguo junhun: Sun Liren jiangjun fengshan lianjun shilu* [Soul of the Chinese Army: Sun Li-jen's Fengshan Training Camp Experience] (Taipei: Xuesheng shuju, 1993), v; Zheng Jinju, *Yi dai zhanshen: Sun Liren*, [A Generation's War Hero: Sun Liren] (Taipei: Shuiniu chuban youxian gongsi, 2004), 69–70.

115. Zheng, *Yi dai zhanshen: Sun Liren*, 70.
116. Chu Hongyuan, *Sun Liren yanlun xuanji* [Collected Speeches of Sun Liren] (Taipei: Zhongyang yanjiuyuan jindaishi yanjiusuo, 2000), 3.
117. Zheng, *Yi dai zhanshen: Sun Liren*, 5.

Chapter 2. A Party Army, 1927–1942

1. See William Kirby, *Germany and Republican China* (Stanford, Calif.: Stanford University Press, 1984); Van de Ven, "The Military in the Republic," 352–74; Donald Sutton, "German Advice and Residual Warlordism in the Nanking Decade: Influences on Nationalist Military Training and Strategy," *China Quarterly* 91 (September 1982): 386–410; Robyn Rodriguez, "Journey to the East: The German Military Mission to China, 1927–1938" (PhD diss., Ohio State University, 2011).
2. Billie Walsh, "The German Military Mission in China, 1928–38," *Journal of Modern History* 46, no. 3 (September 1974): 503.
3. Yuan and Huang, *Huangpu Jianjun*, 74
4. Sutton, "German Advice and Residual Warlordism in the Nanking Decade: Influences on Nationalist Military Training and Strategy," 389.
5. Ibid.
6. Ibid., 392.
7. *Luda Yuekan* [Military Academy Monthly] (Nanjing: Luda yuekan bianji weiyuan hui, 1935–1937).
8. Walsh, "The German Military Mission in China, 1928–38," 504.
9. Ibid., 506.
10. Sutton, "German Advice and Residual Warlordism," 390–91.
11. Memorandum for Major Magruder, Peking, 2 May 1929, U.S. Military Intelligence Reports, 1911–1941 (Frederick, Md.: University Publications of America, 1983).
12. Kirby, *Germany and Republican China*, 221; Liu, *A Military History of Modern China, 1924–1949*, 102.
13. Dreyer, *China at War, 1901–1949*, 184.
14. Walsh, "The German Military Mission in China, 1928–38," 504–5.
15. Wang Qisheng, "Wuzhu wencong bei jing xia de duozhong bianzou: zhanshi guomindang jundui de zhenggong yu dangwu" [Political and Party Work during the War Period], *Kangri zhanzheng yanjiu* 4 (2007): 67.
16. Heinlein, "Political Warfare: The Chinese Nationalist Model," 300–301.
17. Frederic Wakeman, "A Revisionist View of the Nanjing Decade: Confucian Fascism," *China Quarterly* 150 (June 1997): 395–432.
18. Jiang Pei, "Zhongguo guomindang zaoqi jundui zhenggong zhidu de yanbian: 1924–1928" [The Evolution of the Political System of the Early Chinese Kuomintang Army: 1924–1928], *Anhui shixue* 4 (2008): 66; Goufangbu zong zhengzhi bu, *Guojun zhenggong shigao*, 519, 426.

19. *Huangpu Yuekan*, 1, no. 2 (1930): iii.
20. Cheng, *Party-Military Relations*, 21.
21. Heinlein, "Political Warfare: The Chinese Nationalist Model," 315.
22. Hu Yi, "Guomindang jundui zhenggong de fazhan lichen jiqi guji (1924–1949)" [The Evolution and Development of the KMT's Political Work, 1924–1949], *Dandshi yanjiu yu jiaoxue* 4 (2010): 83; Shaokun, *Guo junzheng zhan shi*, 79.
23. Deng Wenyi, *Jundui zhong zhengzhi gongzuo* [Political Work in the Army] (Nanjing: Zhongyang lujun xuexiao zhengzhi xunlian chu, 1930), 10–13.
24. Julia Strauss, "Xingzheng Sanlianshi and Xunlian: Modes of Government of Administration during the Sino-Japanese War," *Zhonghua junshi li xuehui huikan* 1, no. 3 (December 1997): 565–95.
25. Ren Minhai, "Jianshou zhengzhi gongzuo de gangwei" [Upholding Political Works Position], *Xin Jun* 1, no. 2 (1938): 32; Mei Yang, "Liang nian lai: Wo zuo jundui zhengzhi gongzuo de jingyan" [Two Years' Absence: My Political Work in the Military], *Xin Jun* 1, no. 4 (1938): 169; Huang Yao, "Lun zhengzhi gongzuo de jiben xiuyang" [A Discussion of Political Work Basic Accomplishments], *Xin Jun* 2, no. 12 (1939): 82.
26. He Ren, "Xian jieduan de jundui zhenggong wenti," *Xin Jun* 1, no. 2 (1938): 27.
27. *Junshi Yuekan* (Kunming: Yunnan kaizhi yin shua gongsi, 1936–1940).
28. Xia Weihai, "Yindu geming de xian jieduan" [The New Stage of the Indian Revolution], *Huangpu Yuekan* 1, no. 3 (October 1930).
29. Kirby, *Germany and Republican China*, 102–44.
30. Zhang Zhenmin, "Xiangli qiaozhi zhi dizu lilun" [An Understanding of Land and Rent Issues], *Huangpu Yuekan* 1, no. 6 (November 1930).
31. Zhong Yang, "Zhongguo gongchandang de liang da jingdi-tongyi yu jianshe" [The Chinese Communist Party Two Difficult Factors: Agreement and Development], *Huangpu Yuekan* 1, no. 3 (October 1930).
32. Zhang Zhizhong, "Women yinggai zenyang xiuyang" [How Should We Reform?], *Huangpu Yuekan* 1, no. 6 (November 1930).
33. Zhu Peide, *Junguan de xin shenghua* [Military Officers' New Life] (Nanjing: Zhongzheng shuju, 1934), 32–50.
34. "Meiguo lujun feihang jiaolian" [U.S. Army Flight Training], *Huangpu Yuekan* 1, no. 3 (October 1930); "Yi jiu er jiu nian shijie ge guo hangkong gaikuang" [1929 Global Aviation Report], *Huangpu Yuekan* 1, no. 6 (November 1930).
35. *Junshi Xunkan*, Beiping jun fenhui junshi xunlian weiyuanhui, 1934–1940.
36. "Guofang yu jundui guijiahua," *Huanian* 4 (1935): 46.
37. "Jundui xuexiaohua" [Military Education], *Tongyi pinglun* 2, no. 24 (1936): 13–14.
38. Deng Weimei, *Zhongyang lu jun junguan xueyuan tebie ban jiangyi* [Special Class of the Central Military Academy Lectures] (ca. 1937), 3.
39. Lloyd Eastman, *Seeds of Destruction: Nationalist China in War and Revolution, 1937–1949* (Stanford, Calif.: Stanford University Press, 1984), 133.

40. Report: Statement on Commissioned Personnel Strength and Classification as to Training, 28 January 1936. U.S. Military Intelligence Reports, Reel 5, 521–24; Eastman, *Seeds of Destruction*, 145.
41. Liu, *A Military History of Modern China, 1924–1949*, 147–49.
42. Ibid., 149.
43. Yuan and Huang, *Huangpu Jianjun*, 99.
44. Chi, *Nationalist China at War*, 65.
45. Ibid.
46. Chang Jui-te, "Nationalist Army Officers during the Sino-Japanese War, 1937–1945," *Modern Asian Studies* 30, no. 4 (October 1996): 1034–35.
47. Charles Romanus and Charles Sunderland, *Stilwell's Mission to China* (Washington, D.C.: Office of the Chief of Military History Department, 1953), 153.
48. Chang, "Nationalist Army Officers during the Sino-Japanese War, 1937–1945," 1041.
49. Ibid., 1053.
50. "China Executes Eight High Officers and Hails Victorious Generals," *Washington Post*, 15 April 1938.
51. "China to Execute Shirking Officers," *New York Times*, 11 October 1937.
52. "China Executes Eight High Officers and Hails Victorious Generals," *Washington Post*, 15 April 15, 1938.
53. Shaokun, *Guo junzheng zhan shi*, 127.
54. Goufangbu zong zhengzhi bu, *Guojun zhenggong shigao*, 683–87; Heinlein, "Political Warfare: The Chinese Nationalist Model," 391; Shaokun, *Guo junzheng zhan shi*, 129.
55. Zhong Hua, "Kangzhan shiqi guomindang jundui zhengzhi gongzuo shulun" [Anti-Japanese Period Kuomintang Military Political Work], *Lishi xue yanjiu* 4 (2005): 53.
56. Heinlein, "Political Warfare: The Chinese Nationalist Model," 419.
57. Yuan and Huang, *Huangpu Jianjun*, 259–60.
58. Franco David Macri, *Clash of Empires in South China: The Allied Nations' Proxy War with Japan, 1935–1941* (Lawrence: University of Kansas Press, 2012).
59. Liu, *A Military History of Modern China, 1924–1949*, 164–68.
60. Maochun Yu, *The Dragon's War: Allied Operations and the Fate of China, 1937–1947* (Annapolis: Naval Institute Press, 2006), 15–16.
61. Liu, *A Military History of Modern China, 1924–1949*, 169.
62. *Huangpu Yuekan* 8, nos. 1–2 (1937).
63. Jiang Baili, "Kangzhan de jiben guannian" [Basic Concepts of a Resistance War], *Huangpu Yuekan* 9, no. 1 (1938): 47–48.
64. Shen, Qingchen, "Chi jiu kangzhan de jiben gainian" [Basic Concepts for a Long-Lasting War of Resistance], *Huangpu Yuekan* 9, no. 2 (1938): 17–20.
65. Shen, *Sun Liren zhuan*, 45.
66. Ibid., 48.
67. Shen Jingyong, *Zhongguo jungui*, v.

68. Shen, *Sun Liren zhuan*, 53.
69. Zheng, *Yi dai zhanshen: Sun Liren*, 71.
70. Shen, *Sun Liren zhuan*, 57.
71. Shen, *Zhongguo jungui*, v.
72. Zheng, *Yi dai zhanshen: Sun Liren*, 74.
73. Ibid., 75.

Chapter 3. Americans and Officers, 1942-1945

1. Louis Morton, "Army and Marines on the China Station: A Study in Military and Political Rivalry," *Pacific Historical Review* 29, no. 1 (February 1960): 51–73.
2. Charles Finney, *The Old China Hands* (Westport, Conn.: Greenwood Press, 1973), 15–21; John N. Hart, *The Making of an Army "Old China Hand:" A Memoir of Colonel David D. Barrett* (Berkeley: Center for Chinese Studies, 1985), 7–25.
3. Matthew Moten, *Presidents and Their Generals: An American History of Command in War* (Cambridge, Mass.: Harvard University Press, 2014), 169–70.
4. James A. Huston, *The Sinews of War: Army Logistics 1775–1953* (Washington, D.C.: U.S. Government Printing Office, 1997), 296.
5. James Hewes, *From Root to McNamara: Army Organization and Administration, 1900–1963* (Washington, D.C.: Government Printing Office, 1975), 11–13.
6. Edward Coffman, *The Regulars: The American Army, 1898–1941* (Cambridge, Mass.: Harvard University Press, 2004), 203, 234.
7. Ibid., 281.
8. Ibid.
9. Hewes, *From Root to McNamara*, 54.
10. Coffman, *The Regulars*, 284.
11. Marc Gallicchio, "The Other China Hands: U.S. Army Officers and America's Failure in China, 1941–1950," *Journal of American-East Asian Relations* 4, no. 1 (1995): 50.
12. Coffman, *The Regulars*, 246.
13. Ibid.
14. Tuchman, *Stilwell and the American Experience in China*, 180–87.
15. Romanus and Sunderland, *Stilwell's Mission to China*, 7.
16. Ibid., 15–19.
17. Frank Kluckhorn, "U.S. Army Mission to Assist China," *New York Times*, 27 August 1941.
18. Romanus and Sunderland, *Stilwell's Mission to China*, 36.
19. The Military Mission in China to the War Department, 10 February 1942, in *Foreign Relations of the United States [FRUS], 1942*, vol. 5, *China*, 13–15.
20. Paul Kesaris, *U.S. Military Intelligence Reports: China 1911–1941* (Frederick, Md.: University Publications of America, 1983).
21. Romanus and Sunderland, *Stilwell's Mission to China*, 74.

22. Ibid., 73.
23. Ibid., 256.
24. "Message: HQ, U.S. Army Forces China, Burma and India," 22 September 1942, Microfilm M1419, Reel 5, National Archives and Record Administration (NARA).
25. "Liaison Memorandum Number Five," 1 October 1943, Record Group (RG) 493, Stack 290, Box 6, NARA.
26. Gallicchio, "The Other China Hands," 52.
27. "Instructions for Liaison Officers from this Headquarters to Chinese Units," 14 October 1943, RG 493, Stack 290, Box 6, NARA.
28. Col. Henry M. Spengler, "American Liaison Groups," *Military Review* 27, no. 1 (April 1947).
29. Romanus and Sunderland, *Stilwell's Mission to China*, 293–94.
30. W. J. Peterkin, *Inside China, 1943–1945: An Eyewitness Account of America's Mission in Yenan* (Baltimore: Gateway Press, 1992), 10.
31. Romanus and Sunderland, *Stilwell's Mission to China*, 296.
32. James Lilley, *China Hands: Nine Decades of Adventure, Espionage, and Diplomacy in Asia* (New York: Public Affairs, 2004), 50.
33. Yang Chenguan, "Guojun weiwan cheng de junshi shiwu daige (1943–1945) yi guojun meishi zhuangbeihua budui wei zhongxin de shentan" [American military equipment and aid during the last part of the Anti-Japanese War], *Zhonghua junshi xue huiyi huikan* 10 (April 1995): 166–68; Charles Romanus and Riley Sunderland, *Stilwell's Command Problems* (Washington, D.C.: Government Printing Office, 1985), 334.
34. Romanus and Sunderland, *Stilwell's Command Problems*, 340.
35. Memorandum for Gen. Hsiao I-Hsu from Gen. Frank Dorn, 18 May 1944, Box 87, Frank Dorn Papers, Hoover Institution Archives.
36. *Distribution of the Chinese Army by War Zones as of 4/27/1944*, Office of Strategic Services (Farmington Hills, Mich.: Gale Publishing, 2011), 1–9.
37. "Stillwell to Marshall–Eyes Alone," 26 September 1944, M1419, Reel 5, NARA.
38. George Marshall, *The Papers of George Catlett Marshall*, vol. 4, *Aggressive and Determined Leadership, June 1, 1943–December 31, 1944*, ed. Larry I. Bland and Sharon Ritenour Stevens (Baltimore: The Johns Hopkins University Press, 1996), 503–6.
39. Charles E. Kirkpatrick, *An Unknown Future and a Doubtful Present: Writing the Victory Plan of 1941* (Washington, D.C.: Center for Military History, 1992), 6.
40. "Priority Message: Secret, McClure to Wedemeyer," 10 February 1945, RG 493, Box 1, NARA.
41. "T/O for Chinese Army Group Troops: Organization of the Division," 22 February 1944, RG 493, Box 13, NARA.
42. Romanus and Sunderland, *Stilwell's Command Problems*, 233.
43. "Black Book on China: Chinese Training Command," 6 November 1944, RG 493, Box 15, NARA.

44. "China: The New Army," *Time Magazine*, 4 June 1945.
45. Charles F. Romanus and Riley Sunderland, *Time Runs Out in CBI* (Washington, D.C.: Government Printing Office, 1958), 374.
46. "U.S. Army Officers Run China School," *New York Times*, 8 January 1945.
47. Schedule, Command and General Staff School, March 1945, RG 493, NARA.
48. F. W. Boye, "Operating with a Chinese Army Group," *Military Review* 27, no. 2 (May 1947): 3–8.
49. Romanus and Sunderland, *Time Runs Out in CBI*, 267.
50. Ibid., 372.
51. The Secretary of War (Patterson) to the Secretary of State (Byrnes), 18 February 1946, *FRUS, 1946*, vol. 10, *China*, 733.
52. *Training of Foreign Nationals by the AAF*, Army Air Forces Historical Research Agency, no. 64 (August 1947): 30.
53. Romanus and Sunderland, *Time Runs Out in CBI*, 235.
54. "Information Book: China Theater," 6 November 1944, RG 493, Box 15, NARA.
55. "Roster of American Personnel with Chinese Alpha Units," 11 February 1945, RG 493, Box 15, NARA.
56. "World Battlefronts: Battle of Asia: Farewell Performance," *Time Magazine*, 9 July 1945.
57. Second Secretary of Embassy of China (Rice) to Secretary of State, 2 October 1944, *FRUS, 1944*, vol. 6, *China*, 163–64.
58. Edward Coffman, "The American 15th Infantry Regiment in China, 1912–1928: A Vignette in Social History," *Journal of Military History* 58, no. 1 (January 1994): 71–72.
59. Jean Pei and William Wang, *Under the Same Army Flag: Recollections of the Veterans of World War II* (Beijing: Wuzhou zhuanbo chubanshe, 2005), 11.
60. Correspondence from Maj. Gen. H. S. Aurand to Lt. Gen. A. C. Wedemeyer, 13 August 1945, RG 493, NARA; Peterkin, *Inside China, 1943–1945*, 9.
61. Memorandum, Chinese Combat Command, 27 May 1945, RG 493, NARA.
62. Ibid.
63. The Consul General at Kunming (Langdon) to the Ambassador in China (Hurley), Kunming, 12 February 1945, *FRUS, 1945*, vol. 7, *China*, 48–49.
64. "World Battlefronts: Battle of Asia: Farewell Performance," *Time Magazine*, 9 July 1945.
65. Joseph Stilwell, *The Stilwell Papers* (New York: Sloane and Associates, 1948), 190.
66. "Message: Chennault to Wedemeyer," 15 February 1945, RG 493, Box 1, NARA.
67. Memorandum for Record: Capabilities of the Ninth War Area, 11 July 1945, RG 493, NARA.
68. Ibid.
69. Zheng, *Yi dai zhanshen: Sun Liren*, 87–89.

70. William Slim, *Defeat into Victory* (New York: David McKay Company, Inc. 1961), 47.
71. Ibid., 119.
72. Romanus and Sunderland, *Stilwell's Command Problems*, 32.
73. Ibid., 48.
74. Ibid., 253.
75. "General Joseph Stillwell to General Sun Liren," 20 October 1944, Microfilm M1419, Reel 5, NARA; Shen, *Sun Liren zhuan*, 305.

Chapter 4. A National Army for China, 1945-1949

1. Memorandum by Brig. Gen. C. V. R. Schuyler, of the Department of the Army, to the Under Secretary of the Army (Draper), 1 November 1947, *FRUS, 1947*, vol. 7, *China*, 905.
2. The Ambassador in China (Hurley) to the Secretary of State, 1 September 1945, *FRUS, 1945*, vol. 7, *China*, 546.
3. Ibid., 547.
4. "Message, U.S. Forces China Command," 21 August 1945, RG 493, NARA.
5. "Message, COMGENCHINA to WARCOS," 11 August 1945, RG 493, NARA.
6. "Message, WARCOS," 3 September 1945, RG 493, NARA.
7. "China to Get U.S. Mission to Reorganize Her Armies," *New York Times*, 3 November 1945.
8. "Report by the State-War-Navy Coordinating Committee," 22 October 1945, RG 493, Box 20, NARA.
9. Ibid., Appendix B; *FRUS, 1945*, vol. 7, *China*, 589.
10. Report by the Joint Chiefs of Staff, Annex to Appendix, 22 October 1945, *FRUS, 1945*, vol. 7, *China*, 594.
11. Ibid., 595.
12. Memorandum by the Director of the Office of Far Eastern Affairs (Vincent) to the Secretary of State, 12 November 1945, *FRUS, 1945*, vol. 7, *China*, 617.
13. Memorandum by the Secretary of State to the State Department Member on the State-War-Navy Coordinating Committee (Dunn), 5 January 1946, *FRUS, 1946*, vol. 10, *China*, 811.
14. The Joint Chiefs of Staff to the Commanding General, United States Forces, China Theater (Wedemeyer), 14 December 1945 in *FRUS, 1945*, vol. 7, *China*, 699.
15. Memorandum of the Joint Chiefs of Staff to the State-War-Navy Coordinating Committee, 13 February 1946, *FRUS, 1946*, vol. 10, *China*, 817–20.
16. The Chief of the Army Advisory Group in China (Lucas) to the Ambassador in China (Stuart), 28 June 1947, *FRUS, 1947*, vol. 7, *China*, 860.
17. "Message: From COMGEN China to Warcos," 16 April 1946, RG 493, Box 1, NARA.
18. Ibid.

19. "Message: From COMGEN China to Warcos," 7 May 1946, NARA, RG 493.
20. The Chief of the Army Advisory Group in China (Lucas) to the Ambassador in China (Stuart), 28 June 1947, *FRUS, 1947*, vol. 7, *China*, 861.
21. Donald Starr, "U.S. Army Group Advising China Called Failure," *Chicago Daily Tribune*, 14 June 1948.
22. General Order 22, Chinese Combat Command, 25 October 1945, RG 493, NARA.
23. Establishment and Organization of JUSMAGCHINA, 1 November 1948, RG 334, NARA.
24. Memorandum by the Chief of the Division of Chinese Affairs (Sprouse) to the Director of the Office of Far Eastern Affairs (Butterworth), 15 June 1948, *FRUS, 1948*, vol. 8, *China*, 257–59.
25. See Eastman, *Seeds of Destruction*; Suzanne Pepper, *Civil War in China: The Political Struggle, 1945–1949* (New York: Rowman and Littlefield, 1999); Odd Westad, *Decisive Encounters: The Chinese Civil War, 1946–1950* (Stanford, Calif.: Stanford University Press, 2003).
26. Chinese Army India–Burma Campaign, http://cbi-theater-1.home.comcast.net/~cbi-theater-1/cai/genSun.html.
27. Zheng, *Yi dai zhanshen: Sun Liren*, 224.
28. United Nations, Military Staff Committee Resolution 1 (1946), 25 January 1946.
29. Zheng, *Yi dai zhanshen: Sun Liren*, 223.
30. Shen, *Zhongguo jungui*, vi.
31. See Ernest R. May, *The Truman Administration and China, 1945–1949* (Philadelphia: Lippincott, 1975); Larry Bland, ed., *George C. Marshall's Mediation Mission to China, December 1945–January 1947* (Lexington, Va.: George C. Marshall Foundation, 1998); William Stueck, *The Wedemeyer Mission: American Politics and Foreign Policy during the Cold War* (Athens: University of Georgia Press, 1984).
32. Zheng, *Yi dai zhanshen: Sun Liren*, 265–68.
33. Shen, *Zhongguo jungui*, vii.
34. Shen, *Sun Liren zhuan*, 455–56.
35. Guojun shiliao yeshu, *Lujun junguan xuexiao di su junguan xunlianban guansheng fangwen jilu* [Army Officer School: Fourth Training Class Oral Histories] (Taipei: guofangbu shi zhengbian yishi, 2003), 2; Wang Liben, "Taiwan junshi diwei weisheng-Sun Liren Fengshan zhengjun yu guningtou zhanshe" [Taiwan's Military Recovery: Sun Li-jen's Training Center at Fengshan and the Guningtou Battle], *Zhonghua junshi xuehui* 14 (September 2009): 369.
36. Zheng Jieguang, "Zhonghua minguo zhi zhengshi, fei zhengshi junshi jiaoyu-yi sun liren zhuchi zhi zhengshi junshi jiaoyu wei zhuzhou," *Zhonghua junshi xuehui huikan* (October 2006): 97.
37. Guojun shiliao yeshu, *Lujun junguan xuexiao di su junguan xunlianban guansheng fangwen jilu*, 6.
38. Ibid., 34.

39. Wang, "Taiwan junshi diwei weisheng-Sun Liren Fengshan zhengjun yu guningtou zhanshe," 371–72.
40. Chu Hongyuan, "Taiwan xinjun de yaolan: Fengshan di su junguan xunlian ban" [Taiwan's new army cradle: Fengshan's fourth class of training], *Zhongyang yanjiu yuan zhongshan renwen shehui kexue yanjiu suo zhuanshu* 31 (November 1993): 443–47, 454.
41. Meng Guanghan, *Minguo shiqi de lujun da xue* [Republican Period Military Academy] (Jiangsu: Di er lishi dong an guan, 1994), 16–21.
42. Wikisource, "Lujun daxuexiao zhuzhifa [Military Academy Organization Act]," https://zh.wikisource.org/zh/%E9%99%B8%E8%BB%8D%E5%A4%A7%E5%AD%B8%E6%A0%A1%E7%B5%84%E7%B9%94%E6%B3%95_(%E6%B0%91%E5%9C%8B34%E5%B9%B4).
43. Xu Peigen, *Xiandai Junshi* 1 (1945): 2.
44. Zhou Quji, "Meiguo lujun dimian budui zhi zuzhi yu xunlian" [U.S. Army Ground Forces Organization and Training], *Xiandai Junshi* 4 (1947): 44.
45. Bai Chongxi, "Xiandai lujun junshi jiaoyu zhi qushi," *Xiandai Junshi* 5 (1945), 4.
46. Ibid., 5.
47. Gan Yi, "Yi jiu su san nian zhi meiguo canmou daxue," *Xiandai Junshi* 4 (1945): 96.
48. Luo Hongyan, "Xi dian junxiao canguanji" [West Point Military Academy], *Xiandai Junshi* 6 (1945): 88–89.
49. Jia Yibin, "Lun Yubei ganbu zhidu" [The Reserve Cadre System], *Xiandai Junshi* 5 (1947): 23.
50. *Xiandai Junshi* 9 (1946): 41–43.
51. Bai Chongxi, "Xiandai lujun junshi jiaoyu zhi qushi," *Xiandai Junshi* 5 (1945): 3.
52. Fan Chengyuan, "Lun Xiandai junshi jiaoyu yingyou zhi gaijin" [Modern Military Education Assessment and Reforms], *Xiandai Junshi* 7 (1947): 10.
53. Yang De, "Lun Yangjie de guofang sixiang" [A Discussion of Yang Jie's Military Thought], *Junshi lishi yanjiu* (2012): 43.
54. Yang Jie, "Jianshe xiandai guofang yingyou de renshi" [An Assessment of National Defense], *Xiandai Junshi* 6 (1947): 1–2.
55. Xu Peigen, *Xiandai Junshi* 9 (1946): 11.
56. *Xiandai Junshi* 7 (1947).
57. Daheng B. Pike, "Huachengdun neng fangyu yuanzibaodan zhi gongjihu" [A Hypothetical Atomic Strike on Washington], *Xiandai Junshi* 11 (1947): 27.
58. Zhou Quji, "Yuanzidan shuizhong baofa chengli zhi shiyan" [The Successful Atomic Test at Sea], *Xiandai Junshi* 7 (1947): 30–37; Liu Fuling, "Bijini dao yuanzi dan, shiyan de wenda" [Bikini Island Atomic Test], *Xiandai Junshi* 7 (1947): 28–29.
59. Li Tianduan, "Feidan jiqi fangheng" [Aerial Bombing and Defense], *Xiandai Junshi* 1 (1948): 48.
60. Zheng Naihou, "Ruhe baozhang woguo anquan" [How to Protect our National Security], *Xiandai Junshi* 2 (1948): 13.
61. Lu Fengge, "Zhanshi" [Historical Warfare], *Xiandai Junshi* 10–12 (1946): 9–25.

62. Ibid.
63. You Fengchi, "Ruhe shishi guofang junshi jianshe" [How to Test National Military Development], *Xiandai Junshi* 5 (1945): 7–9.
64. Xu Peigen, "Mingri zhi zhanzheng" [Tomorrow's War], *Xiandai Junshi* 1 (1948): 11.
65. Fu Chaojie, "Benxiao di ershiyi qi sanshi wu niandu yanxi" [Military Academy Twenty First Class, Five-Year Anniversary Ceremony], *Xiandai Junshi* 1 (1947): 36.
66. Ye Du, "Ruhe jiaojian gongfei" [How to Stop Communist Bandits], *Xiandai Junshi* 7 (1948): 30.
67. Ibid., 33.
68. Ibid., 34.
69. "Yuanzi neng shida" [The Atomic Age], *Lujun junguan xuexiao Xianduxun chu er shi yi qi jianshi* (September–October 1947): 22–26.
70. "Zenyang zuo yi ge xiandai junren he shijie junren" [How to be a Modern and Global Military Officer], *Lujun junguan xuexiao Xianduxun chu er shi yi qi jianshi* (September–October 1947): 14–16.
71. Captain Ray Huang, "Letter from Nanking," *Military Review* 28, no. 9 (December 1948): 24–30.
72. See for example works produced by Chinese officers at U.S. schools from 1945 to 1949: Wu Shih-weh, "History, Organization and Operation of the Armored School and Chinese Military Academy," Military Monograph, Advanced Officers Class #1, The Armored School (Fort Knox, Ky., 25 February 1947); C. S. Chang, "Logistical Service of Chinese Army in the Last War," Monograph of Analytical Study (Fort Leavenworth, Kans.: Command and General Staff College, 1947); Peng Chen-Kai, "Proposals for Improvement of the Chinese Army Supply System" (Fort Leavenworth, Kans.: Command and General Staff College, 24 May 1949); Y. K. Yang, "The Supply Service of the Chinese Army" (Fort Leavenworth, Kans.: Command and General Staff College, 1 November 1948).
73. Huang Chan-Kuei, "The Logistical Organization of the Chinese Army," Analytical Study (Fort Leavenworth, Kans.: Command and General Staff College, 12 November 1947), 9.
74. Ibid., 12.
75. "Meiguo de zhanfei bijiao-genju meiguo fangmian de tongji" [American War Costs, a Statistical Comparison], *Zhongguo junren zhoukan*, 2 February 1946.
76. Ji Cheng "Cong zhanzheng bianzhi shuadao guofang jianshe" [An Assessment of National Defense from Compiled Wartime Data], *Zhongguo junren zhoukan*, 2 March 1947.
77. "Weilai zhanzheng de yuce" [Predicting Future Warfare], *Zhongguo junren zhoukan*, 9 March 1947.
78. Shaokun, *Guo junzheng zhan shi*, 147–48; Goufangbu zong zhengzhi bu, *Guojun zhenggong shigao*, 845.

79. "Jundui dangbu de shiming" [The Mission of the Military Political Department], *Jundang yu zhenghu*, no. 1.
80. "Gaijin zhengxun gongzuo de jiben yaowu" [Reforming Political Administration], *Jundang yu zhenghu*, no. 5, Tebie dang bu, Zhengzhi xunlian chu.
81. Junshi weiyuan hui, *Gaojin ge junshi xuexiao zhengxun gongzuo jihua* [Reforming Political Work in Military Schools] (Chongqing: Zhengzhi bu, 1943).
82. Heinlein, "Political Warfare: The Chinese Nationalist Model," 432.
83. Ministry of Information, *The China Handbook, 1937–1945* (New York: Macmillan, 1947), 52.
84. Wang, "Wuzhu wencong beijing xia de duozhong bianzou: zhanshi guomindang jundui de zhenggong yu dangwu," *Kangri zhanzheng yanjiu* 4 (2007): 2.
85. Liu, *A Military History of Modern China*, 235.
86. Ibid., 238.
87. Marshall, *The Papers of George Catlett Marshall*, Document #5–341.
88. *Shenbao*, 17 January 1946; Zhang Shiying, "Kang zhan shengli hou guomin zhengfu jundui guojiahua de nuli" [Army Nationalization by the National Government after World War II], *Zhonghua junshi xuehui huikan* 1, no. 5 (December 1999), 199.
89. *Shenbao*, 12 January 1946; *United States Relations with China* (Washington, D.C.: Department of State, 1949), 138.
90. Ministry of Information, *The China Handbook, 1937–1945*, 745.
91. Ibid.
92. Memorandum prepared by the Plans Staff of Lieutenant General Albert C. Wedemeyer, 13 January 1946, *FRUS, 1946*, vol. 9, *China*, 181.
93. Lieutenant General Albert C. Wedemeyer to General Marshall, 5 February 1946, *FRUS, 1946*, vol. 9, *China*, 207–9.
94. Ibid.
95. Zhou Enlai, *Zhou Enlai junshi wenxuan* [Zhou Enlai Military Thought] (Beijing: Renmin chuban she, 1997), 52.
96. Minutes of Meeting between General Marshall and General Chang Chi-chung, 25 January 1946, *FRUS, 1946*, vol. 9, *China*, 200.
97. Meng Guanghan, *Zhengzhi xieshang huiyi jishi* [Political Consultative Conference History] (Chongqing: Chongqing chuban she, 1989), 1002.
98. Minutes of Meeting of the Military Sub-Committee of the Three, 18 February 1946, *FRUS, 1946*, vol. 9, *China*, 249.
99. Minutes of Meeting between General Marshall and General Zhou Enlai, 15 February 1946, *FRUS, 1946*, vol. 9, *China*, 223–24.
100. George Catlett Marshall, Minutes of Military Subcommittee, 18 February 1946, *Marshall's Mission to China, December 1945–January 1947*, vol. 2 (College Park, Md.: University Publications of America, 1976), document 5d.

101. Guo Rugui, *Guo rugui huiyi lu* (Beijing: gongchandang shi chuban she, 2009), 131; Minutes of Meeting of the Military Subcommittee of the Three, 16 February 1946, *FRUS, 1946*, vol. 9, *China*, 244.
102. Minutes of Meeting of the Military Subcommittee of the Three, 21 February 1946, *FRUS, 1946*, vol. 9, *China*, 268.
103. Meng, *Zhengzhi xieshang huiyi jishi*, 981.
104. Ministry of Information, *The China Handbook, 1937–1945*, 755; Chin Hsiao-yi, ed., *Zhonghua minguo zhongyao shiliao chubian: dui ri kangzhan shiqi* [Compilation of Important Historical Material: Period of Anti-Japanese War] (Taipei: Zhong yang wen wu gong ying she, 1981), 78.
105. *Shenbao*, 26 February 1946, 1; Ministry of Information, *The China Handbook, 1937–1945*, 755.
106. Chin, *Zhonghua minguo zhongyao shiliao chubian*, 74.
107. *United States Relations with China* (Washington, D.C.: Department of State, 1949), 141.
108. Ministry of Information, *The China Handbook, 1937–1945*, 755.
109. Ibid., 757.
110. *United States Relations with China*, 142–43.
111. Zhang, "Kang zhan shengli hou guomin zhengfu jundui guojiahua de nuli," 197.
112. *Guofang yue kan* 1, no. 3 (November 1946): 1.
113. Chiang Kai-shek, *Xian zongtong Jiang Gong quanji*, vol. 2, edited by Zhang Qiyu (Taipei: Zhongguo wenhua daxue chuban she, 1984), 1805–13, 2184–87.
114. Zhou, *Zhou Enlai junshi wenxuan*, 67.
115. Liu, *A Military History of Modern China*, 235.
116. *Shenbao*, 3 June 1946; Chien, *The Government and Politics of China*, 189; Chief of Military History, *Civil War in China* (Taipei: Department of the [U.S.] Army, n.d.), 8.
117. "Minzhu jundui junren" [Soldiers in the People's Military], *Zhongguo junren zhoukan*, 23 February 1947.
118. "Dangqian junshi jiaoyu" [Contemporary Military Education], *Zhongguo junren zhoukan*, 9 March 1947.
119. Charles Barber, "China's Political Officer System," *Military Review* 33, no. 4 (July 1953): 11; Zhong, "Kangzhan shiqi guomindang jundui zhengzhi gongzuo shulun," 53; Shaokun, *Guo junzheng zhan shi*, 160.
120. Goufangbu zong zhengzhi bu, *Guojun zhenggong shigao*, 1053.
121. Ibid., 1045.
122. Tan Jiquan, *Jundui zhengzhi gongzuo de lilun yu shishi* (Nanjing: Xin zhongguo chubanshe, 1948), 1–2.
123. Shaokun, *Guo junzheng zhan shi*, 173–76.

Chapter 5. Refining the Army Profession, 1950–1953

1. Wu Zhenzheng, *Qun ying yi wang: Lujun xiao di su junguan xunlian ban ruwusheng zongdui koushu lishi* [Qunying's Recollections: Army Officers of the Fourth Training Class Oral Histories] (Taipei: Guofangbu shizheng bianyishi. 2011), 83–84.
2. *Lujun junguan xuexiao xiaoshi* [Military Academy School History] (n.p., 1969), 2:59.
3. Yuan and Huang. *Huangpu Jianjun*, 123–24.
4. *Lujun junguan xuexiao xiaoshi* (n.p., 1969), 2:31–34.
5. Jay Taylor, *The Generalissimo's Son, Chiang Ching-kuo and the Revolutions in China and Taiwan* (Cambridge, Mass.: Harvard University Press, 2000), 195.
6. Ibid., 454.
7. *Junshi zazhi* 3, no. 6–4, no. 1 (Taipei: Junshi zazhi chuban she, 1953–1955).
8. Sun Chengcheng, *Yuanzi shidai yu yuanzi zhanzheng* [The Atomic Age and Atomic Warfare] (Taipei: Fangong chuban she, 1950).
9. Bo Yin, "Meijun zuozhan zhihui yuanze yu canmou yewu" [The American Military Command and Staff System] *Binglu Zazhi* 26 (September, 1953): 11–16.
10. "Meiguo lujun yubei junguan zhidu" [The American Reserve Officer System] *Binglu Zazhi* 27 (October 1953): 113–16.
11. She Fang, "Yuxiang yuanzi zhanzheng de budui zuzhi he lianyong" [Atomic Warfare Organization and Use], *Binglu zazhi* 27 (October 1953): 24–30.
12. Wang Junzhao, "Di erci shijie dazhan dejun zuozhan zhidao zhi tese" [Characteristics of the German Military in the Second World War], *Binglu zazhi* 26 (September 1953): 31–32.
13. *Guofang yekan* 8–14 (Taipei: Guofang yefang she, 1950–52).
14. The China Handbook Editorial Board, *China Handbook, 1952–1953* (Taipei: China Publishing Company, 1952), 186–87.
15. Ibid.
16. "Meiyuan shoupai pen sheji" [America Dispatches Missiles], *Lianhe Baodao*, 16 March 1953, 1.
17. "Zhu mao fei bangru qinfei Taiwan" [Mao Bandit Gang Attacks Taiwan], *Lianhe Baodao*, 5 March 1952, 1.
18. Gong Jianguo, "Zhonghua minguo zhengfu qiantai hou lujun zhengbian guocheng yu chengxiao chushen (1950–1961)" [The Army Reorganization Process after the Move to Taiwan], *Zhonghua junshi xuehui huikan* (September 2007): 240–41.
19. Ibid., 247.
20. Sun Jianzhong, *Guojun zhuangjia bin fazhan shi* [A History of the ROC Armored Forces] (Taipei: Guofang bus hi zhengbian yishi, 2005), 525–76.
21. Ibid., 323.
22. Zheng, *Yi dai zhanshen: Sun Liren*, 292–94.
23. Liu Hongxiang, "Zhenggong zhengbu xuexiao zhi yanjiu (1950–1970)" [Political Work Department School Research] (PhD diss., Guoli zhongyang daxue, 2006), 145–47.

24. Chu Hongyuan, *Sun Liren yanlun xuanji*, 53.
25. Ibid., 44.
26. Ibid., 22.
27. Ibid., 50.
28. Ibid., 10.
29. Ibid., 21.
30. Ibid.
31. Chen, Hung-hsien, *1950 niandai chuqi guojun junshi fangong zhi yan jiu* (Taipei: Guoshiguan, 2015), 88.
32. Joseph Ballantine, *Formosa: A Problem of United States Foreign Policy* (Washington, D.C.: The Brookings Institution, 1952), 118–19.
33. Robert Accinelli, *Crisis and Commitment: United States policy toward Taiwan, 1950–1955* (Chapel Hill: University of North Carolina Press, 1996), 20.
34. Ballantine, *Formosa: A Problem of United States Foreign Policy*, 139; "Truman Bars Military Help for Defense of Formosa; British End Nationalist Tie," *New York Times*, 6 January 1950, 1.
35. Lin Hsiao-ting, "Taiwan's Secret Ally," *Hoover Digest* 2 (2012).
36. William Chase, *Front Line General: The Commands of William C. Chase* (Houston: Pacesetter Press, 1975), 168; Lin, "Taiwan's Secret Ally."
37. Ballantine, *Formosa: A Problem of United States Foreign Policy*, 127.
38. "Ordered to Formosa, U.S. Names 2 Aides to Chiang Regime," *New York Times*, 29 July 1950, 5.
39. Ballantine, *Formosa: A Problem of United States Foreign Policy*, 129.
40. Ibid., 141.
41. Memorandum by Mr. Richard E. Johnson of the Office of Chinese Affairs to the Director of the Office of Chinese Affairs, 8 December 1950, *FRUS, 1950*, vol. 6, *China*, 593.
42. Ibid.
43. Ibid., 591, 596.
44. Karl Rankin, *China Assignment* (Seattle: University of Washington Press, 1964), 81; Memorandum for Record, Mr. Merchant, Subject: Military Advisory Personnel for Formosa, 19 January 1951, *U.S. State Department Confidential Files, Formosa–Republic of China, 1950–1954*, Reel 5 (Frederick, Md.: University Publications of America, 1986).
45. Ballantine, *Formosa: A Problem of United States Foreign Policy*, 142.
46. The Under Secretary of State (Webb) to the Director of the Bureau of the Budget (Lawton), 17 April 1951, *FRUS, 1951*, vol. 7, *China*, 1631–37.
47. Ibid., 1634.
48. Ibid., 1634–35.
49. Memorandum by the Director of International Security Affairs (Cabot) to the Assistant to the Secretary of Defense for International Security Affairs (Burns), 31 March 1951, *FRUS, 1951*, vol. 7, *China*, 1614–15.

50. The Secretary of State to the Embassy in the Republic of China, 25 April 1951, *FRUS, 1951*, vol. 7, *China*, 1648–51.
51. Henry R. Lieberman, "U.S. Advisory Work in Formosa Drags: Delayed Arrival of Training Equipment Retards Task of Military Aid Mission," *New York Times*, 11 November 1951.
52. Chase, *Front Line General*, 2–3.
53. Ibid., 21–23.
54. Ibid., 164–67.
55. Ibid., 170.
56. Ibid.
57. Report Submitted by the Senior Defense Member of the NSC Staff (Nash) to the Sterling Committee on NSC 128, 13 June 1952, *FRUS, 1952–1954*, vol. 14, *China and Japan*, 67.
58. "Chase Says Nationalists in 'Last Half of Ninth,'" *Pacific Stars and Stripes*, 29 August 1951, 4.
59. Headquarters, Military Assistance Advisory Group Formosa, Activity Report for November, 1953, Reel 6, *U.S. State Department Confidential Files, Formosa–Republic of China, 1950–1954* (Frederick, Md.: University Publications of America, 1986).
60. Ibid., 3.
61. "Chase Says Nationalists in 'Last Half of Ninth,'" *Pacific Stars and Stripes*, 29 August 1951, 4.
62. "Appraisal of Formosa: Chiang's Island Has Big Potential Power But It Must be Developed and Directed," *New York Times*, 2 April 1951, 4; Chase, *Front Line General*, 171.
63. Chase, *Front Line General*, 170.
64. From FE, Merchant, to Department of State, Subject: Progress in MDAP in Formosa, Reel 5, 17 September 1951, *U.S. State Department Confidential Files, Formosa–Republic of China, 1950–1954* (Frederick, Md.: University Publications of America, 1986).
65. Chase, *Front Line General*, 196.
66. Memorandum of Conversation by Leonard H. Price of the Office of the Special Assistant for Mutual Security Affairs, 20 February 1952, *FRUS, 1952–1954*, vol. 14, *China and Japan*, 10.
67. Selected Executive Session Hearings of the Committee 1951–56, Mutual Security Program, Part 2, U.S. House of Representatives (Washington, D.C.: GPO, 1980), 574.
68. Ministry of National Defense, *MAAG's Decade in the Republic of China* (Taipei: Ministry of National Defense, 1961), 18; Headquarters, Military Assistance Advisory Group, Taiwan, Subject: Revision-Country Statement on MAP, Non-NATO Countries, 10 August 1957, 8.
69. "An Army Man of Note: Mr. Music Maker," *Stars and Stripes Pacific Edition*, 7 April 1956, 24.
70. William Chou, "MAAG—Saga of Service," *Taiwan Review*, 6 June 1966, 2.

71. Charles Barber, "Military Assistance Advisory Group Formosa," *Military Review* 34, no. 9 (December 1954): 54.
72. Telegram: From: Taipei (Rankin) To: Secretary of State, 15 June 1951, Reel 5, *U.S. State Department Confidential Files, Formosa–Republic of China, 1950–1954* (Frederick, Md.: University Publications of America, 1986).
73. Records of the Joint U.S. Military Advisory Group to the Republic of China, RG 334, Box 1, NARA.
74. Headquarters: Military Assistance Advisory Group, Formosa, Subject: Country Statement on MDAP, Non-NATO Countries, 18 January 1955, 2.
75. Hearings before the Committee on Appropriations, United States Senate, 83rd Cong., 16 July 1953, Washington, D.C.
76. "Nationalist China's Army," *Star and Stripes, Pacific Edition*, 9 March 1955, 9.
77. "Free China's Gunners," *Stars and Stripes Pacific Edition*, 23 April 1953, 8.
78. Guoshiguan, Wai Jiaobu Files, Military Assistance Advisory Group, Formosa, 19 June 1952, "Invitation to Travel;" Guoshiguan, "Junren bu Mei yanxi kaocha," Waijiao Bu, 11 July 1952; *The China Post*, "Gen. Chou Leads Military Mission to US at Invitation of General Taylor," 15 April 1958.
79. Barber, "Military Assistance Advisory Group Formosa," 54.
80. Ministry of Information, *The China Handbook, 1937–1945*, 287.
81. "Chiang Calls Men Born on Formosa," *New York Times*, 17 February 1955, 1.
82. Jennifer Liu, "Indoctrinating the Youth: Guomindang Policy on Secondary Education in Wartime China and Postwar Taiwan, 1937–1960" (PhD diss., University of California, Irvine, 2010), 177.
83. Far East-Drumright to Chinese Affairs, W. P. McConaughy, Subject: An Evaluation of the Military Situation in Formosa, 8 December 1955, Top Secret, Reel 6, 4, *U.S. State Department Confidential Files, Formosa–Republic of China, 1950–1954* (Frederick, Md.: University Publications of America, 1986).
84. Liu, "Indoctrinating the Youth," 177.
85. "MAAG Activity Report for Month of September 1954," 24 November 1954, Records of the Office of Chinese Affairs, 1945–1955, RG 59, Reel 37, NARA.
86. "Message: CHMAAG Formosa 190614Z," November 1954, Records of the Office of Chinese Affairs, 1945–1955, RG 59, Reel 37, NARA; Memorandum by the Director of the Office of Chinese Affairs (McConaughy) to the Assistant Secretary of State for Far Eastern Affairs (Robertson), Secret, 13 December 1954, *FRUS, 1952–1954*, vol. 14, *China and Japan*, 1025; Rankin, *China Assignment*, 275–76.
87. Far East-Drumright to Chinese Affairs, W. P. McConaughy, Subject: An Evaluation of the Military Situation in Formosa, 8 December 1955, Top Secret, Reel 6, 8, *U.S. State Department Confidential Files, Formosa–Republic of China, 1950–1954* (Frederick, Md.: University Publications of America, 1986); Chase, *Front Line General*, 165.
88. Frank Holober, *Raiders of the China Coast: CIA Covert Operations During the Korean War* (Annapolis, Md.: Naval Institute Press, 1999).

89. "Ike to Let Chiang Attack Red China: 7th Fleet Reported Set to Lift Barriers to Raids on Mainland," *Los Angeles Times*, 31 January 1953, 1.
90. The Chief of the Military Assistance Advisory Group, Formosa (Chase) to the Chief of General Staff, Republic of China (Chow), 5 February 1953, *FRUS, 1952–1954*, vol. 14, *China and Japan*, 144–45.
91. The Charge in the Republic of China (Rankin) to the Department of State, Secret, 23 March 1953, *FRUS, 1952–1954*, vol. 14, *China and Japan*, 160.
92. "A Report to the National Security Council by the NSC Planning Board on United States Objectives and Courses of Action with Respect to Formosa and the National Government of China," 27 March 1953, *Digital National Security Archive* (Proquest), 3.
93. The Charge in the Republic of China (Rankin) to the Department of State, 23 March 1953, *FRUS, 1952–1954*, vol. 14, *China and Japan*, 161.
94. Ibid.
95. Rankin, *China Assignment*, 290–91; Chase, *Front Line General*, 184.
96. Embassy-Taipei to Department of State, Subject: Report on the Mutual Security Program in Formosa, 21 July 1954, Secret, Reel 6, 6, *U.S. State Department Confidential Files, Formosa–Republic of China, 1950–1954* (Frederick, Md.: University Publications of America, 1986).
97. The Ambassador in the Republic of China (Rankin) to the Department of State, 8 March 1954, *FRUS, 1952–1954*, vol. 14, *China and Japan*, 383.
98. "Briefing Data on Chinese National Armed Forces," 30 September 1954, Records of the Office of Chinese Affairs, 1945–1955, Microfilm Reel 36, NARA; The Ambassador in the Republic of China (Rankin) to the Department of State, 8 March 1954, *FRUS, 1952–1954*, vol. 14, *China and Japan*, 385.
99. The Ambassador in the Republic of China (Rankin) to the Department of State, 8 March 1954, *FRUS, 1952–1954*, vol. 14, *China and Japan*, 385.
100. Rankin, *China Assignment*, 271; The Ambassador in the Republic of China (Rankin) to the Department of State, 8 March 1954, *FRUS, 1952–1954*, vol. 14, *China and Japan*, 385.

Chapter 6. Restoring the Party to Dominance, 1953-1955

1. Chen, *1950 niandai chuqi guojun junshi fangong zhi yan jiu*, 88.
2. Heinlein, "Political Warfare: The Chinese Nationalist Model," 558.
3. Jiang Zhongzhang, *Ruhe gaizao women geming de fangfa* [How to Reform our Revolutionary Methods] (Taipei: Zhongyang gaizao weiyuan hui wugong yingshe, 1951); Bruce Dickson, "The Lessons of Defeat: The Reorganization of the Kuomintang on Taiwan, 1950–1952," *China Quarterly* 133 (March 1993): 65–67.
4. Bullard, *The Soldier and the Citizen*, 82.
5. Dickson, "The Lessons of Defeat," 68.

6. The Charge in the Republic of China (Jones) to the Department of State, 19 September 1952, *FRUS, 1952–1954*, vol. 14, *China*, 108.
7. Heinlein, "Political Warfare: The Chinese Nationalist Model," 510–11.
8. Ramon Myers and Hsiao-ting Lin, *Breaking with the Past: The Kuomintang Central Reform Committee on Taiwan, 1950–1952* (Stanford, Calif.: Hoover Institution Press, 2007), 10.
9. Goufangbu zong zhengzhi bu, *Guojun zhenggong shigao*, 1415.
10. Bullard, *The Soldier and the Citizen*, 80–81.
11. Gongzuo Gangling, "Minguo sanjiu nian zhenggong gaizhi de jiben fagui-guojun zhengzhi," cited in Shaokun, *Guo junzheng zhan shi*, 238.
12. Ibid.
13. Heinlein, "Political Warfare: The Chinese Nationalist Model," 579.
14. Ibid., 580.
15. Bullard, *The Soldier and the Citizen*, 121.
16. General Political Department, Ministry of National Defense, *Briefing on the Political Establishment in the Chinese Armed Forces* (Taipei, 1959), 60.
17. Michael Szonyi, *Cold War Island: Quemoy on the Front Line* (Cambridge, UK: Cambridge University Press, 2008), 151–58; Heinlein, "Political Warfare: The Chinese Nationalist Model," 584.
18. Gongzuo Gangling, "Minguo sanjiu nian zhenggong gaizhi de jiben fagui-guojun zhengzhi," cited in Shaokun, *Guo junzheng zhan shi*, 235.
19. Ibid., 237.
20. General Political Department, *Briefing on the Political Establishment in the Chinese Armed Forces*, 28.
21. Heinlein, "Political Warfare: The Chinese Nationalist Model," 590.
22. Goufangbu zong zhengzhi bu, *Guojun zhenggong shigao*, 1853–62.
23. Bullard, *The Soldier and the Citizen*, 97.
24. Heinlein, "Political Warfare: The Chinese Nationalist Model," 599–601.
25. Ibid., 611.
26. Ibid.
27. George Reid, "The Political Commissar in the Red Army," *Military Review* 28, no. 1 (April 1948): 20.
28. Cheng, *Party-Military Relations*, 83.
29. Zhengzhi zuozhan xuexiao xiaoshi weiyuanhui, *Zhengzhi zuozhan xuexiao xiaoshi* [History of the Political Warfare Military School] (Taipei: Zhenzhi zuozhan xuexiao, 1980), 7.
30. Jiang Nan, *Jiang Jingguo zhuan* [Chiang Kai-shek Biography] (Taipei: Qianwei chubanshe, 1997), 268–69.
31. Zhengzhi zuozhan xuexiao xiaoshi weiyuanhui, *Zhengzhi zuozhan xuexiao xiaoshi* [History of the Political Warfare Military School], 9–10.

32. Thomas Marks, *Counterrevolution in China: Wang Sheng and the Kuomintang* (London: Frank Cass Publishers, 1998), 152–56.
33. General Political Department, *Briefing on the Political Establishment in the Chinese Armed Forces*, 112; Marks, *Counterrevolution in China*, 153–55; Bullard, *The Soldier and the Citizen*, 101.
34. General Political Department, *Briefing on the Political Establishment in the Chinese Armed Forces*, 112.
35. Zhengzhi zuozhan xuexiao xiaoshi weiyuanhui, *Zhengzhi zuozhan xuexiao xiaoshi* [History of the Political Warfare Military School], 14, 257–78, 316–26.
36. Ibid., 261.
37. Ibid.; Marks, *Counterrevolution in China*, 176–77.
38. Liu, "Indoctrinating the Youth," 112–68.
39. Ibid., 185.
40. Jiang Jingguo, *Jiang Jingguo xiansheng fuxinggang jiang ciji* [Chiang Ching-kuo Speeches at Fuxinggang], vol. 2 (Taipei: Zhonggong ganbu xuexiao chubanshe, 1963), 123.
41. Zhengzhi zuozhan xuexiao xiaoshi weiyuanhui, *Zhengzhi zuozhan xuexiao xiaoshi* [History of the Political Warfare Military School], 34.
42. Jiang Jingguo, *Jiang Jingguo xiansheng quanji* [Collected Works of Chiang Ching-kuo], edited by Li Denghui (Taipei: Xin zheng yuan xinwen ju, 1992), 544.
43. Bullard, *The Soldier and the Citizen*, 101.
44. Chen Hung-hsien, "1950 niandai chuqi guojun zhenggong zhidu de chongjian" [1950s Era Political Work System], *Guoshiguan guankan* 42 (December 2014): 5.
45. Jiang Jingguo, *Jiang Jingguo xiansheng fuxinggang jiang ciji* [Chiang Ching-kuo Speeches at Fuxinggang], vol. 1 (Taipei: Zhonggong ganbu xuexiao chubanshe, 1963), 9.
46. Jiang, *Jiang Jingguo xiansheng quanji* [Collected Works of Chiang Ching-kuo], 504.
47. Jiang Jingguo, *Jiang Jingguo xiansheng fuxinggang jiang ciji*, [Chiang Ching-kuo Speeches at Fuxinggang], vol. 3 (Taipei: Zhonggong ganbu xuexiao chubanshe, 1963), 22–23.
48. Jiang, *Jiang Jingguo xiansheng quanji* [Collected Works of Chiang Ching-kuo], 528.
49. Jiang, *Jiang Jingguo xiansheng fuxinggang jiang ciji* [Chiang Ching-kuo Speeches at Fuxinggang], 3:42–43.
50. Cai Xianghui, ed., *Jiang zhongzheng xiansheng zai tai junshi yan lunji* [Chiang Kai-shek Military Speeches on Taiwan] (Taipei, Guomindang hui chubanshe, 1994), 188.
51. Jiang, *Jiang Jingguo xiansheng quanji* [Collected Works of Chiang Ching-kuo], 89.
52. Jiang, *Jiang Jingguo xiansheng quanji* [Collected Works of Chiang Ching-kuo], 1:505.
53. Wang Xun, *Ziyou zhongguo san jun* [Three Armies of Free China] (Hong Kong: Shidai chuban she, 1957), i–iii.
54. Taylor, *The Generalissimo's Son*, 215.
55. Shen, *Sun Liren zhuan*, 714.
56. Ibid.
57. Ibid., 215.

58. "President Chiang's Views on the Political Officer System in Armed Forces," 29 April 1954, Records of the Office of Chinese Affairs, 1945–1955, Microfilm Reel 36, NARA.
59. Goufangbu zong zhengzhi bu, *Guojun zhenggong shigao*, 1499.
60. The Charge in the Republic of China (Rankin) to the Department of State, 6 July 1951, *FRUS, 1951*, vol. 7, *China*, 1730–32.
61. Ibid.
62. Chase, *Front Line General*, 180.
63. The Charge in the Republic of China (Rankin) to the Department of State, 6 July 1951, *FRUS, 1951*, vol. 7, *China*, 1730–32.
64. Subject: Activities of the Political Department, Major General William C. Chase, Headquarters Military Assistance Advisory Group, December 28, 1953, RG 334, NARA.
65. Memorandum by the Officer in Charge of Chinese Economic Affairs (Barnett) to the Assistant Secretary of State for Far Eastern Affairs (Rusk), 3 October 1951, *FRUS, 1951*, vol. 7, *China*, 1816–27.
66. "Morale Within Chinese Armed Forces," 30 December 1953, Records of the Office of Chinese Affairs, 1945–1955, RG 59, Reel 36, NARA.
67. Memorandum by the Officer in Charge of Chinese Economic Affairs (Barnett) to the Assistant Secretary of State for Far Eastern Affairs (Rusk), 3 October 1951, *FRUS, 1951*, vol. 7, *China*, 1820.
68. The Charge in the Republic of China (Rankin) to the Department of State, 11 December 1951, *FRUS, 1951*, vol. 7, *China*, 1865.
69. Ibid., 1866.
70. Memorandum by the Chief of the Navy Section of the Military Assistance Advisory Group, Formosa (Beyerly) to the Chief of the Military Assistance Advisory Group, Formosa (Chase), 9 November 1951, *FRUS, 1951*, vol. 7, *China*, 1868.
71. The Assistant Secretary of Defense for International Security Affairs (Nash) to the Deputy Assistant Secretary of State for Far Eastern Affairs (Drumright), 23 February 1954, *FRUS, 1952–1954*, vol. 14, *China and Japan*, 365.
72. Ibid.
73. Goufangbu zong zhengzhi bu, *Guojun zhenggong shigao*, 1500.
74. Message: Karl Rankin to Walter McConaughy, 2 February 1954, Records of the Office of Chinese Affairs, 1945–1955, RG 59, Reel 36, NARA.
75. National Intelligence Estimate, NIE-43-54, 14 September 1954, *FRUS, 1952–1954*, vol. 14, *China*, 628.
76. Memorandum for Record: From Advisor to General Political Department, NGRC to K. Rankin (Ambassador), Subject: MAAG Personnel for General Political Department, 1 August 1953, *U.S. State Department Confidential Files, Formosa–Republic of China, 1950–1954*, Reel 4, 6 (Frederick, Md.: University Publications of America, 1986).
77. Chase, *Front Line General*, 181.

78. Supporting MAAG Formosa Request for Officers to be Attached to Political Department and Peace Preservation Corps, 18 February 1954, Records of the Office of Chinese Affairs, 1945–1955, RG 59, Reel 36, NARA.
79. Political Department, Ministry of National Defense, *Briefing on Political Establishment in the Chinese Armed Forces* (Taipei, 1959); Memorandum by the Director of the Office of Chinese Affairs (McConaughy) to the Assistant Secretary of State for Far Eastern Affairs (Robertson), 13 December 1954, *FRUS, 1952–1954*, vol. 14, *China*, 1026.
80. "Sunliren ren zongtong fucan junzhang," *Zhongyang Ribao*, 25 June 1954, 1.
81. Comments on Some Recent Presidential Appointments in the NGRC Armed Forces, 16 September 1954, Records of the Office of Chinese Affairs, 1945–1955, Microfilm Reel 36, NARA.
82. *Current Intelligence Bulletin*, 21 October 1955, Central Intelligence Agency, Freedom of Information Act Reading Room.
83. Ibid.
84. "Sun Liren Incident," *Encyclopedia of Taiwan*, http://taiwanpedia.culture.tw/en/content?ID=3868.
85. Shen, *Sun Liren zhuan*, 961.
86. "Lingdao wencui" [Leadership Collections], *Nan Shifang*, July 2011, 75.
87. *Current Intelligence Bulletin*, 21 October 1955, Central Intelligence Agency, FOIA.
88. Ibid.
89. "Taipei Holds General, Ex-Governor Testifies," *Washington Post*, 15 February 1958.
90. Chen Cungong, *Sun Liren an xiangguan renwu fangwen jilu* [Recollections of the Sun Li-Jen Incident] (Taipei, Zhongyang yanjiu suo koushu lishi congshu, 2007).
91. Article 6, Mutual Defense Treaty between the United States of America and the Republic of China, http://avalon.law.yale.edu/20th_century/phil001.asp.
92. Monte Bullard, *Strait Talk: Avoiding a Nuclear War between the U.S. and China over Taiwan*, appendix 16 (Monterey, Calif.: Monterey Institute of International Studies, 2004), 284, http://cns.miis.edu/straittalk/.
93. "Taiwan Defense Command Is Set Up by U.S. Forces," *Washington Post*, 23 October 1955, A4.
94. "Report: Gen. Chase Will Retire as Head of MAAG," *Chicago Tribune*, 19 June 1955, 9.
95. Andrew Headland, "Chiang to Honor U.S. Military Aid Group," *Stars and Stripes, Pacific Edition*, 28 April 1971, 28.

Conclusion

1. Tzeng Yi-suo, "Civil-Military Relations in Democratizing Taiwan, 1986–2007" (PhD diss., George Washington University, 2009), 55–56.
2. Ibid., 65.

3. Steve Tsang, ed., *In the Shadow of China: Political Developments in Taiwan since 1949* (Honolulu: University of Hawaii Press, 1993), 26.
4. Analysis of the Internal Security Situation in Taiwan, Operations Coordinating Board, November 23, 1956, RG 59, Box 3, NARA.
5. Ibid.
6. "Taiwan's Police Force," State Department Cable, June 15, 1962, RG 59, Gale Declassified Item No. CI01476, NARA.
7. Sheena Chestnut Greitens, *Dictators and Their Secret Police: Coercive Institutions and State Violence* (Cambridge, UK: Cambridge University Press, 2016), 203.
8. K. C. Wu, "Your Money Is Building a Police State in Taiwan," *Look Magazine*, June 29, 1954
9. Bai Xili, *Guofang junshi guanli* [National Defense Management] (Taipei: Guofang bu shizheng ju, 1959), i–ii
10. *Guofang guanli shouce* [Defense Management Handbook] (Taipei: Guofang guanli xuexiao, 1973), 1.
11. *Dang zheng jun lianhe zuozhan gangyao* [Party, Nation, Army Joint Operations Outline] (Taipei: Yangmingshan, 1956).
12. Chen Chia-sheng, "Taiwan and the Development of a Late-Modern Military" (PhD dissertation, University of Buffalo, 2009), 145.
13. Ibid., 146.
14. GRC Efforts to Gain U.S. Support for an Invasion of the Mainland, United States Joint Chiefs of Staff, October 22, 1959, RG 218, Gale Declassified, CI01367, NARA; Leonard Gordon, "United States Opposition to the Use of Force in the Taiwan Straits, 1954–1962," *Journal of American History* 72, no. 3 (Dec. 1985): 654–55; "GRC Operations Against the Mainland," Memorandum from the Director of the Bureau of Intelligence and Research (Hilsman) to Secretary of State Rusk, 29 May 1962 (*FRUS 1961–1963*, vol. 22, *Northeast Asia*, document 113.)
15. Joint State/Defense Message, Telegram from the Department of State to the Embassy in the Republic of China, 9 March 1966 (*FRUS, 1964–1968*, vol. 30, *China*, document 131.)
16. U.S. Department of Defense, Defense Security Cooperation Agency, DSCA Data and Statistics.
17. Taiwan Relations Act, H.R. 2479, 96th Congress (1979–1980), https://www.congress.gov/bill/96th-congress/house-bill/2479.
18. James Mann, *About Face: A History of America's Curious Relationship with China, from Nixon to Clinton* (New York: Vintage Books, 1998), 264.
19. Taylor Fravel, "Towards Civilian Supremacy: Civil-Military Relations in Taiwan's Democratization," *Armed Forces and Society* 29, no. 1 (Fall 2002): 59.
20. Foreign Broadcast Information Service (FBIS) Taipei, HEIPAI HSINWEN [TAIWAN WEEKLY]—1995-07-08 'Taiwanization' of Military 'Unstoppable;' Daily Report, China, FBIS-CHI-95-169 on 1995-08-31, 71.

21. David Kuehn, "Democratization and Civilian Control of the Military in Taiwan," *Democratization* 15, no. 5 (November 2008): 881.
22. Ibid., 879.
23. Bruce Jacobs, *Democratizing Taiwan* (New York: Brill, 2012), 55–58.
24. Foreign Broadcast Information Service (FBIS), Taipei Domestic Service—1983-09-20, "General Wang Sheng Appointed Ambassador to Paraguay," Daily Report, China, FBIS-CHI-83-186 on 1983-09-23, VI.
25. Tzeng, "Civil-Military Relations in Democratizing Taiwan, 1986–2007," 76–82.
26. Fravel, "Towards Civilian Supremacy," 59.
27. Jacobs, *Democratizing Taiwan*, 60.
28. Ibid., 77.
29. Lee Teng-hui, *Li zongtong denghui xiansheng bas hi yi nian yanlun xuanji* [Lee Teng-hui Collected Speeches, 1992] (Taipei: Xingzhengyuan xinwen ju, 1993), 15–16.
30. Ibid., 68.
31. York Chen, "The Modernization of Taiwan's National Security Council," *The China Brief* 10, no. 22 (November 5, 2010): 1–2.
32. Michael Thim, "Complete Collection of Taiwan's Defence Policy Documents," https://michalthim.files.wordpress.com/2015/08/2000-national-defense-report.pdf.
33. Republic of China, National Defense Law, Article 11 and Article 12.
34. Fravel, "Towards Civilian Supremacy," 69.
35. Cheng Ta-Chen, "Guofang erfa zhi pingjia" [An Evaluation of the Two National Defense Laws], *Guojia fazhan yanjiu* 2, no. 2 (June 2003): 107–33.
36. Cheng, *Party Military Relations*, 140.
37. Ibid., 141.
38. Su Jinqiang, "Guojun zhengzhi jiaoyu yu jundui guojiahua de yanjin" (PhD diss., Fuxxinggang College, 1998), 86–87.
39. Cultural and Political Affairs Division, "About the General Political Warfare Bureau," https://www.mnd.gov.tw/english/Publish.aspx?cnid=420&p=51001.
40. Sofia Wu, "President Urges Political Warfare Officers To Keep Up with Changes," Central News Agency, 6 January 2002.
41. Editorial, "Partisanship in the Military," *Taipei Times*, 1 December 2006, 8.
42. Edward Chen, "Defense Ministry to Complete Restructure in 3 Years," Central News Agency, 9 January 2000.
43. David Hsu, "Restructuring Making ROC Military Smaller but Stronger," Central News Agency, 29 November 2001; Michael Chase, "Defense Reform in Taiwan: Problems and Prospects," *Asian Survey* 45, no. 3 (May/June 2005): 369–70.
44. Sarah Mishkin, "Taiwan prepares for end of conscription," *Financial Times*, 21 November 2012.
45. Michael Chase, *Taiwan's Security Policy: External Threats and Domestic Politics* (Boulder, Colo.: Lynne Reiner Publishers, 2008), 33–37.

46. David Vernal, "Overseas Education for Taiwanese Military Officers: Policy, Practice and Effects" (Master's thesis, National Chengchi University, July 2006), 27.
47. Ibid., 29.
48. Shirley Kan, "Taiwan: Major U.S. Arms Sales Since 1990," Congressional Research Service, 29 November 2012, 2.
49. Ibid., 66–69.
50. Chu Chao-Hsiang, "Wo guo 'Junwen guanxi' fazhan de lichen yu xiankuang zhi yanjiu, yi guofang erfa dingding wei fenxi jidian" [My Country's Civil-Military Relations Development and Contemporary Situation in Relation to the Two National Defense Laws] (PhD diss., Guoli Taiwan shifan daxue, 2008), 123–25.

Bibliography

Archival Sources

Central Intelligence Agency
  Freedom of Information Act Reading Room
Dwight D. Eisenhower Presidential Library, Abilene, Kansas
  Ann Whitman Papers
  John Foster Dulles Papers
Hoover Institution Archives, Stanford, California
  Frank Dorn Papers
  Haydon L. Boatner Papers
  Joseph W. Stilwell Papers
Institute of Modern History Archives, Academia Historica Archives, Taipei, Taiwan
Kuomintang Party Archives, Taipei, Taiwan
Library of Congress, Washington, D.C.
  General Nathan F. Twining Papers
Mudd Manuscript Library, Princeton University, New Jersey
  Karl Rankin Papers
  John Foster Dulles Papers
National Archives Administration (Taiwan, Guoshiguan), Taipei, Taiwan
National Archives and Records Administration (U.S.), College Park, Maryland
  RG 59 General Records of the Department of State
  RG 218 Records of the Joint Chiefs of Staff
  RG 319 Records of Military Attaché in Nanking
  RG 334.5.3 Records of the Joint U.S. Military Advisory Group to the Republic of China (JUSMAG China)
  RG 493.5 Records of Headquarters U.S. Forces, China Theater (HQ USF CT) 1941–46
  RG 493.8 Records of the Peiping Headquarters Group 1946–47

"Eyes Alone" Correspondence of General Joseph W. Stilwell, January 1942–October 1944 (Microfilm)
Records of the U.S. State Department, Office of Chinese Affairs, 1945–55. (Microfilm)
Ronald W. Reagan Presidential Library, Simi Valley, California
David Laux Papers
Harry S. Truman Presidential Library, Independence, Missouri
U.S. Army Heritage and Education Command, Carlisle, Pennsylvania
U.S. Army Center of Military History, Washington, D.C.

Published Sources: Chinese

Bai, Chongxi. *Bai Chongxi xiansheng fangwen jilu* [Oral History of General Bai Chongxi]. Taipei: Zhongyang Yanjiu Suo, 1989.
Bai, Xili. *Guofang junshi guanli* [National Defense and Military Management]. Taipei: Guofang bu shizheng ju, 1959.
Cai, Xianghui, ed. *Jiang zhongzheng xiansheng zai tai junshi yan lunji* [Military Speeches of Chiang Kai-shek in Taiwan]. Taipei: Guomindang hui chubanshe, 1994.
Cao, Xueping. *Xuexiao xundao yu jun xun* [School Guidance and Military Training]. Taipei: Minguang, 1962.
Cao, Yang. "Lun woguo guofang er fa wenren lingjun zhi sheji" [Discussion of the Two National Defense Laws and Civilian Control of the Military]. *Fuxinggang Xuebao* 93 (2009): 201–20.
Chang, Meng-huan. *Fangong dalu de xin jun* [New Army for Counter-Attack on the Mainland]. Hong Kong: Ziyou chubanshe, 1952.
Chen, Cungong. *Sun Liren an xiangguan renwu fangwen jilu* [Recollections of the Sun Li-jen Incident]. Taipei: Zhongyang yanjiu suo koushu lishi congshu, 2007.
Chen, Dongbo. "Junshi lunli yanjiu tujing zhi tantao" [An Exploration of Military Ethics Studies]. *Fuxinggang Xuebao* 60 (June 1997): 208–20.
Chen, Du. *Guomindang gaoji jiangling zhuanlue* [Guomindang Senior Officer Biographies]. Beijing: Zhongwen chubanshe, 2005.
Chen, Hung-hsien. *Lu jun guan xue xiao di si jun guan xun lian ban guan sheng fang wen ji lu* [Army Officer School, Fourth Officer Training Detachment Official Visits]. Taipei: Guofangbu, 2003.
———. *1950 niandai chuqi guojun junshi fangong zhi yan jiu* [A Study of the National Army's Counter-Attack in the Early 1950s]. Taipei: Guoshiguan, 2015.
———. "1950 niandai chuqi guojun zhenggong zhidu de chongjian" [Reconstruction of the political system in the army in the early 1950s]. *Guoshiguan guankan* 42 (December 2014).
Chen, Jianhua, ed. *Huangpu junxiao yanjiu* [Whampoa Academy Research]. Guangzhou: Zhongshan daxue chubanshe, 2006–2007.
Chen, Shoushan. *Taiji shou wei shang jiang zongsiling: chen shoushan koushu lishi* [Chen Shoushan Oral History]. Taipei: Guoshiguan, 2002.

Chen, Yu. *Muse Huangpu: Huangpu junxiao zai dalu zuihou yiqi xie zhen* [Whampoa at Twilight: The Last Photos of Whampoa on the Mainland]. Beijing: Jiefangjun chuban she, 2013.

Cheng, Ta-Chen. "Guofang erfa zhi pingjia" [An Evaluation of the Two National Defense Laws]. Guojia fazhan *Yanjiu* 2, no. 2 (June 2003).

Chiang, Chien-jen. *Kuo-chun chengkung shih-kao* [A History of Political Work in the National Army]. Taipei: Office of Military History, 1960.

Cheng, Jung-Hsin. "Woguo guofang lingdao zhihui tizhi de zhuanxing: wenren lingjun mianxiang de fenxi" [The Transformation of ROC National Defense System: An Analysis from the Perspective of Civilian Control of the Military]. *Fuxinggang Xuebao* 100 (2010): 107–34.

Chiang, Ching-kuo. *Jiang Jingguo xiansheng fuxinggang jiang ciji* [Chiang Ching-kuo Speeches at Fuxinggang]. Vol. 2. Taipei: Zhonggong ganbu xuexiao chubanshe, 1963.

Chiang, Kai-shek. *Chiang zong tong si xiang yan lun ji* [Chiang Kai-shek Collected Thoughts]. Taipei: Zhongyang wenwu gongying she, 1966.

———. *Xian zongtong jiang gong quanji* [First President's Collected Speeches]. Vols. 1–2. Zhongguo wenhua daxue chuban bu, 1984.

Chiang, Wei-kuo. *Taiwan zhi zhanlue jiazhi yu guangfu dalu* [Taiwan's Strategic Value and Recovery of the Mainland]. Taipei: Sanjun daxue, 1974.

Chin, Hsiao-yi, ed. *Zhonghua minguo zhongyao shiliao chubian: dui ri kangzhan shiqi* [Compilation of Important Historical Material: Period of Anti-Japanese War]. Taipei: Jing xiao zhe Zhong yang wen wu gong ying she, 1981.

Chu, Chao-Hsiang. "Wo guo 'Junwen guanxi' fazhan de lichen yu xiankuang zhi yanjiu, yi guofang erfa dingding wei fenxi jidian" [My Country's Civil-Military Relations Development and Contemporary Situation in Relation to the Two National Defense Laws]. PhD diss., Guoli Taiwan shifan daxue [National Taiwan Normal University], 2008.

Chu, Hongyuan. "Taiwan xinjun de yaolan: Fengshan di su junguan xunlian ban" [Taiwan's new army cradle: Fengshan's fourth class of training]. *Zhongyang yanjiu yuan zhongshan renwen shehui kexue yanjiu suo zhuanshu* [Academia Sinica] 31 (November 1993).

———. *Sun Liren yanlun xuanji* [Collected Works of Sun Li-jen]. Taipei: Zhongyang yanjiuyuan jundai yanjiusuo, 2000.

———. *Sun Liren shangjiang zhuan an zhui zong fang tan lu* [Tracing the Facts: Oral Histories of the Sun Li-jen Case]. Taipei: Taiwan xuesheng shuju, 2012.

Dang zheng jun lianhe zuozhan gangyao [Party, Nation, Army Joint Operations Outline]. Taipei: Yangmingshan, 1956.

Deng, Weimei. *Zhongyang lu jun junguan xueyuan tebie ban jiangyi* [Special Class of the Central Military Academy Lectures]. Ca. 1937, copy at Stanford University, OCLC: 122260666.

Deng, Wenyi. *Jundui zhong zhengzhi gongzuo* [Political Work in the Military]. Nanjing: Zhongyang lujun xuexiao zhengzhi xunlian chu, 1930.

———. *Jun dui zhong zheng zhi gong zuo* [Political Work in the Military]. Beijing: Beijing zhong xian tuo fang ke ji fa zhan you xian gong si, 2012.

Du, Congrong. *Huangpu jun xiao zhi chuang jian ji dong zheng bei fa zhi hui yi* [Recollection of the Whampoa Academy and Northern Expedition]. Taipei, 1975.

Du, Xinru. *Xianfa nei guan fang junshi zhi cankao ziliao* [Constitutional Articles Concerning Military Affairs]. Nanjing: Zhongyan xunlian tuan, 1946.

Du, Yuming. *Guo gong neizhan milu* [A Secret History of the KMT-CCP Civil War]. Taipei: Babilun chubanshe, 1991.

Duan, Fuchu. "Zhonghua minguo minzhu huaxia de wenwu guanxi jundui guojia hua de jincheng" [Republic of China Civil-Military Relations and Army Nationalization Process]. *Fuxinggang Xuebao* 104 (June 2014): 1–24.

Duan, Fuchu, and Luxun Hong. *Jundui yu shehui guanxi* [Military-Society Relations]. Taipei: Shiying chubanshe, 2002.

Fan, Sheng-Meng. "Lun fazhi guo yuanze xia de jundui yu zuzhi" [A Discussion of Army Organization in Developing Countries]. *Guofang Zazhi* [National Defense Magazine] 29, no. 4 (July 2014): 97–112.

Fang, Pengcheng. "Jundui gonggong guanxi: meiguo yu woguo de bijiao yanjiu" [Military Public Relations: A Comparison of U.S. and Our Nation]. *Fuxinggang Xuebao* 87 (September 2006): 27–51.

Feng, Shaokun. *Guo junzheng zhan shi* [National Civil-Military History]. Taipei: Zhengzhi zuozhan xuexiao bianying, 1972.

Fuxinggang lunwen ji [Fuxinggang Academy Collected Works]. Taipei: Zhengzhi zuozhan xuexiao, 1979–1984.

Fuxinggang Wenji [Fuxinggang Collected Words]. Taipei: Zhengzhi zuozhan xuexiao yanjiu bu bianying, 1979.

Gao, Yongguang. "Woguo junshi yuanxiao zhengzhi jiaoyu kecheng zhi yanjiu-jundui yu guojia, jundui yu shehui guanxi quexiang de neirong fenxi" [Content Analysis of Political Education in Military Academies: An Assessment of Civil-Military and Military-Society Relations]. PhD diss., Guoli zhengzhi daxue [National Chengchi University], 1999.

Geming shi xian yanjiuyuan. "Dang zhengjun ganbu lianhe zuozhan yanjiuban" [Party-government-army cadres combined training]. Taipei: Institute of Revolutionary Practice, 1954.

Gong, Jianguo. "Zhonghua minguo zhengfu qiantai huo lujun zhengbian guocheng yu chengxiao chushen (1950–1961)" [The Early Nationalist Period on Taiwan, Military Reforms]. *Zhonghua junshi xuehui huikan* (September 2007).

Guo, Gongzheng. *Guo jun tong shi jiao yu xue shu yan tao hui lun wen ji* [Army Education System Symposium]. Taipei: Zheng zhan xue xiao jun she zhong xin, 2005.

Guo, Rugui. *Guo rugui huiyi lu* [Recollections of Guo Rugui]. Beijing: gongchandang shi chuban she, 2009.

Guofang Bu. *Junfa shouce* [Military Law Handbook]. Nanjing: Guofang bu, 1947.

———. *Guofang bu shizheng fagui huibian* [Department of Defense Laws and Regulations]. Nanjing: Guofang bu, 1947.
Guofangbu zong zhengzhi bu. *Guojun zhenggong shigao* [National Army Political Work]. Taipei: Guojun zhenggong shibian, 1960.
Guofang guanli shouce [National Defense Management Handbook]. Taipei: Guofang guanli xuexiao, 1973.
Guojun junji jiaoyu jiaoan ji jiang yi [Military Education Teaching Plan and Handout]. Taipei: Guo fang bu Zong zheng zhi bu, 1955.
Guojun shiliao yeshu. *Lujun junguan xuexiao di su junguan xunlianban guansheng fangwen jilu* [Army Officer School: Fourth Training Class Oral Histories]. Taipei: guofangbu shi zhengbian yishi, 2003.
Guojun zhenggong dianfan caoan [Framework of National Army Political Work]. Taipei: Guofangbu zong zhengzhi bu, 1954.
Guojun zhenggong shigao [Military Political Work History]. Taipei: Guojun zhenggong shigao biansuan weiyuanhui, 1960.
Guomin da hui mishu ju. *Xianzheng ducai yu jun zhengfu* [Constitutional Dictatorship and Military Government]. Taipei: Guomin da hui mishu ju, 1965.
Han, Jingfu. "Woguo jundui de shehui anquan zidu" [Our Nation's Military Social Security System]. *Fuxinggang Xuebao* 62 (December 1997): 301–24.
———. "Woguo zhiyuan yi junren fuli zhidu gaishu" [An Overview of the Military Welfare System]. *Fuxinggang Xuebao* 64 (September 1998): 175–200.
Hau, Pei-tsun. *Ba nian canmou zongzhang riji* [Eight Years as Chief of Staff Diary]. Taipei: Tianxia yuanjian wenhua chuban she, 2000.
———. *Jingguo xiansheng wan nian* [Chiang Ching-kuo's Later Years]. Taipei: Tianxia wenhua chuban she, 1995.
———. *Xing zheng yuan bas shi yi nian yanlun ji* [Collected Works of 1992]. Taipei: Xingzheng yuan xinwen ju, 1993.
He, Lixing, and Wei Qingchao. "Guojun xianxing zhengzhi jiaoyu dui guanbing jundui guojiahua guannian jianli zhi qiantan" [Current Military Education of Officers and Soldiers and the Development of the "Army Nationalization" Concept]. *Fuxinggang Xuebao* 92 (2008): 103–30.
He, Ren. "Xian jieduan de jundui zhenggong wenti" [Current Period Military-Political Issues]. *Xinjun* [New Army] 1, no. 2 (1938).
He, Zhihao. *Jun zheng yu jun ling* [Civil-Military Relations and Military Orders]. Taipei: Lian qin chu ban she, 1957.
Hong, Luxun. "Minzhu zhengti zhong de wenren tongzhi-junren fuxong yu jundui zhengzhi jiaoyu de quanshi." *Fuxinggang Xuebao* 68 (December 1999).
Hu, Yi. "Guomindang jundui zhenggong de fazhan lichen jiqi guji (1924–1949)" [Guomindang Military Political Work Development Records]. *Dangshi yanjiu yu jiaoxue* [Contemporary Research and Education] 4 (2010).

Huang, Yao. "Lun zhengzhi gongzuo de jiben xiuyang" [Discussing Political Work Basic Principles]. *Xin jun* 2, no. 12 (1939).

Huang, Zhongwen. *Minguo yushang jiangmounian* [Republic of China General Officers Chronology]. Taipei: Qiye chubanshe, 1990.

Jiang, Pei. "Zhongguo guomindang zaoqi jundui zhenggong zhidu de yanbian: 1924–1928" [China's Guomintang Early Period Military-Political System]. *Anhui shixue* 4 (2008).

Jiang, Shuiping. "Cong lujun daxue yange shitan lujun zhican jiaoyu jingjin zhi fangxiang" [From the perspective of the War College, a Discussion of Army Education and Improvements]. *Lujun xueshu shuangyuekan* [Army Bimonthly] 43, no. 496 (December 2007).

Jiang, Zhongzhang. *Ruhe gaizao women geming de fangfa* [How to Reform Our Revolutionary Methods]. Taipei: Zhongyang gaizao weiyuan hui wugong yingshe, 1951.

Jiang, Zhongzheng. *Junshi jiguan budui jianli zhidu gaijin yewu zhi yaodian bing shuoming jundui kexuehua de zhongyao* [Military Organizational Changes to Improve the Quality of Military Science]. Taipei: Zhongyang gaizao weiyuanhui wenwu gongying she, 1951.

Jundang yu zhenghu [Party-Army and Government]. Tebie dang bu, Zhengzhi xunlian chu, 1939–1940.

Junguan geming lilun duben [A Handbook on Military Revolutionary Theory]. Taipei: Guo fang bu zong zheng zhi bu, 1956.

Junsheng. "Guomin geming jun" [The People's Revolutionary Army]. Guangzhou: Guomin gemingjun di yi ji tuan jun zongsiling bu zhengzhi xunlian chu, 1927.

Junshi weiyuan hui [Central Military Commission]. *Gai jin ge jun shi xue xiao zheng xun gong zuo ji hua* [A Plan to Reform Military Schools' Political Training]. Chongqing: Junshi weiyuan hui zhengzhi bu, 1942.

———. *Gao jin ge junshi xuexiao zhengxun gongzuo jihua* [Outline of Military School Political Work Training Program]. Chongqing: Zhengzhi bu, 1943.

Junxue bianji ju. *Jundui duiyu hangkongji zhi xingdong* [Military Policies toward Aircraft]. Beijing, ca. 1912–30.

Junxue jikan [Journal of Military Science]. Shanghai: Shangwu yinshu guan, 1908.

Kung, Ling-sheng. *Kong Ling-sheng xiansheng fangtan lu* [An Interview with Kong Ling-Sheng]. Taipei: Guoshiguan, 2002.

Lai, Yingwen, and Hong Luxun. "Zhuge Liang de zhengjun sixiang ji qi zheng jun guanxi de juese" [Zhuge Liang's Political-Military Thought and Civil-Military Relations]. *Fuxinggang Xuebao* 85 (2005): 137–66.

Lee, Teng-hui. *Li zongtong denghui xiansheng bas hi yi nian yanlun xuanji* [Lee Deng-hui Collected Speeches, 1992]. Taipei: Xingzhengyuan xinwen ju, 1993.

———. *Lizongtong deng hui xiansheng bashi nian yanlun xuanji* [President Lee Collected Speeches]. Taipei: Xinzheng yuan xin wen ju, 1992.

———. *Lee Teng-hui zhi zheng gao bai shixian* [Lee Administration Executive Record]. Taipei: Yinke chuban youxian gongke, 2001.

———, ed. *Jiang Jingguo xiansheng quanji* [Collected Works of Chiang Ching-kuo]. Taipei: Xingzheng yuan xinwen ju, 1991.

Li, Baoming. "Jiang Jieshi zai jundui hua wenti shang de jiangxiang he shixian" [Chiang Kai-shek on Army Nationalization, thought and practice]. *Zhengda shiza* 10 (June 2006).

Li, Chengxun. *Xian zheng ti zhi xia guo fang zu zhi yu jun dui jue se zhi yan jiu* [Research on the Role of National Defense Organizations under Constitutional Government]. Taipei: Yongran falue shiwu suo, 1993.

Li, Disheng. *Guomindang xia ji junguan de riji* [Goumindang Lower Ranking Officer Diary]. Beijing: Huaben chubanshe, 2012.

Li, Xiang. "Guomindang yinren jundui zhenggong zhidu yuanyin kao" [The Kuomintang Imported the Army's Political Work System's Reasons Study in 1920s]. *Guizhou wenshi congshu* [Guizhou Academic Collection] 2 (2009): 24–27.

Li, Zhen. *Liao yaoxiang jiangjun shi zhounian jinian zhuanji* [Tenth Anniversary of the Death of Lao Yaoxiang]. Miaoli: Liaohuang borong, 1978.

Liliang [Strength]. Taiwan, 1950.

Lin, Yuanqi. *Gong fei zen yang zuo jun dui dang gong* [How the Communists Conduct Military Political Work]. Taipei: Fangong yi shi jiu ye, 1954.

Liu, An-chi. *Liu Anchi xiansheng fangwen jilu* [Oral History of General Liu Anchi]. Taipei: Zhongyang Yanjiu Suo, 1991.

Liu, Feng-han. *Xinjian jun* [The New Founded Army]. Taipei: Institute of Modern History, Academia Sinica, 1967.

Liu, Hongxiang. "Zhenggong zhengbu xuexiao zhi yanjiu (1950-1970)" [Political Work Department School Research]. PhD diss., Guoli zhongyang daxue [National Chengchi University], 2006.

Liu, Yang. *Guomindang jianjun yanyi* [Guomindang Army Development]. Beijing: Zhongqing yinju guang, 2012.

Liu, Zhi. *Huangpu junxiao yu guomin geming jun* [Whampoa Academy and the National Revolutionary Army]. Nanjing: Duli chubanshe, 1947; Taipei: wen hai chubanshe, 1972.

Lu, Yi. "Guomindang jundui zhenggong de fazhan licheng jiqi guji 1924–1949" [Kuomintang Military Political System Development, 1924–1949]. *Dangshi yanjiu yu jiaoyu* 4 (2010): 81–88.

Luda Yuekan [Luda Military Academy Monthly]. Nanjing: Luda yuekan bianji weiyuan hui, 1935–37.

Lujun junguan xuexiao xiaoshi [Army Officer Academy Digest]. Vol. 2. Taiwan, 1969.

"Lun zhongguo junzheng" [China's Civil-Military Relations]. *Shiwu Bao* 50 (1897): 13–14.

Luo, Youlun. *Luo Youlun xiansheng fangwen jilu* [Oral History of General Luo Youlun]. Taipei: Zhongyang Yanjiu Suo, 1994.

Mei, Yang. "Liang nian lai: Wo zuo jundui zhengzhi gongzuo de jingyan" [The Past Two Years: My Experiences of Political Work in the Army]. *Xin Jun* 1, no. 4 (1938).

Meng, Guanghan. *Zhengzhi xieshang huiyi jishi* [Political Consultative Congress Recollections]. Chongqing: Chongqing chuban she, 1989.

Minguo shiqi de lujun da xue [The Nationalist-era Military Academy]. Jiangsu: Di er lishi dang an guan, 1994.

Mo, Shaoke. *Sun Liren: beiqing* [Sun Li-jen: An Epic Military Tragedy]. *Renmin Wenzhai* 46 (June 2011).

Ni, Luo. *Wang Sheng*. Taipei: Shijie wenwu chuban she, 1995.

Qian, Shufen. "Cong jundui de juese xunlian zhidu lun juese renshi dui jundui shenghuo shiying de yingxiang" [The Role of Training and Critical Thinking in the Military Lifestyle]. *Fuxinggang Xuebao* 45 (December 1990): 443–62.

———. "Jundui zuzhi de lingdao yu fudao zhi yanjiu" [Military Leadership and Guidance]. *Fuxinggang Xuebao* 48 (December 1992): 349–78.

Ren, Minhai. "Jianshou zhengzhi gongzuo de gangwei" [Political Work Outline]. *Xin jun* 1, no. 2 (1938).

Shei, You-Lin. "Lun guojun zuzhi biange zhi yanjiu yu yinying" [An Analysis of Army Organizational Reform]. *Guofang zazhi* 29, no. 2 (March 2014): 1–20.

Shen, Jingyong. *Zhongguo jungui: Sun Liren jiangjun fengshan lianjun shilu* [China's Warrior: Sun Li-jen at Fengshan Training Center]. Taipei: xuesheng shuju, 1993.

Shen, Younian. *Gongfei zenyang zuo jundui zhenggong* [Communist Bandits' Political Work Methods]. Taipei: Fangong yishi jiuye fu dao chu, 1954.

Si fa yuan. *Chuli zai huamei junren xingshi an jian* [Handling of Criminal Cases Involving U.S. Personnel in China]. Taipei: Sifa yuan xingzheng bu, 1967.

Su, Jinqiang. "Guojun zhengzhi jaioyu yu jundui guojiahua de yanjin" [Political Education in the National Army and Army Nationalization]. PhD diss., Fuxinggang College, 1998.

Su, Keli. "Ershi shiji de junshi geming-yi ri'ezhanzheng (1904–1905) weili" [Twentieth Century Military Revolution and Russo-Japanese War]. *Zhonghua junshi xuehui huikan* [China Military Study Society Journal], April 2005.

———. *Jundui yu shehui* [The Military and Society]. Taipei: Yeqiang chuban she, 1997.

Sun, Chengcheng. *Yuanzi shidai yu yuanzi zhanzheng* [The Atomic Age and Atomic Warfare]. Taipei: Fangong chubanshe, 1950.

Sun, Jianzhong. *Guojun zhuangjia bin fazhan shi* [A History of the ROC Armored Forces]. Taipei: Guofang bus hi zhengbian yishi, 2005.

Sun, Li-jen, and Jingyong Shen. *Zhongguo junhun: Sun Liren* [China's Military Hero: Sun Li-jen]. Taipei: Taiwan xuesheng shuju, 1993.

Tan, Yiqing. *Guomindang jianjun yanyi* [An Assessment of the Guomindang's Army-Building]. Beijing: Zhongguo qingnian chubanshe, 2012.

Tang, Yilu, ed. *Zhongguo renmin jiefangjun quanguo jiefangzhanzhengshi* [The Complete History of the Chinese People's Liberation Army's Liberation of the Entire Country]. Beijing: Guofang kexue chubanshe, 1993.

Tsai, Chen-Wei. "Zhongguo chuantong zhengti de wenwu guanxi ji junshi shiye chutan" [Chinese Traditional Civil-Military Relations and the Military Establishment]. *Fuxinggang Xuebao* 90 (2007): 105–28.

Tsui, Ai-Mei. "Junxiao xingbie jiaoyu de fancuo: Cong xingbie jiaodu fansi liangxing ying guizhidu" [Backlash of Gender Education in Military Schools: Reflecting on Military Gender Rules]. *Tongshi jiaoyu xuekan* 12 (December 2013): 91–113.

Tzeng, Yisuo. "Taiwan minzhuhua yu guoan bumen zhengce yingxiang li zhi zhuangbian" [Taiwan's Democratization and Nationalization Reorganization Policy]. *Fuxinggang Xuebao* 89 (2007): 489–510.

Wang, Ermin. *Qing ji junshi shi lunji* [Qing Period Military History]. Taipei: Lian jing chu ban shi ye gong si, 1980.

Wang, Liben. "Taiwan junshi diwei weisheng-Sun Liren Fengshan zhengjun yu guningtou zhanshe" [Taiwan's Military Recovery: Sun Li-jen's Training Center at Fengshan and the Guningtou Battle]. *Zhonghua junshi xuehui* [China Military Studies] 14 (September 2009).

Wang, Qisheng. "Wuzhu wencong bei jing xia de duozhong bianzou: zhanshi guomindang jundui de zhenggong yu dangwu" [Political and Party Work during the War Period]. *Kangri zhanzheng yanjiu* [Anti-Japanese War Journal] 4 (2007).

———. "Zhanshi guomindang jundui de zhenggong yu dangwu" [Kuomintang Political Work during the Anti-Japanese War]. *Kangri zhanzheng yanjiu* [Anti-Japanese War Journal] 4 (2007).

Wang, Xun. *Ziyou zhongguo san jun*. Taipei: chang feng 1954.

———. *Ziyou zhongguo san jun*. Hong Kong: Shidai chuban she, 1957.

Wang, Yuankun. *Junshi shenpan fa shi yong* [Military Trial Law Reader]. Taipei, 1959.

Wang, Zhenhua. *Kangzhan shiqi waiguo dui Hua junshi yuanzhu* [Military Aid to China During the Anti-Japanese War]. Taipei: Huanqiu shuju, 1987.

Wen, Haxiong. *Wen Haxiong xiansheng fangwen lilu* [Oral History of General Wen Haxiong]. Taipei: Zhongyang Yanjiu Suo, 1997.

Wen, Wen. *Guomindang zhongyang lujun xuexiao yu junshi zhuangke xuexiao* [Kuomintang Central Military Academy and Military Science School]. Beijing: Wenshi chuban she, 2009.

———. *Guomindang zhongyang xunlian tuan yu junshi ganbu xunlian tuan* [Kuomintang Central Military Training Group and Cadre Training Group]. Beijing: Wenshi chuban she, 2010.

Wu, Xuexiao. *Zuo xin yezhan zhu cheng* [Modern Field Fortifications]. Taipei: Wuxue, 1953.

Wu, Zhenzheng. *Qun ying yi wang: Lujun xiao di su junguan xunlian ban ruwusheng zongdui koushu lishi* [Oral histories of the Officer Training Academy]. Taipei: Guofangbu shizheng bianyishi, 2011.

Xi, Jingheyan (Hosoi, Kazuhiko). "Nanjing guomin zhengfu shiqi de lujun daxue" [Nanjing Government Period Army Academy]. *Wuhan kexue daxue bao* 13, no. 2 (April 2011): 219–20.

Xiao, Minsong. *Lun zhengzhi minzhu hua yu jundui guojia hua* [Regarding Political Democratization and Military Nationalization]. Hong Kong: Zhiyuan chuban she, 1946.

Xing, Zhengyuan. *Li zongtong denghui xiansheng bashi yi nian yan lun xuanji* [President Lee Teng-hui Collected Works, 1992]. Taipei: Xing zhengyaun xinwen ju, 1992.

———. *Li zongtong deng hui xian sheng ba shi yi nian yan lun xuanji* [President Lee Teng-hui Collected Works]. Taipei: Xing zhengyuan xinwen ju, 1993.

———. *Zhongmei hezuo jingyuan gaiyao* [Summary of Sino-American Trade and Economic Cooperation]. Taipei: Xingzheng yuan meiyuan yun yong wei yuan hui, 1960.
Xu, Peigen. *Zhongguo guofang sixiang shi* [Chinese National Defense Thought]. Taipei: Zhongyang wenwu gong ying she, 1983.
Yang, Bokai. *Meirisu san guojun junbei* [America, Japan, Russia: Three Countries' Military Preparations]. Shanghai: Shenbao, 1933.
Yang, Chenguang. "Guojun lai tai chuqi de zhongzheng yu meiguo junyuan (1949–1953)" [American Military Assistance to the National Army after the Move to Taiwan]. *Zhonghua junshi xuehui huikan* [Journal of the Chinese Military History Society], October 2011.
———. "Guojun weiwan cheng de junshi shiwu daige (1943–1945)-yi guojun meishi zhuangbeihua budui wei zhongxin de shentan" [American Military Equipment and Aid during the Last Part of the Anti-Japanese War]. *Zhonghua junshi xue huiyi huikan* [Journal of the Chinese Military History Society] (April 1995).
———. "Kangzhan shiqi zhongguo mayinjun de jiaoyu xunlian" [The Experience of the Chinese Army in India during the Anti-Japanese War]. *Zhonghua junshi xuehui huikan* [Journal of the Chinese Military History Society] (October 1996).
Yang, Juyin. "Shehui fuli zhengce zhixing shang de kunjing yu tiaozhan" [Social Welfare Policies Implementation Challenges and Difficulties] *Fuxinggang Xuebao* 60 (June 1997): 295–305.
Yin, Guoxiang. *Yin Guoxiang xiansheng fangwen jilu* [Oral History of General Yin Guoxiang]. Taipei: Zhongyang Yanjiu Suo, 1994.
Ying, Du. *Junshi xue tong lun: Guofang zuo zhan zhi yaoling* [Military Science: The Essentials of National Defense]. Tianjin: Tianjing shangbaoguan, 1933.
Yong, Xu. *Jindai zhongguo junzheng guanxi yu junfa huayu yanjiu* [Modern Chinese Civil-Military Relations and Military Law Research]. Beijing: Zhonghua shuju, 2009.
You, Yang. *Junxiao shenghuo de huiyi* [Recollections of Military Academy Life]. Jiulong: Xin shiji cubanshe, 1950.
Yu, Da. *Yu da xiansheng fangwen jilu* [Oral History of General Yu Da]. Taipei: Zhongyang Yanjiu Suo, 1989.
Yu, Zidao. "Cong junshi jihua, guofang lun dao guofang xinlun: Lun Cai E, Jiang Baili, Yang Jie de guofang sixiang" [From a Perspective of National Defense Thought, an Exploration of Lun Cai E, Jiang Baili, and Yang Jie]. *Junshi lishi yanjiu* [Military Historical Research] 4 (2002).
Yuan, Shouqian, and Huang Jie. *Huangpu Jianjun* [Whampoa Army Training]. Taipei: Jiang zongton dui zhongguo yu shijie zhi gongxian congbian bianzhi hui, 1971.
"Yuanzi neng shidai zhucheng zhi chuxiang yu jiazhi." *Lujun junguan xuexiao* [Army Military Academy Journal] (September–October 1947).
Yue, Bingnan. *Zheng jiemin jiangjun shengping* [The Life of General Zhen Jiemin]. Taipei: Shiying, 2010.

Zenyang ba junzhong wenhua zuo de hao [What Military Culture Does Well]. Taipei: Guofangbu zong zhengzhi bu, 1952.
"Zenyang zuo yi ge xiandai junren he shijie junren" [How to Be a Modern Officer and a Global Officer]. *Lujun junguan xuexiao Xianduxun chu er shi yi qi jianshi* (September–October 1947).
Zhang, Fakui. *Zhang Fakui koushu zi zhuan: Guomindang lujun zong siling huiyi lu* [Zhang Fakui Oral History Memoirs: Memories of a Guomindang General Officer]. Beijing: Dandai zhongguo chubnshe, 2012.
Zhang, Faqian. *Zhang Faqian xiansheng fangwen jilu* [Oral History of General Zhang Faqian]. Taipei: Zhongyang Yanjiu Suo, 1992.
Zhang, Pengyuan. "Qingmo minchu Hunan de junshi biange" [Military Reforms in Hunan in the late Qing and Early Republic]. *Zhongyang yanjiuyuan jindai shi yanjiusuo jikan* 11 (July 1982): 101–16.
Zhang, Qiyuan, ed. *Xian zong tong jiang gong quan ji* [President Chiang Kai-shek Collected Works]. Taipei: Zhonghua wenhua chuban she, 1984.
Zhang, Ruide. *Kangzhan shiqi de guojun renshi* [Anatomy of the Nationalist Army, 1937–45]. Taipei: Zhongyang Yanjiu Suo, 1993.
Zhang, Shiying. "Kang zhan shengli hou guomin zhengfu jundui guojiahua de nuli" [Military Nationalization after the Victory over Japan]. *Zhonghua junshi xuehui huikan* [China Military Study Journal] 1, no. 5 (December 1999).
Zhang, Youhua. *Li Denghui baquan weiji* [Lee Teng-Hui's Authority Crisis]. Taipei: Xingaodi chuban, 1994.
Zhang, Yufa. "Erci geming: Guomindang yu Yuan Shikai de junshi duikang (1912–1914)" [The Second Revolution: Military Confrontation of the Kuomintang and Yuan Shikai]. *Zhongyang yanjiuyuan jindai shi yanjiusuo jikan* [Bulletin of the Institute of Modern History, Academia Sinica], no. 15 (1986): 239–97.
Zhang, Zhizhong. *Zhang Zhizhong huiyi lu* [Recollections of Zhang Zhizhong]. Beijing: Huawen chuban she, 2007.
Zheng, Dongguo. *Wo de rong ma sheng ya* [My Military Career]. Beijing: Tuanjie chubanshe, 2008.
Zheng, Jieguang. "Zhonghua minguo zhi zhengshi, fei zhengshi junshi jiaoyu-yi sun liren zhuchi zhi zhengshi junshi jiaoyu wei zhuzhou" [Chinese Political/Apolitical Military Education]. *Zhonghua junshi xuehui huikan* [China Military Study Journal] (October 2006).
Zheng, Jinju. "Yi dai zhanshen: Sun Liren" [A Generation's War Hero: Sun Li-jen]. Taipei: Shuiniu chuban youxian gongsi, 2004.
Zheng, Xueyu. "Wo guo dui wai junshi jichu jiaoyu zhi jiaoliu (1904–2005)" [Our country's military education from foreign countries]. *Zhonghua junshi xuehui huikan* [Journal of the Chinese Military History Society] (October 1996).

Zheng, Zhiting, and Qiushan Zhang. *Baoding lujun xuetang ji junguan xue xiao shi lue*. Beijing: Renmin chubanshe, 2005.

Zhenggong xuexiao. *Junzhong xinwen*. Taipei: Zheng gong gan bu xue xiao xin wen yan jiu zu, 1955.

Zhengzhi zuozhan xuexiao xiaoshi weiyuanhui [Political Warfare School Administration Committee]. *Zhengzhi zuozhan xuexiao xiaoshi* [History of the Political Warfare Military School]. Taipei: Zhenzhi zuozhan xuexiao, 1980.

Zhong, Hua. "Kangzhan shiqi guomindang jundui zhengzhi gongzuo shulun" [An Analysis of Kuomintang Military-Political Work during the Anti-Japanese War]. *Nanjing shehui kexue* [Nanjing Social Studies] 4 (2005).

Zhongguo guomindang zhenggang zhengce zhi yanjiu [China's Guomindang Political Platform, Policies, and Research]. Taipei: Guofangbu zong zhengzhi bu, 1952.

"Zhongguo junren jiaoyu zhi xianxiang" [Chinese Military Personnel Education and Appearance]. *Dongfang Zazhi* 10 (1904): 220–24.

"Zhongguo junquan jizhong zhi yiban" [Chinese Military Authority]. *Da Tong Bao* 14, no. 10 (1910).

"Zhongguo junzhi gaige" [China's Military Reforms]. *Dongya Bao* (7) 1898.

Zhongyang Junxiao. *Zhongyang junxiao tushu guanbao* [Bulletin of Central Military Academy Library] 2 (April 1933).

Zhongyang lu jun guan xuexiao. *Zhongyang lujun guan xuexiao shi gao* [History of the Central Military Academy]. Nanjing: Zhongyang lu jun guan xuexiao, 1936.

Zhou, Enlai. *Jundui guijia hua* [Military Nationalization]. Xin sijun junqu [New Fourth Army Base Area] (1946).

———. *Zhou Enlai junshi wenxuan* [Zhou Enlai Military Thought]. Beijing: Renmin chuban she, 1997.

Zhou, Meihua. *Minguo zhengfu junzheng zuzhi ziliao* [National Government Military Administration Organizational Historical Data]. Taipei: Guo shiguang, 1996.

Zhonghua minguo guofangbu [Ministry of National Defense Republic of China]. *2006 Guofang baogao shu* [National Defense Report]. Taipei: Ministry of National Defense, 2006.

———. *2004 Guofang baogao shu* [National Defense Report]. Taipei: Ministry of National Defense, 2004.

———. *1992 Guofang baogao shu* [National Defense Report]. Taipei: Ministry of National Defense, 1992.

Zhu, Bingyi, and Yang Xuefang. *Lujun daxue yan geshi* [History of Army University]. Taipei: Sanjun daxue, 1990.

Zhu, Peide. *Junguan de xin shenghuo* [Military Officers New Lifestyle]. Nanjing: Zhongzheng shuju, 1934.

Ziyou zhongguo de zhengjun jingshi [Free China Political Officer Manual]. Taipei: Guofang bu zong zhengzhi bu yinxing, 1956.

Published Sources: English

Abbott, Andrew. *The System of Professions: An Essay on the Division of Expert Labor.* Chicago: University of Chicago Press, 1988.

Accinelli, Robert. *Crisis and Commitment: United States Policy toward Taiwan, 1950–1955.* Chapel Hill: North Carolina Press, 1996.

Adams, Thomas Knight. "Military Doctrine and Organization Culture of the United States Army." PhD diss., Syracuse University, 1990.

Adelman, Jonathan R. "The Formative Influence of the Civil Wars: Societal Roles of the Soviet and Chinese Armies." *Armed Forces and Society* 5, no. 1 (November 1978): 93–116.

Alexander, Jeffrey C. *Action and Its Environments: Towards a New Synthesis.* New York: Columbia University Press, 1988.

Babb, Joseph G. "The Harmony of Yin and Yank: The American Military Advisory Effort in China, 1941–1951." PhD diss., Kansas State University, 2012.

Bai, Chongxi. *Military Education and Training in China.* Shanghai: International Publishers, 1946.

Ballantine, Joseph W. *Formosa: A Problem of United States Foreign Policy.* Washington, D.C.: The Brookings Institution, 1952.

Barber, Charles H. "China's Political Officer System." *Military Review* 33, no. 4 (July 1953): 10–21.

———. "Military Assistance Advisory Group Formosa." *Military Review* 34, no. 9 (Dec. 1954): 53–59.

Bedeski, Robert. *State-Building in Modern China: The Kuomintang in the Prewar Period.* Berkeley, Calif.: Center for Chinese Studies, Research Monograph 18, 1981.

Bell, Mark S. *China: Being a Military Report on the Northeastern Portions of the Provinces of Chih-Li and Shan-Tung; Nanking and its Approaches; Canton and its Approaches; etc.* Vols. 1 and 2. Simla, India: Government Central Branch Press, 1884.

Bell, Montague, and H. G. W. Woodhead. *The China Yearbook, 1916.* London: Routledge and Sons, 1916.

Bergère, Marie-Claire. *Sun Yat-sen.* Stanford, Calif.: Stanford University Press, 1998.

Bjorge, Gary. *Moving the Enemy: Operational Art in the Chinese PLA's Huai Hai Campaign.* Fort Leavenworth, Kans.: U.S. Army Command and General Staff College, 2004.

Black, Jeremy. *War and the Cultural Turn.* Cambridge, UK: Polity, 2012.

———. "Military Organizations and Military Change in Historical Perspective." *Journal of Military History* 62, no. 4 (October 1998): 871–92.

Bland, Larry, ed. *George C. Marshall's Mediation Mission to China, December 1945–January 1947.* Lexington, Va.: George C. Marshall Foundation, 1998.

Board of Review, Branch office of the Judge Advocate General, China-Burma-India. *Holdings and Opinions.* Vol 3. Washington, D.C.: Office of the Judge Advocate General, 1946.

Bobrow, Davis. "The Good Officer: Definition and Training." *China Quarterly* 18 (April-June 1964): 141–52.

Boot, Max. *War Made New: Technology, Warfare and the Course of History, 1500 to Today.* New York: Gotham Press, 2006.

Bourdieu, Pierre. "Rites as Acts of Institution." Chapter 4 in *Honor and Grace in Anthropology*, edited by J. G. Peristiany and Julian Pitt-Rivers. Cambridge, UK: Cambridge University Press, 1992.

Boye, F. W. "Operating with a Chinese Army Group." *Military Review* 27, no. 2 (May 1947): 3–8.

Brown, Jeremy, ed. *Dilemmas of Victory: The Early Years of the People's Republic of China.* Cambridge, Mass.: Harvard University Press, 2008.

Brunero, Donna. *Britain's Imperial Cornerstone in China: The Chinese Maritime Customs Service, 1854–1949.* London: Routledge Press, 2006.

Bullard, Monte R. *China's Political-Military Evolution: The Party and the Military in the PRC, 1960–1984.* Boulder, Colo.: Westview Press, 1985.

———. *The Soldier and the Citizen: The Role of the Military in Taiwan's Development.* London: M. E. Sharpe, 1997.

———. *Strait Talk: Avoiding a Nuclear War between the U.S. and China over Taiwan.* Monterey, Calif.: Monterey Institute of International Studies, 2004.

Carlson, Evans Fordyce. *The Chinese Army: Its Organization and Military Efficiency.* New York: Institute of Pacific Relations, 1940.

———. *Twin Stars of China.* Westport, Conn.: Hyperion Press. 1940.

Cassin, Lionel. *The Communist Conquest of China; A History of the Civil War, 1945–1949.* Cambridge, Mass.: Harvard University Press, 1965.

Chang, C. S. *Logistical Service of Chinese Army in the Last War.* Monograph of Analytical Study. Fort Leavenworth, Kans.: Command and General Staff College, 1947.

Chang, Jiu-te. "Nationalist Army Officers during the Sino-Japanese War, 1937–1945." *Modern Asian Studies* 30, no. 4 (October 1996): 1033–56.

Chase, Michael. *Taiwan's Security Policy: External Threats and Domestic Politics.* Boulder, Colo.: Lynne Rienner Publishers, 2008.

———. "Defense Reform in Taiwan: Problems and Prospects." *Asian Survey* 45, no. 3 (May/June 2005): 362–82.

Chase, William C. *Front Line General: The Commands of William C. Chase.* Houston: Pacesetter Press, 1975.

Chen, Chia-sheng. *Taiwan and the Development of a Late Modern Military.* PhD diss., University of Buffalo, 2009.

Chen, Chun-Ming. "Party Alternation, Civil-Military Relations and the Democratic Consolidation in Taiwan." *Taiwan Journal of Political Science* 24 (June 2005): 77–109.

Chen, Shui-bian. *A New Era of Peace and Prosperity: Selected Addresses and Messages.* Vol. 1. Taipei: Government Information Office, 2001.

Chen, York. "The Modernization of Taiwan's National Security Council." *The China Brief* 10, no. 22 (November 5, 2010).

Cheng, Hsiao-shih. *Party-Military Relations in the PRC and Taiwan: Paradoxes of Control.* Boulder, Colo.: Westview Press, 1990.
Cherepanov, A. I. *As Military Adviser in China.* Moscow: Progress Publishers, 1982.
———. *As Military Adviser in China.* Taipei: Office of the Military Historian, 1970.
Chestnut Greitens, Sheena. *Dictators and Their Secret Police: Coercive Institutions and State Violence.* Cambridge, UK: Cambridge University Press, 2016.
Chi, Hsi-cheng. *The Much-Troubled Alliance: U.S.-China Military Cooperation during the Pacific War, 1941–1945.* Hackensack, N.J.: World Scientific, 2015.
———. *Nationalist China at War: Military Defeats and Political Collapse, 1937–1945.* Ann Arbor: University of Michigan Press, 1982.
Chief of Military History. *Civil War in China.* Taipei: Department of the [U.S.] Army, 1966.
Chien, Tuan-sheng. *The Government and Politics of China, 1912–1949.* Stanford, Calif.: Stanford University Press. 1970.
The China Handbook Editorial Board. *China Handbook, 1952–1953.* Taipei: China Publishing Company, 1952.
Ministry of Information, Republic of China. *The China Handbook, 1937–1945.* New York: Macmillan, 1947.
Chou, William. "MAAG—Saga of Service." *Taiwan Review,* 6 June 1966.
Chu, Shiming. *A Comparison of Divisional Organization in Several Armies.* Fort Leavenworth, Kans.: U.S. Army Command and General Staff College, 1936.
Coffman, Edward. *The Regulars: The American Army, 1898–1941.* Cambridge, Mass.: Harvard University Press, 2004.
———. "The American 15th Infantry Regiment in China, 1912–1938: A Vignette in Social History." *Journal of Military History* 58, no. 1 (January 1994): 57–74.
Collier, Harry. *Organizational Changes in the Chinese Army, 1895–1950.* Taipei: Office of the Military Historian, 1969.
Colton, Timothy J. *Commissars, Commanders and Civilian Authority: The Structure of Soviet Military Politics.* Cambridge, Mass.: Harvard University Press, 1979.
Condit, Kenneth. *The Joint Chiefs of Staff and National Policy, 1947–1949.* Washington, D.C.: U.S. Government Printing Office, 1996.
Cox, Samuel. *The China Theater, 1944–1945: A Failure of Joint and Combined Operations Strategy.* Fort Leavenworth, Kans.: U.S. Army Command and General Staff College, 1993.
Crossley, Pamela. *Orphan Warriors: Three Manchu Generations and the End of the Qing World.* Princeton, N.J.: Princeton University Press, 1991.
Davidson-Houston, J. V. *Field Service Regulations of the Chinese National Army.* Beijing: Henri Vetch Publisher, 1934.
Dewey, Thomas E. *Journey to the Far Pacific.* New York: Doubleday, 1952.
Dickson, Bruce. "The Lessons of Defeat: The Reorganization of the Kuomintang on Taiwan, 1950–1952." *China Quarterly* 133 (March 1993): 56–84.

Dimaggio, Paul, and Walter Powell. "The Iron Cage Revisited: Institutional Isomorphism and Collective Rationality in Organizational Fields." *American Sociological Review* 48, no. 2 (April 1983): 147–60.

Domes, Jurgen. *Peng Te-Huai: The Man and the Image.* London: Hurst and Company, 1985.

Dorn, Frank. *The Sino-Japanese War, 1937–1941: From Marco Polo Bridge to Pearl Harbor.* New York: Macmillan, 1977.

———. *Walkout: With Stilwell in Burma.* New York: Thomas Y. Crowell, 1971.

Dray-Novey, A. J. "The Twilight of the Beijing Gendarmerie, 1920–1924." *Modern China* 33, no. 3 (July 2007): 349–76.

Dreyer, Edward L. *China at War, 1901–1949.* New York: Longman Press, 1995.

Duara, Prasenjit. *Rescuing History from the Nation.* Chicago: University of Chicago Press, 1995.

Eastman, Lloyd. *The Abortive Revolution: China under Nationalist Rule, 1927–1937.* Cambridge, Mass.: Harvard University Press, 1974.

———. *Seeds of Destruction: Nationalist China in War and Revolution, 1937–1949.* Stanford, Calif.: Stanford University Press, 1984.

Eberspacher, Cord. "To Arm China: Sino-German Relations in the Military Sphere Prior to the First World War." *Berliner China-Hefte/Chinese History and Society* 33 (2008): 54–74.

Edwards, Martin, and Michael Tsai, eds. *Defending Taiwan: The Future Vision of Taiwan's Defence Policy and Military Strategy.* New York: RoutledgeCurzon, 2003.

———. *Taiwan's Defense Reform.* New York: Routledge Press, 2006.

Ehrman, James M. "Ways of War and the American Experience in the China-Burma-India Theater, 1942–1945." PhD diss., Kansas State University, 2006.

Elleman, Bruce. *Modern Chinese Warfare, 1795–1989.* London: Routledge Press, 2001.

Elliott, Mark. *The Manchu Way: The Eight Banners and Ethnic Identity in Late Imperial China.* Stanford, Calif.: Stanford University Press, 2001.

Esherick, Joseph. *Reform and Revolution in China: The 1911 Revolution in Hunan and Hubei.* Berkeley: University of California Press, 1976.

Feit, Edward. *The Armed Bureaucrats: Military-Administrative Regimes and Political Development.* Boston: Houghton Mifflin Company, 1973.

Finer, S. E. *The Man on Horseback: The Role of the Military in Politics.* Baltimore: Penguin Books, 1975.

Finney, Charles G. *The Old China Hands.* Westport, Conn.: Greenwood Press, 1973.

Fogel, Joshua, and William Rowe, eds., *Perspectives on a Changing China.* Boulder, Colo.: Westview Press, 1979.

Fravel, Taylor. "Towards Civilian Supremacy: Civil-Military Relations in Taiwan's Democratization." *Armed Forces and Society* 29, no. 1 (Fall 2002): 57–84.

Fu, Zhengyuan. *Autocratic Conditions and Chinese Politics.* Cambridge, UK: Cambridge University Press, 1993.

Fung, Allen. "Testing the Self-Strengthening: The Chinese Army in the Sino-Japanese War of 1894–1895." *Modern Asian Studies* 30, no. 4 (October 1996): 1007–31.

Fung, Edmund. *The Military Dimension of the Chinese Revolution.* Vancouver: University of British Columbia Press, 1980.

———. "Military Subversion in the Chinese Revolution of 1911." *Modern Asian Studies* 9, no. 1 (1975): 103–23.

General Political Department, Ministry of National Defense. *Briefing on the Political Establishment in the Chinese Armed Forces.* Taipei, 1959.

Germani, Ian. "Terror in the Army: Representatives on Mission and Military Discipline in the Armies of the French Revolution." *Journal of Military History* 75 (July 2011): 733–68.

Gibson, Michael. "Chiang Kai-shek's Central Army, 1924–1938." PhD diss., George Washington University, 1985.

Gillespie, Richard. "Whampoa and the Nanking Decade (1924–1936)." PhD diss., American University, 1971.

Gittings, John. *The Role of the Chinese Army.* Oxford, UK: Oxford University Press, 1967.

Gong, Ting. "The Party Discipline Inspection in China: Its Evolving Trajectory and Embedded Dilemmas." *Crime Law and Social Change* 49, no. 2 (2008): 139–52.

Graff, David A., and Robin Higham eds. *A Military History of China.* Boulder, Colo.: Westview Press, 2002.

Greenwald, Howard P. *Organizations: Management without Control.* Los Angeles: Sage Publications, 2008.

Grieve, William G. *The American Military Mission to China, 1941–1942: Lend-Lease Logistics, Politics and the Tangles of Wartime Cooperation.* Jefferson, N.C.: McFarland, 2014.

Hall, Peter, and Rosemary Taylor. "Political Science and the Three New Institutionalisms." *Political Studies* 44, no. 5.

Hansen, Victor Davis. *Carnage and Culture: Landmark Battles in the Rise of Western Power.* New York: Doubleday, 2001.

Harries-Jenkins, Gwyn, and Jacques van Doorn. *The Military and the Problem of Legitimacy.* Beverly Hills: Sage Publications, 1976.

Hart, John N. *The Making of an Army "Old China Hand": A Memoir of Colonel David D. Barrett.* Berkeley, Calif.: Institute of East Asian Studies, 1985.

Hau, Pei-tsun. *Strait Talk.* Taipei: Government Information Office, 1993.

Headquarters: Military Assistance Advisory Group, Formosa. Subject: Country Statement on MDAP, Non-NATO Countries, 1955.

Heinlein, Joseph. "Political Warfare: The Chinese Nationalist Model." PhD diss., American University, 1974.

Hewes, James. *From Root to McNamara: Army Organization and Administration, 1900–1963.* Washington, D.C.: U.S. Government Printing Office, 1975.

Hibbert, George. "Reminiscences of the China Theater." *Military Review* 26, no. 12 (March 1947): 22–28.

Holober, Frank. *Raiders of the China Coast: CIA Covert Operations during the Korean War.* Annapolis, Md.: Naval Institute Press, 1999.

How, Julie Lian-Ying. *Soviet Advisors with the Kuominchun, 1925–1926: A Documentary Survey.* Armonk, N.Y.: M. E. Sharpe, 1986.

Hu, Pu-yu. *A Brief History of the Chinese National Revolutionary Forces.* Taipei: Chung Wu Publishing, 1973.

———. *A Brief History of the Sino-Japanese War, 1937–1945.* Taipei: Chung Wu Publishing, 1974.

Huang, Chan-Kuei. "The Logistical Organization of the Chinese Army." Fort Leavenworth, Kans.: Command and General Staff College, 12 November 1947.

Huang, Phil. "Public Sphere"/"Civil Society" in China? The Third Realm between State and Society." *Modern China* 19, no. 2 (April 1993): 216–40.

Huang, Ray. "Letter from Nanking." *Military Review* 28, no. 9 (December 1948): 24–30.

Huntington, Samuel P. *The Soldier and the State: The Theory and Politics of Civil-Military Relations.* Cambridge, Mass.: Harvard University Press, 1957.

Huston, James A. *The Sinews of War: Army Logistics 1775–1953.* Washington, D.C.: U.S. Government Printing Office, 1997.

Jacobs, Bruce. *Democratizing Taiwan.* New York: Brill, 2012.

Janowitz, Morris. *The Professional Soldier: A Social and Political Portrait.* New York: The Free Press, 1960.

Jaures, Jean, Liu Wendao, and Liao Shishao. *Xin Junlun* [New Military Law]. Shanghai: Shangwu yinshu guan, 1924.

Joffe, Ellis. *Party and Army: Professionalism and Political Control in the Chinese Officer Corps, 1949–1964.* Cambridge, Mass.: Harvard University Press, 1965.

Jordan, Donald A. *The Northern Expedition: China's National Revolution of 1926–1928.* Honolulu: University of Hawaii Press, 1976.

Jowett, Philip. *Chinese Warlord Armies 1911–1930.* London: Osprey Publishing, 2010.

———. *Chinese Civil War Armies 1911–1949.* London: Osprey Publishing, 1997.

Kagan, Frederick. *Finding the Target: The Transformation of American Military Policy.* New York: Encounter Books, 2006.

Kalyagin, Aleksandr. *Along Alien Roads.* New York: Columbia University Press, 1983.

Kan, Shirley. "Taiwan: Major U.S. Arms Sales Since 1990." *Congressional Research Service,* 29 November 2012.

Kennedy, Thomas L. "The Peiyang Arsenal and the Evolution of Warlord Logistics, 1895–1911." *Bulletin of the Institute of Modern History* (Academia Sinica) 10 (July 1981): 417–31.

Kirby, William. *Germany and Republican China.* Stanford, Calif.: Stanford University Press, 1984.

———. "Continuity and Change in Modern China: Economic Planning on the Mainland and on Taiwan, 1943–1958." *Australian Journal of Chinese Affairs* 24 (July 1990): 121–41.

Kuehn, David. "Democratization and Civilian Control of the Military in Taiwan." *Democratization* 15, no. 5 (November 2008): 870–90.

Kuhn, Philip A. *Rebellion and Its Enemies in Late Imperial China: Militarization and Social Structure, 1796–1864.* Boston: Harvard University Press, 1970.

———. *Origins of the Modern Chinese State*. Stanford, Calif.: Stanford University Press, 2002.
Landis, Richard. "Institutional Trends at the Whampoa Military School: 1924–1926." PhD diss., University of Washington, 1969.
———. "Training and Indoctrination at the Whampoa Academy." In *China in the 1920s: Nationalism and Revolution*, edited by F. Gilbert Chan and Thomas Etzold, 73–93. New York: New Viewpoints Press, 1996
Lary, Diana, and Stephen MacKinnon. *Scars of War: The Impact of Warfare on Modern China*. Vancouver: University of British Columbia Press, 2001.
Lary, Diana. *Warlord Soldiers: Chinese Common Soldiers, 1911–1937*. Cambridge, UK: Cambridge University Press, 1985.
Lee, Teng-Hui. *Creating the Future: Towards a New Era for the Chinese People*. Taipei: Government Information Office, 1992.
Leng, Shao-chuan, ed. *Chiang Ching-kuo's Leadership in the Development of the Republic of China on Taiwan*. New York: University Press of America, 1993.
Levine, Stephen. *Anvil of Victory: The Communist Revolution in Manchuria*. New York: Columbia University Press, 1987.
Levine, Steven I., and James Hsiung. *China's Bitter Victory: The War with Japan, 1937–1945*. London: M. E. Sharpe, 1992.
Li, Nan, ed. *Chinese Civil-Military Relations: The Transformation of the People's Liberation Army*. London: Routledge, 2006.
Li, Zongren. *The Memoirs of Li Tsung-Jen*. Boulder: Westview Press, 1979.
Lin, Hsiao-ting. "Taiwan's Secret Ally." *Hoover Digest*, no. 2 (2012).
Liu, F. F. *A Military History of Modern China*. Princeton, N.J.: Princeton University Press, 1956.
———. "The Nationalist Army of China: An Administrative Study of the Period 1924–1946." PhD diss., Princeton University, 1951.
Liu, Jennifer. "Indoctrinating the Youth: Guomindang Policy on Secondary Education in Wartime China and Postwar Taiwan, 1937–1960." PhD diss., University of California, Irvine, 2010.
Lu, Yan. *Re-Understanding Japan: Chinese Perspectives, 1895–1945*. Honolulu: University of Hawaii Press, 2004.
Lynch, Michael. *The Chinese Civil War, 1945–1949*. London: Osprey Publishing, 2009.
Lynn, John A. *Battle: A History of Combat and Culture*. New York: Basic Books, 2003.
———. "The Evolution of Army Style in the Modern West, 800–2000." *International History Review* 18, no. 3 (August 1996): 505–45.
MacKinnon, Stephen. "The Peiyang Army: Yuan Shi-k'ai and the Origins of Modern Chinese Warlordism." *Journal of Asian Studies* 32, no. 3 (May 1973): 405–23.
Marks, Thomas A. *Counterrevolution in China: Wang Sheng and the Kuomintang*. Portland, Oreg.: Frank Cass Publishers, 1998.
Marshall, George Catlett. *The Papers of George Catlett Marshall*, edited by Larry I. Bland and Sharon Ritenour Stevens. Lexington, Va.: George Marshall Foundation, 1981.

Martin, Bryan. *The Shanghai Green Gang: Politics and Organized Crime, 1919–1937*. Berkeley: University of California Press, 1996.

May, Ernest R. *The Truman Administration and China, 1945–1949*. Philadelphia: Lippincott, 1975.

McCord, Edward. *The Power of the Gun: The Emergence of Modern Chinese Warlordism*. Berkeley: University of California Press, 1993.

McCormack, Gavan. *Chang Tso-lin in Northeast China, 1911–1928*. Stanford, Calif.: Stanford University Press, 1977.

McCoy, Katherine E. "Organizational Frames for Professional Claims: Private Military Corporations and the Rise of the Military Paraprofessional." *Social Problems* 59, no. 3 (August 2012).

Miles, Milton E. *A Different Kind of War: The Little-Known Story of the Combined Guerrilla Forces Created in China by the U.S. Navy and the Chinese During World War II*. Garden City, N.Y.: Doubleday, 1967.

Ministry of National Defense, Republic of China. *MAAG's Decade in the Republic of China*. Taipei: Ministry of National Defense, 1961.

———. *U.S. MAAG-Taiwan*. Taipei: Military History and Translation Office, 2008.

Morton, Louis. "Army and Marines on the China Station: A Study in Military and Political Rivalry." *Pacific Historical Review* 29, no. 1 (February 1960): 51–73.

Moten, Matthew. *Presidents and Their Generals: An American History of Command in War*. Cambridge, Mass.: Harvard University Press, 2014.

Mutual Defense Treaty between the United States of America and the Republic of China. United States Treaties and Other International Agreements. Vol. 6. Washington: Government Printing Office, 1955.

Myers, Ramon, and Hsiao-ting Lin. *Breaking with the Past: The Kuomintang Central Reform Committee on Taiwan, 1950–1952*. Stanford, Calif.: Hoover Institution Press, 2007.

Noble, Dennis. *The Eagle and the Dragon: The United States Military in China, 1901–1937*. New York: Greenwood Press, 1990.

Notes on China. Washington, D.C.: U.S. War Department, Adjutant General's Office, August 1900.

O'Brien, Anita. "Military Academies in China, 1885–1915." In *Perspectives on a Changing China*, edited by William T. Rowe and Joshua Fogel, 157–81. Boulder, Colo.: Westview Press, 1979.

Pei, Jean, and William Wang. *Under the Same Army Flag: Recollections of the Veterans of World War II*. Beijing: Intercontinental Press, 2005.

Peng, Chen-Kai. *Proposals for Improvement of the Chinese Army Supply System*. Fort Leavenworth, Kans.: Command and General Staff College, 24 May 1949.

Pepper, Suzanne. *Civil War in China: The Political Struggle, 1945–1949*. Berkeley: University of California Press, 1978.

———. *Radicalism and Education Reform in Republican China: The Search for an Ideal Development Model*. Cambridge, UK: Cambridge University Press, 1996.

Peterkin, W. J. *Inside China, 1943–1945: An Eyewitness Account of America's Mission to Yenan*. Baltimore: Gateway Press, 1992.

Powell, Ralph L. *The Rise of Chinese Military Power, 1895–1912*. Princeton, N.J.: Princeton University Press, 1955.

Qu, Hua. *Review and Analysis of Our Military's Implementation of the Political Commissars System*. Nanjing: Military Historical Research, 2007.

Rankin, Karl Lott. *China Assignment*. Seattle: University of Washington Press, 1964.

Rankin, Mary B. "The Origins of a Chinese Public Sphere." *Etudes Chinoises* 9, no. 2 (Autumn 1990): 147–75.

Reid, George H. "The Political Commissar in the Red Army." *Military Review* 28, no. 1 (April 1948): 14–20.

"A Report to the National Security Council by the NSC Planning Board on United States Objectives and Courses of Action with Respect to Formosa and the National Government of China." 27 March 1953. Proquest Digital National Security Archive.

Rigg, Robert. *Red China's Fighting Hordes*. Harrisburg, Pa.: Military Service Publishing Company, 1952.

Rodriguez, Robyn. "Journey to the East: The German Military Mission to China, 1927–1938." PhD diss., Ohio State University, 2011.

Romanus, Charles, and Riley Sunderland. *Stilwell's Mission to China*. Washington, D.C.: Center for Military History, 1953.

———. *Stilwell's Command Problems*. Washington, D.C.: Center for Military History, 1956.

———. *Time Runs Out in CBI*. Washington D.C.: Center for Military History, 1958.

Rowe, William T. "The Public Sphere in Modern China." *Modern China* 16, no. 3 (July 1990): 309–29.

Sacca, John Wanda. "Like Strangers in a Foreign Land: Chinese Officers Prepared at American Military Colleges, 1904–1937." *Journal of Military History* 70 (July 2006): 703–42.

Sackman, Sonia. "Culture and Subcultures: An Analysis of Organizational Knowledge." *Administrative Science Quarterly* 37, no. 1 (March 1992), 140–61.

Schillinger, Nicholas. *The Body and Military Masculinity in Late Qing and Early Republican China: The Art of Governing Soldiers*. Lanham, Md.: Lexington Books, 2016.

Schnabel, James. *The Joint Chiefs of Staff and National Policy, 1945–1947*. Washington, D.C.: U.S. Government Printing Office, 1996.

Selected Executive Session Hearings of the Committee, 1951–56. Mutual Security Program, Part 2. U.S. House of Representatives. Washington, D.C.: U.S. Government Printing Office, 1980.

Shambaugh, David. "Civil-Military Relations in China: Party-Army or National Military." *Copenhagen Journal of Asian Studies*, no. 16 (2002): 10–29.

———. "The Soldier and the State in China: The Political Work System in the People's Liberation Army." *China Quarterly*, no. 127 (September 1991): 527–68.

———. "Taiwan's Security: Maintaining Deterrence amid Political Accountability." *China Quarterly*, no. 148 (December 1996): 1284–318.

Simon, Herbert A. "Bounded Rationality and Organizational Learning." *Organization Science* 2, no. 1 (February 1991): 125–34.

Slim, William. *Defeat into Victory*. New York: David McKay. 1961.

Smith, Richard. *Mercenaries and Mandarins: The Ever-Victorious Army in the Nineteenth Century*. New York: KTO Press, 1978.

———. "The Reform of Military Education in Late Ch'ing China, 1842–1895." *Journal of the Royal Asiatic Society, Hong Kong Branch* 18 (1978): 15–38.

Spector, Ronald. *In the Ruins of Empire: The Japanese Surrender and the Battle for Postwar Asia*. New York: Random House, 2007.

Spector, Stanley. *Li Hung-chang and the Huai Army; A Study in Nineteenth Century Chinese Regionalism*. Seattle: University of Washington Press, 1964.

Spence, Jonathan. *To Change China: Western Advisers in China, 1620–1960*. Boston: Little Brown, 1969.

Spengler, Henry M. "American Liaison Groups." *Military Review* 27, no. 1 (April 1947): 61–64.

Stilwell, Joseph. *The Stilwell Papers*. New York: Sloane and Associates, 1948.

Strand, David. *Rickshaw Beijing: City, People and Politics in the 1920s*. Berkeley: University of California Press, Berkeley, 1993.

Strauss, Julia. *Strong Institutions in Weak Polities: State Building in Republican China, 1927–1940*. Oxford, UK: Clarendon Press, 1998.

———. "The Evolution of Republican Government." *China Quarterly*, no. 150 (June 1997): 329–51.

———. "Xingzheng Sanlianshi and Xunlian: Modes of Government Administration during the Sino-Japanese War." *Zhonghua junshi li xuehui huikan* [Bulletin of the Chinese Society for Military History Studies] 1, no. 3 (December 1997): 565–95.

Stueck, William. *The Wedemeyer Mission: American Politics and Foreign Policy during the Cold War*. Athens: Georgia University Press, 1984.

Sutton, Donald. *Provincial Militarism and the Chinese Republic: The Yunnan Army, 1905–1925*. Ann Arbor: University of Michigan Press, 1980.

———. "German Advice and Residual Warlordism in the Nanking Decade: Influences on Nationalist Military Training and Strategy." *China Quarterly* 91 (September 1982): 386–410.

Sweeney, Red. *Ramgarh: Now It Can Be Told*. Privately published, 1952.

Taylor, Brian D. *Politics and the Russian Army: Civil-Military Relations, 1689–2000*. Cambridge, UK: Cambridge University Press, 2003.

Taylor, Jay. *The Generalissimo's Son: Chiang Ching-kuo and the Revolutions in China and Taiwan*. Cambridge, Mass.: Harvard University Press, 2000.

Terriff, Terry, and Theo Farell, eds. *The Sources of Military Change: Culture, Politics, Technology*. Boulder, Colo.: Lynne Rienner Publishers, 2002.

Tien, Hung-Mao. *The Great Transition: Political and Social Change in the Republic of China*. Stanford, Calif.: Hoover Institution Press, 1989.

Tsang, Steve, ed. *In the Shadow of China: Political Developments in Taiwan since 1949.* Honolulu: University of Hawaii Press, 1993.
Tsou, Tang. *America's Failure in China, 1941–1950.* Chicago: University of Chicago Press, 1963.
Tuchman, Barbara. *Stilwell and the American Experience in China, 1911–1945.* New York: Macmillan, 1970.
Tzeng, Yi-suo. "Civil-Military Relations in Democratizing Taiwan, 1986–2007." PhD diss., George Washington University, 2009.
U.S. State Department. *Confidential Files, Formosa–Republic of China, 1950–1954.* Frederick, Md.: University Publications of America, 1986.
———. *Foreign Relations of the United States.* Washington, D.C.: U.S. Government Printing Office.
———. *United States Relations with China: With Special Reference to the Period 1944–1949.* Washington, D.C.: U.S. Government Printing Office, 1949.
Upton, Emory. *The Armies of Asia and Europe.* Portsmouth, N.H.: Griffin and Company, 1878.
van de Ven, Hans. "Public Finance and the Rise of Warlordism." *Modern Asian Studies* 30, no. 4 (October 1996): 829–68.
———. "Stilwell in the Stocks: the Chinese Nationalists and the Allied Powers in the Second World War." *Asian Affairs* 34, no. 3 (November 2003): 243–59.
———. "The Military in the Republic." *China Quarterly* 150 (June 1997): 352–74.
Vernal, David. "Overseas Education for Taiwanese Military Officers: Policy, Practice and Effects." MA thesis, National Chengchi University, July 2006.
Von Bernardi, Friedrich, and Gao Lao. *Zhanzheng zhexue* [Military Theory]. Shanghai: Shangwu xinwu guan, 1924.
Von Plinsky, Alexander. *General Albert C. Wedemeyer's Missions in China, 1944–1947: An Attempt to Achieve the Impossible.* Fort Leavenworth, Kans.: U.S. Army Command and General Staff College, 1991.
Wakeman, Frederic. *Policing Shanghai, 1927–1937.* Berkeley: University of California Press, 1996.
———. "A Revisionist View of the Nanjing Decade: Confucian Fascism." *China Quarterly* 150 (June 1997): 395–432.
Walsh, Billie. "The German Military Mission in China, 1928–38." *Journal of Modern History* 46, no. 3 (September 1974): 502–13.
Wedemeyer, Albert C. *Wedemeyer Reports!* New York: Henry Holt, 1958.
———. *Wedemeyer on War and Peace.* Edited by Keith Eiler. Stanford, Calif.: Hoover Institution Press, 1987.
Wendt, Alexander, and Barnett, Michael. "Dependent State Formation and 3rd World Militarism." *Review of International Studies* 19, no. 4 (October 1993): 321–47.
Westad, Odd Arne. *Decisive Encounters: The Chinese Civil War, 1946–1950.* Stanford, Calif.: Stanford University Press, 2003.

Wilbur, C. Martin, and Julie Lien-ying How. *Missionaries of Revolution: Soviet Advisors and Nationalist China, 1920–1927.* Cambridge, Mass.: Harvard University Press, 1989.

Williamsen, Marvin. "The Military Dimension, 1937–1941." Chapter 6 in *China's Bitter Victory: The War with Japan, 1937–1945,* edited by James C. Hsiung and Steven Levine. New York: M. E. Sharpe, 1992.

Wilson, Peter H. "Defining Military Culture." *Journal of Military History* 72 (January 2008): 1–41.

Worthing, Peter. "The Road Through Whampoa; The Early Career of He Yingqin." *Journal of Military History* 69 (October 2005): 953–85.

Wou, Odoric. *Militarism in China: The Career of Wu P'ei-Fu, 1916–1939.* Dawson: Australian National University Press, 1977.

Wu, Shih-weh. *History, Organization and Operation of the Armored School and Chinese Military Academy.* Military Monograph, Advanced Officers Class #1. Fort Knox, Ky.: The Armored School, 25 February 1947.

Xu, Xiaoqun. *Chinese Professionals and the Republican State: The Rise of Professional Associations in Shanghai, 1912–1937.* Cambridge, UK: Cambridge University Press, 2001.

Yang, Y. K. "The Supply Service of the Chinese Army." Fort Leavenworth, Kans.: Command and General Staff College, 1 November 1948.

Younghusband, Francis. *British Military Report; Coast Defense of China, The Construction of Chinese Railways, etc.* Simla, India: Government Central Branch, 1887.

Yu, Maochun. *The Dragon's War: Allied Operations and the Fate of China, 1937–1947.* Annapolis, Md.: Naval Institute Press, 2006.

Zelin, Madeline. *The Merchants of Zigong: Industrial Entrepreneurship in Early Modern China.* New York: Columbia University Press, 2006.

Zhang, Xiaoming. "Towards Arming China: United States Arms Sales and Military Assistance, 1921–1941." PhD diss., University of Iowa, 1994.

Zhu, Fang. *Gun Barrel Politics: Party-Army Relations in Mao's China.* Boulder, Colo.: Westview Press, 1998.

Magazines and Newspapers

Beiyang bingshi zazhi [Beiyang Soldier Magazine]
Binglu Zazhi [Soldier Magazine]
Chicago Daily Tribune
Current Intelligence Bulletin
Foreign Broadcast Information Service (*FBIS*)
Fuxinggang Xuebao [Fuxinggang Journal]
Guofang yuekan [National Defense Monthly]
Guofang yuekan [National Defense Monthly]
Guofang zazhi [National Defense Magazine]
Guofang Zhoubao [National Defense Weekly]

Huanian [China Year]
Huangpu Yuekan [Whampoa Monthly]
Jiancheng zhoukan [Development Weekly]
Junfa zhuankan [Military Law Journal]
Junshi Xunkan [Military Affairs]
Junshi Yuekan [Military Monthly]
Junshi zazhi [Military Magazine]
Lianhe Baodao [United Daily]
Lingdao Wen Cui [Leaders' Speeches]
Life Magazine
Los Angeles Times
Nanyang junshi zazhi [Nanyang Military Magazine]
New York Times
Pacific Stars and Stripes
Shenbao [Shanghai News]
Taipei Times
Time Magazine
Tongyi pinglun
Washington Post
Xinhua News Agency
Yunnan junshi zazhi [Yunnan Military Magazine]
Zhongguo junren zhoukan [Chinese Soldier Weekly]
Zhongyang Ribao [Central News Agency]

Index

Page numbers in *italics* indicate photographs.

Abbott, Andrew, *The Systems of Professions: An Essay on the Division of Expert Labor*, 11
Aerospace Industrial Development Corporation, 165
agent provocateur activities, 162
aircraft operations training, 67
Alpha Program, 65, 69–70, 84, 86
American Bridge Company, 37
American Economic Mobilization and Economic Warfare (Xu), 97
American Executive Headquarters, Beijing, 113
American Export-Import Bank, 59
American Institute in Taiwan, 165
American Military Mission to China, 59–60
Anti-Communist Youth Corps, 141
anti-smuggling paramilitary force, 52, 72–73
Armed Forces Staff College, 133
armored warfare, 101, 119–20, 121–22
army-building, American involvement in, 3–4
army nationalization. *See* national army
Army Officer Academy, 30. *See also* Whampoa Academy
Army of the Future, The (French plan), 102
artillery training, 66, 134

Asian Games, 37
atomic bomb, 97, 99–100, 105, 120
atomic testing, 100
aviation, military, 26, 105

Bai Chongxi, 98, 99
ballistic missile defense, 100
bannermen, 17
Baoding Military Academy, 21–22, 27–28, 30, 47, 52–53
base locations, 112
Battle of Yenangyaung, 72–73, 91
Beijing Military Academy, 24
Beiyang Army, 19–20, 21, 22, 24, 52–53
Beiyang bingshi zazhi journal, 24
Bernardi, Friedrich von, *On War of Today*, 28
best practices adaptation, 6
"Big Army" program, 64–70
Bikini Atoll atomic test, 100
Blitzkrieg warfare, 101
Blue Shirt Society, 42
Boatner, Hayden, 58, 62, 69
border defense, 101
Borodin, Michael, 35
Boxer Indemnity scholarship fund, 37
Boxer Protocol, 56
Boye, F. W., 67
Bradley, Omar, 58

233

branch qualification schools, 88
brothel network, 144
Buck, Pearl, 59
bureaucratic military systems, 10–11
Burma campaign, 64–65, 66; Sun Li-jen in, 72–73
Byrnes, James F., 87

cadre force, 56
Cai E, 23
Cairo Conference, 63
Cai Tingkai, 52
Carter, Jimmy, 164
cavalry forces, 101; Manchu, 17
CCP Central Military Commission, 13
Central Military Academy, 39–41, 44, 47, 50; at Fengshan, 118, 122
Central Party School, 141
Central Political Academy, 41
Central Reform Commission, 141
Chang Tso Lin, 76
character development, 45
Chase, William, 82, 136, 160; Formosa MAAG and, 129–31; on Kai Plan, 138; officer education emphasis of, 133; on political officers, 153–54, 156; on ROC military school system, 134
Chen Cheng, 49, 157
Cheng Hsiao-shih, *Party-Military Relations in the PRC and Taiwan: Paradoxes of Control*, 14
Cheng Jiemin, 162
Chen Hung-hsien, 148
Chen Jiongming, 30
Chennault, Claire Lee, 71
Chen Shui-bian, 166, 170
Chiang Ching-kuo, 15, 116, 167; China Youth Corps and, 147; civil-military relations and, 147–50; criticism of military officers by, 149; death of, 161; on foreign military models, 149; Formosa MAAG and, 138; Fuxinggang College and, 145–47; in Fuxinggang ideological development, 148, 150, 174; on KMT and ROC development, 149; in KMT resurgence on Taiwan, 140–41; as political officer patron, 141; in political officer training development, 139; as ROC president, 166; on role of individual, 150; Sun Li-jen and, 149, 158
Chiang Kai-shek, 61, 77, 79, 82, 92, 95, 114, 118, 127, 149, 164; American public opinion of, 59; Central Military Academy involvement, 40; Central Reform Commission and, 141; on collective responsibility, 34–35; death of, 166; Formosa MAAG and, 138; Fuxinggang Staff College and, 147; German partnership and, 39; journal articles by, 120; on KMT defeat in civil war, 150; New Life movement of, 45; opposition to apolitical military, 116; party reform and, 152; on peacetime American military advisory board, 85; political and military role of, 35; on political officer system, 41–42, 107, 141; Second Sino-Japanese War and, 46, 52; on senior officers' competency, 48; Stilwell and, 60, 65, 90; Sun Li-jen and, 122, 152, 156, 157; on Sun Li-jen Incident, 157–58; as Whampoa commandant, 34; Xue Yue and, 71; Y Force and, 63
Chiang Wei-kuo, 122
Chiang Yunchin, 157
Chicago Herald Tribune, 89, 92
China: as Allied power, 95; American criticism of, 68; diplomatic recognition of PRC as, 164; in "Four Policemen" paradigm, 60–61, 70; imperial civil service exams, 36; military regions in, 112; role of professionals in, 10; U.S. postwar position on, 84–89. *See also* People's Republic of China; Republic of China
China Aid Act (1948), 127
China Lobby, 60
China Reconstruction Society, 42
China Youth Corps, 139, 147
Chinese Army in India, 61, 64, 65, 66, 73, 89, 90, 125
Chinese civil war: Chiang Kai-shek on KMT defeat in, 150; KMT performance in, 125; military

reorganization necessitated by, 108–9; Sun Li-jen on KMT action in Manchuria, 91–92
Chinese Combat Command, 67, 69
Chinese Communist Party, 30–31, 148, 149; military journals on responses to, 102; military responsibilities of, 3; postwar military strength of, 110; U.S. diplomatic strategy for engagement with, 108–9
Chinese Expeditionary Army, 62, 64, 90
Chinese Expeditionary Force in Burma, 72
Chinese 19th Army, 52
Chinese Professionals and the Republican State: The Rise of Professional Associations in Shanghai, 1912–1937 (Xu), 10
Chinese Soldier Weekly, 105
Chinese Training Command, 66
Chou Chih-jou, 134
Chungtai Hotel incident, 167
Citadel, the, 172
civilian authority, 123
civilian-military cooperation, 123–24
civil-military relations, 147–50
civil service exams, 36
civil society/public sphere debates, 6–7
Clark, Mark, 151
Cold War, 12
collective responsibility, 34–35
Command and General Staff School, 66–67, 121, 133
communications, 137
Communism, analysis of in journals, 44–45
Communist Revolution, 89
conscription, 16
constabulary forces, 17
Constitution. *See* Republic of China Constitution of 1947
Control Yuan, 158
Cooke, Charles M., 127
coordination groups, 108
cruise missile defense, 100
cultural values in support of military profession, 22–23

Dai Li, 70
Da Tong Bao newspaper, 23–24
defense doctrines, 119–20
Defense Ministry Organization Law, 169–70
Democracy and Military Service (Jaures), 28
Democratic League, 109
Democratic Progressive Party, 167, 168–69, 170
Deng Wenyi, 116
diplomatic policy, 101
domestic security, 154, 161, 162–63, 167–68
Dongfang Zazhi (Oriental Times), 23–24
Dongya Bao (East Asia Times), 24
Dorn, Frank, 58, 62
draft, military, 135–36
Dray-Novey, A.J., 10
Du Yuming, 73, 91–92
dynamic competition, 6

East Asia Times, 24
École Militaire, 134
education. *See* military education and training
education centers, 8–9
Effect of the Atomic Bomb on Chinese Military Affairs, The (Xu), 97
Eisenhower, Dwight, 90, 136, 159, 164
Ever Victorious Army, 19
exchange students, 37–38, 93, 104–6, 171–72
Executive Yuan, 108, 169

Fan Chengyuan, 99
Far East Games, 37
Feng Yuxiang, 28
F-16 fighter, 165
Field Artillery Training Center, 66
financial system, of Chinese army, 26
5 May cease-fire agreement, 52
fluidity of force concept, 120
force posture, 112
force reductions, 110, 171
Foreign Army Corps, 19
foreign-language training, 24
Formosa MAAG: chains of command in, 129–31; command structure of, 129,

Formosa MAAG (*continued*) 136, 137; communications and, 137; diminished mission of, 158–59; direct advisory efforts of, 134–35; in military school system development, 132–34; mission of, 129, 131; offensive posture shift, 137; planning objectives of, 136–37; political officers and, 154–55; Sun Li-jen and, 132, 156; Sun Li-jen Incident and, 156–60

Formosa Resolution, 159

Fort Knox, 134

Fort Sill, 134

Four Policemen paradigm, 60–61, 70

Fox, Alonzo P., 128

France, 28, 134; German invasion of, 101–2; political officers of, 31

Free China journal, 163

free professionals, 10

French High Command, 102

French Revolution, 31

From Here to Eternity (Jones), 56

frontier policies, 101

Fu Chaojie, 101–2

"Future of Military Aviation, The" (*Junhua*), 26

Fuxinggang Journal, 173

Fuxinggang Staff College, 139, 143, 145–48, 150, 170

Gamelin, Maurice, 101

General Political Works Department, 142

General Staff Headquarters, 169

German military system, 20–21

German officers: as instructors in Chinese military schools, 24, 53; as military advisors, 39–41

Germany: exchange students in, 22; invasion of France, 101–2; partnership with Kuomintang, 44, 49; relationship with China, 28

graduate education, 172

Great Britain, 28, 56, 61, 72, 97; Taiping Rebellion and, 19

Great Leap Forward, 164

Green Island prison, 162

Green Standard Army, 17–18

guerilla operations, 121

Guideline to Political Work, 142

Guofang Yuekan journal, 114, 173

Guo Tingliang, 157–58

Gu Youhui, 93

Han Chinese: banner units, 17; Green Standard Army, 17–18; independent forces of, 18–19

Han dynasty, 101

Hart, Robert, 23

Harvard Business School, 58

Hau Pei-tsun, 168, 172–73

Heinlein, Peter, 140

He Yingqin, 60

honor, Sun Li-jen concept of, 125–27

honor code, 125

How, Julie, 13

How to Eliminate Communist Bandits (Ye), 102

Hsieh Yoh, 71–72

Hsiung Shih-fei, *80*

Huai Army, 19–20

Huang Chan-Kuei, 104–5

Huang Jie, 157

Huangpu yuekan journal, 43

Huanian magazine, 46

Hu Hanmin, 31

human rights abuses, 162

Hurley, Patrick, 85

Hu Weike, 146

ideology: as ideal, 126–27; training in at Fuxinggang, 148–50

imitative adaptation, 6

imperial civil service exams, 36

Imperial Japanese Army Academy, 34

Indian independence movement, 44

Indigenous Defense Fighter, 165

infantry school, 88

Information Department, 116, 142

information officers, 153

Institutional instrumentality, 8

isomorphism, 8

Japan, 11; exchange students in, 22; military journals' focus on, 26;

relationship with China in warlord era, 28; Russo-Japanese War, 24, 26; Second Sino-Japanese War, 46–50; Sino-Japanese War, 20
Japanese military academies, 30, 51
Japanese officers, as instructors in Chinese military schools, 24
Japanese surrender, 84–85
Jaures, Jean, *Democracy and Military Service*, 28
Jiang Baili, 24, 50, 99
Jinan German School, 36
Jinmen Island, 137, 144, 145, 159, 168
Joint U.S. Military Advisory Group, 89, 128–29
Jones, James, 56
journals: civilian, 45–46; military newsmagazines, 105. *See also* military journals
Junhua military journal, 23–24; in development of military science focus, 26–27; key topics in, 25; on military schools system, 25–26
junior officer education, 88
Junshi Xunkan journal, 45
Junshi zazhi magazine, 119
Juntong, 70–71
jurisdiction, as element of professionalism, 11

Kai Plan, 137–38
Kang Youwei, 22–23
Kaohsiung incident, 167
Kennedy, John F., 164
Knowland, William F., 127
Korean War, 12, 128, 136
Krupp artillery, 19–20
Kuominchun army, 28
Kuomintang army: Communist defeat of, 89; German reform of, 40; in Manchuria, 91–92; as national army, 39; performance in civil war, 125; postwar strength of, 110; U.S. in shaping identity of, 55–56
Kuomintang Central Standing Committee, 166
Kuomintang Party: American criticism of war effort of, 71; communist purge in, 41, 49; diplomatic recognition of, 39; German partnership with, 44; influence at Fuxinggang, 147; interaction with military officers, 12–14; membership expansion, 141–42; military journals and, 43, 44; on military nationalization, 114; military power and, 29–36; party and political work in, 32–33, 106; party-army and, 12–14, 29, 42; political officer decline under, 41–42; purge of military leaders by, 4; resurgence on Taiwan, 140–41; U.S. diplomatic strategy for engagement with, 108–9; use of Soviet political-military models by, 148

Landis, Richard, 13
Langdon, William R., 69
leaders, as ideal, 126–27, 148
Lee Deng-hui, 168–69
Legislative Yuan, 169
Lend-Lease Act, 59
Liang Qichao, 22–23
Liao Yaoxiang, 61, 75, 90
Li Hongzhang, 19–21, 22
Lilley, Frank, 63
Lin Biao, 91
Liu, F. F., 13
Liu, Henry, 167
Liu Zhi, 32
Lucas, John P., 88
Luce, Henry, 59
Lu Fengge, 101
Luo Hongyan, 98
Luo Zhuoying, 72, 75
Lynn, John, 6

MacArthur, Douglas, 59, 128, 129, 130, 136
Madame Chiang Kai-shek, *79*
Magruder, John, 59–60
Mainland Operations Division, 121
Manchu Bannermen, 17
Manchu dynasty, 18–19
Manchuria, 89, 90–92, 101, 112, 114, 150
Mao Zedong, 100, 114, 164

Maritime Customs Bureau, 23
Marshall, George, 60, *80*, 108, 109, 112, 130
martial law, 161–62, 167
martial values, 22–23
May 4th Movement, 37
Ma Ying-jeou, 14
media, on political involvement in military affairs, 45–46
member networks, 8–9
Mexican Revolution, 130
Miles, Milton, 70
military academies: centralization of, 95; enrollment, 21; foreign instructors at, 24; Kuomintang, 29; post-Qing, 27–28; in publication of professional journals, 24; Sun Li-jen on purpose of, 30. *See also specific institutions*
military advisors: German, 39–41; Soviet, 30, 35. *See also* Formosa MAAG; U.S. Military Assistance Advisory Group
Military Affairs Commission, 48
Military Affairs journal, 45
Military Assistance Program grants, 164
military aviation, 26
military band school, 133
military base location, 112
military books, foreign, 28
military brothel network, 144
military change, 4; cultural approach to, 6–7; World War II impact on, 94–95
military detention centers, 162
military draft, 135–36
military education and training: in character development, 45; Chinese military exchange students, 28, 93, 104–6; in civilian schools, 147; foreign-language training, 24; in German style, 20–21; graduate education, 172; Li Hongzhang in development of, 19–20; NCOs and, 22; primary schools, 21–22; reform program for, 21; during Second Sino-Japanese War, 47; on standards and practices, 25; in Taiwan, 92–93, 117–20; U.S. influence on, 127–29; U.S. military manuals in, 133–34; in U.S. Army, 56–58, 88, 119; War College role in, 24; xenophobic attitude as hindrance to, 21; of Y force units, 62–64
military exercises, 118
Military Information Bureau, 41–42
military journals, 9, 23–29, 93–97; junior officers' contributions to, 94; management studies as focus in, 163; in military science focus development, 26–27; on mobility, 100–101; during Nanjing decade, 43–45; on national army building, 93–97; nonpolitical, 45–46; on organizational models, 104–6; postwar quality of, 94–95; quality during Sino-Japanese War, 50; on responses to CCP operations, 102; role in professionalization, 94; on scientific warfare, 99–100; self-criticism expressed in, 25; Soviet Union as topic in, 98–99; in Taiwan, 119–20, 163; U.S. as topic in, 96–97. *See also specific publications*
military justice, 34–35
Military Law of Collective Responsibility, 34–35
military models: American, 96–98, 134; foreign, Chiang Ching-kuo criticism of, 149; Soviet, 31, 148
military nationalization. *See* national army
military officer societies, 42
military police, 111–12, 146
military power, as factor in Chinese hegemony, 16
military primary schools, 21–22
military professionalism: adoption of bureaucratic system in, 10–11; American, 98; challenges to, 5; character training in, 45; cultural values supporting, 22–23; defined, 4; jurisdictional claims and, 11, 115; KMT challenge to, 160; military nationalization in promoting, 114; political department as challenge to, 139–40; political officer as challenge to, 5; in Qing dynasty, 16; in Republic of China officer corps, 3–4; technical competence as component of, 124–25; U.S. military in shaping, 55

military regions, 112
military school systems: American reforms to, 66, 132–34; creation by Qing Empire, 8–9; Formosa MAAG in development of, 132–34; *Junhua* article on, 25–26; of Political Work Department, 145–46; in ROC, 132–34
military science, 26–27
militia forces, 108, 111–12
Ming dynasty, 16
Ministry of Communication, 111
Ministry of Conscription, 135
Ministry of Defense, 109, 116, 118, 121, 129
Ministry of Defense for the People's Republic of China, 13
Ministry of Finance, 52
Ministry of National Defense, 104–5, 114, 115–16, 137, 147, 153, 154, 169
Ministry of the Interior, 154
missile defense, 100
mission-type orders, 120
Mitchell, William "Billy," 76
mobility, 97, 100–103
Modern Military Affairs journal, 95–99
modern warfare, 99
Mongols, 16
Mongul banner units, 17
Monterey Talks, 172
Morrison, G. E., 23
motorized warfare, 101
Mutual Defense Treaty, 159–60
Myitkyina campaign, 74

Nanjing Military Academy, 24, 28
Nanyang Military Academy, 24
nation, Sun Li-jen concept of, 123
national army, 107–16; consensus building for, 107–8; core concepts for, 108; criticism of, 103; debate concerning need for, 45–46; force reductions in, 110; impact on legal jurisdictional claim, 115; KMT army as, 39; in law and order activities, 113; military base location and, 112; military journals on creating, 93–97; military officers' approval of, 173; organizational models for, 104–6; paramilitary forces and, 111–12; in promotion of professionalism, 114; purpose of, 112–13; ratio of KMT to CCP personnel in, 109–10, 113; regional approach as alternative to, 71–72; reorganization agreement for, 112–13; as small political party wedge issue, 109; in Taiwan, 168; U.S. role in building, 70–71, 108–10
"National Defense and Military Nationalization" (*Huanian*), 46
National Defense Law, 169–70
National Defense Magazine, 120, 173
National Defense Monthly, 114
Nationalist Party of China, 3, 51. *See also* Kuomintang Party
Nationalist Party School, 51
National Military Council, 41, 108, 112, 115–16
National Revolutionary Army's Guidelines of Political Work, 142
National Security Council, 161, 169, 172
National War College, 133
neo-institutionalism studies, 8
New 1st Army, 74–75, 90, 92, 93
New Life civic education movement, 45
Newly Created Army, 20–21
New National Reader textbook, 22
New 6th Army, 75, 90
1911 Revolution, 29, 56, 135
9th Military Region, 71
Nixon, Richard, 131
noncommissioned officers, 22
normative isomorphism, 8
Northern Expedition, 34, 35, 42, 51
North Korea, 128
Norwich University, 28
Nurhaci, 17

occupational competition, 11
officer branch school program, 88
officer combat groups, 121
officer evaluations, 144
officer promotions, 144; in Qing dynasty, 18; during Second Sino-Japanese War, 48
officers: organization role of, 4; as professionals, 9–10

Officers' Moral Endeavor Corps, 42
officer societies, 42
On War of Today (Bernardi), 28
Operation Carbonado, 84
Operation Crossroads, 100
Operation Ichi-Go, 64–65, 71
Organic Law of the National Security Council, 169
organizational change, 7
organizational models, 104–6
organizational studies, 7–8
Oriental Times, 24
Oyama, Isao, 52

paramilitary forces, 111–12
Paris Commune, 42
party-army concept: challenges to in Taiwan, 165–66; as challenge to professionalism, 5; Kuomintang and, 12–14, 29; origin of, 13; tensions within, 34
Party-Military Relations in the PRC and Taiwan: Paradoxes of Control (Cheng), 14
party work, 32; in ROC Army, 143–45
Patriot missile defense system, 172
Peace Preservation Corps, 111–12, 113, 154
Pearl Harbor attack, 54, 60, 72
Peking Embassy, 58
Peng Meng-chi, 154
Peng Mengji, 157
people, Sun Li-jen concept of, 123–24
People's Liberation Army, 102
People's Republic of China, 161, 164
physical training, 118
police/military force, 17
Political Activities Committee, 141
political commissar system, 151, 153–54
Political Consultative Conference, 108–10
Political Department, 31, 49, 106–7, 116, 144, 170; as challenge to military identity, 139–40; Chiang Ching-kuo and, 140–41, 150; Sun Li-jen and, 151–52; U.S. objections to role of, 154–55
political evaluation system, 144
political officers: American officers' view of, 145; chain of command, 33–34,

144; as challenge to professionalism, 5; Chiang Ching-kuo as patron to, 141; creation of, 31; criticism of, 41–42, 107; decline of system in Taiwan, 169–70; decline of system under KMT, 41–42; Fuxinggang Staff College and, 145–49; impact of supply system on, 107; influence of on military commanders, 144; internal security apparatus and, 146; internal tasks in military units, 33; monitoring function of, 170; in Northern Expedition, 34; number of, 143; role of, 13–14, 31–32, 141–45; in Second Sino-Japanese War, 106–7; in Taiwan, 140, 151; training of, 31, 33, 41, 49, 139–40, 151; troop welfare activities, 143–44; U.S. military opposition to, 152–56
political oversight, 140
political training, 106–7
Political Warfare Bureau, 170
political warfare school, 139
political work, 32–33, 116, 143–45, 152
Political Work Department, 142, 145–46
profession, Sun Li-jen concept of, 124–25
professional change, 7
professionalism, jurisdictional definition in, 11. *See also* military professionalism
professional journals. *See* military journals
professional networks, 8–9
professionals: "free," 10; military officers as, 9–10
promotions. *See* officer promotions
public opinion: American, on China, 59; in defining professional jurisdiction, 11
Purdue University, 37, 51

Qi Jiguang, 34
Qing dynasty: end of, 27; military promotion in, 18; military traditions in, 16–18; use of military power by, 16
Qinghe Military Academy, 28

Radford, Arthur, 136
railroad guards, 111
Ramgarh Training Center, 61–62, 69, 73–74, 78

Rankin, Karl, *83*, 118, 129, 138
Reagan, Ronald, 164, 165
recruitment, 135–36
reforms, military, 16; American role in, 65–66, 69–70, 108–9; German role in, 40; military draft and, 135–36; military nationalization and, 46; of ROC Army, 131–32, 166, 168
"Relationship between the Military and Statistics, The" (*Junhua*), 26
Republic of China: American influence in Taiwan, 127–29; army school system, 122; civil-military relations in, 147–50; as deterrent force against PRC, 164; development of military professionalism in, 3–4; internal security apparatus, 146; martial law in, 161–62, 167; political isolation of, 166–67; political leaders' response to American aid, 138; U.S. defense treaties with, 159–60; withdrawal to Taiwan, 117
Republic of China Air Force, 137, 163–64
Republic of China Army, *83*; age of personnel, 135–36; armored forces, 121–22; as "army in exile," 119; changes in mission of, 166; CIA assessment of political officer system, 155–56; composition of, 121; contemporary status, 170–73; in domestic security functions, 162–63, 167–68; Kai Plan, 137–38; KMT political control over, 161; literacy rate of personnel, 143; military school system development in, 132–34; party work and political work in, 143–45; political evaluation system in, 144; political work in, 32–33; recruitment for, 135–36; reform programs for, 131–32; structures and equipment, 120–22; Sun Li-jen's four concepts for, 123–27; Taiwanification of, 166; technical competence in, 124–25; training centers, 117–20; U.S. aid program for, 128–29, 132
Republic of China Constitution of 1947, 84, 117, 153, 169
Republic of China Navy, 137, 163

Republic of China president: Chiang Ching-kuo as, 166; command authority of, 169
Rhode Island National Guard, 130
Rice, Edward, 68
Roosevelt, Franklin D., 60, 65, 70
Roosevelt, Theodore, 57
Root, Elihu, 57
Russo-Japanese War, 24, 26

Salt Inspectorate, 10
Salt Monopoly, 52
scientific warfare, 97, 99–100, 105
Second Revolution, 29
Second United Front, 49
secret police system, 153
self-control, 125
self-criticism, 25
Shandong province, 36
Shen Qingchen, 50
Shih Ming-teh, 167
Sino-American Cooperative Organization, 70–71
Sino-American Mutual Defense Treaty, 159–60
Sino-Japanese War, 20
Sino-Japanese War, Second, 46–50; American liaison officers and, 62–64; foreign support in, 49–50; political officers and, 106
Sino-Soviet Non-Aggression Pact, 49
"Six Assurances" memo, 165
Slim, William, 73–74
Smythe, George, 160
Song dynasty, 101
Soong, T. V., 52, 85
Soong Mei-ling, *79*
South Korea, 128
South Vietnam, 164
Soviet commissar, 31
Soviet political-military models, 148
Soviet Union, 28, 29, 97; assistance during Sino-Japanese War, 49–50; China in global effort against, 165; Chinese officers' view of, 98–99; in "Four Policemen" paradigm, 61; military advisors at Whampoa Academy, 13, 30,

242 INDEX

Soviet Union (*continued*)
   35; political officers of, 31; support of KMT by, 148
Spanish-American War, 57
staff officer system, 119
Stalin, Josef, 148
standards and practices, 25
Stilwell, Joseph, 58, 59, 74, 75, *79*; Chiang Kai-shek and, 60, 65, 90; on Chinese officers' competency, 48; criticism of SACO by, 70–71; goals for Chinese army development, 60–61; on Sun Li-jen, 75; as theater commander, 60
Stilwell and the American Experience in China, 1911–1945 (Tuchman), 12
Stimson, Henry, 59
strategic mobility, 97, 101, 112
Strauss, Julia, 10
Streamlining and Consolidation program, 171
Sun Huanting, 36
Sun Li-jen, 5–6, *79*, *80*; activities during Nanjing Decade, 50–54; battlefield performance of, 73; in Burma campaign, 72–73; Chiang Ching-kuo and, 149; Chiang Kai-shek and, 122, 152, 156, 157; early years and education, 36–38, 73; Formosa MAAG and, 132, 156; on "honor," 125–27; on military academy purpose, 30; as military instructor, 51–52; on "nation," 123; on "people," 123–24; Political Department and, 151–52; on political officer system, 153; post-Burma campaign activities, 89–92; on "profession," 124–25, 173–74; purge of, 140; at Ramgarh Training Center, 61, 73–74; as ROC commander in chief, 122; on ROC weaponry, 121; on self-control, 125; significance of, 14; Stilwell on performance of, 75; at Taiwan Training Command, 92–93, 118; in tax police force, 52–53; at Virginia Military Institute, 14, 37–38, 51, 125
Sun Li-jen Incident, 156–60
Sun Yat-sen, 5, 13, 35, 148, 149; in politicalization of army, 29–30
Sun-Yat-senism, 146

supply system, 107
Systems of Professions, The: An Essay on the Division of Expert Labor (Abbott), 11

tactical mobility, 97, 101
Taichung incident, 166–67
Taiping Rebellion, 18–19, 56
Taiwan. *See* Republic of China
Taiwan Defense Command, 146
Taiwan Garrison Command, 162, 167, 169
Taiwanification, 166
Taiwan Relations Act, 164–65
Taiwan Strait, 132, 136, 165
Taiwan Strait Crisis, 163–64
Taiwan Training Command, 92–93
Tang dynasty, 16, 101
Tang Enbo, 48
Tao Baichuan, 158
Tao Investigation Committee, 158
tax police force, 52
"tea house" network, 144
technical competence, 124–25
Temporary Provisions of the 1947 Constitution, 169
Tenney, Parker, 40
30-Division Plan, 61
38th Division, 72–73, 74
Tiananmen movement, 6–7
Tianjin Military Academy, 19
Time magazine, 66, 68, 69–70
Tongyi Pinglun, 46
Trotsky, Leon, 148
Truman, Harry S., 85, 108, 127, 128, 130
Tsinghua University, 36–37
Tuchman, Barbara, *Stilwell and the American Experience in China, 1911–1945*, 12

Unified Discussion, 46
United Nations Forces Korea, 151
United Nations Organization, 87, 101
United Nations Security Council, 90
United States: aid program for ROC, 128–29, 140; Chinese officers' view of, 97–98; Chinese students in, 37–38, 93, 104–6, 171–72; educational influence of in Taiwan, 127–29; intergovernmental

INDEX   243

partnership with China, 4; military training in, 22, 67, 98; military transfers to ROC, 121–22; postwar partnership with China, 85, 110; public opinion of China in, 59; as topic in military journals, 96–97
United States Taiwan Defense Command, 159–60
universal male conscription, 16
U.S. Air Force, 97
U.S. Air Force Academy, 172
U.S. Armor training center, 134
U.S. Army: in army-building, 3–4, 12; criticism of Chinese habits, 68; cultural education in, 69; General Staff, 57; in interwar period, 58–59; as military advisors, 11–12; Military Intelligence Division, 58; military manuals in ROC officer education program, 133–34; officer education system, 57–58, 88, 119; opinion of China in, 59; opposition to political officers, 152–56; partnership with Chinese military, 5, 55–56; pre-war status of, 56–57; service members' experience in China, 68–69; staff officer system, 119; Tianjin garrison, 56; wartime expansion of, 57–58
U.S. Army Air Force, 67
U.S. Army artillery course, 134
U.S. Army Command and General Staff School, 58, 66, 97
U.S. Army Industrial College, 58
U.S. Army Mission in Nanjing, 88
U.S. Army Signal Corps, 137
U.S. Army War College, 57, 58, 134, 172
U.S. Central Intelligence Agency, 121, 136, 161; report on political officer system, 155–56; on Sun Li-jen Incident, 158
U.S. Commander in Chief, Far East, 136
U.S. Congress, 134, 159, 164
U.S. Defense Language Institute, 172
U.S. Department of Defense, 96–97, 129, 155
U.S. Federal Bureau of Investigation, 167
U.S. 15th Infantry Regiment, 56, 58, 69
U.S. 1st Cavalry Division, 130
U.S. Joint Chiefs of Staff, 127
U.S. liaison officers, 62–64, 67–68

U.S. Military Academy, 57, 58, 97, 98, 134, 148, 172
U.S. Military Assistance Advisory Group, 86–89, 118. *See also* Formosa MAAG
U.S. Military Assistance and Advisory Groups, 12
U.S. military education system, 98
U.S. National Defense University, 172
U.S. National Guard, 130
U.S. National Security Council, 137
U.S. Naval Academy, 172
U.S. Navy, 56, 70, 128, 129, 132, 136, 159
U.S. Navy Staff College, 172
U.S.-PRC Joint Communiqué, 165
U.S. Republican Party, 127
U.S. ROTC program, 47, 119
U.S. Seventh Fleet, 128, 129, 132, 136
U.S. State Department, 127; on Formosa MAAG command structure, 129; "light footprint" approach advocated by, 89, 128; on political officer system, 153–55; role in Sino-American military partnership, 84–89
U.S.-Taiwan Defense Industry Conference, 172
U.S. 38th Infantry Division, 130
U.S. War Department, 86, 87

Versailles Treaty, 37
Vietnam, 16
Vietnam War, 164
Vincent, John Carter, 87
Virginia Military Institute, 14, 28, 37–38, 51, 73, 125, 172

Wang Hsi-ling, 167
Wang Jingwei, 31, 41
Wang Kuan-chow, 134
Wang Sheng, 146, 167, 170, 172–73
War College: foreign-language training, 24; military journals and, 23–24, 95–97; postwar restructuring of, 95–96
War College Education Act, 95
War Council, 20
Ward, Frederick Townsend, 19, 56
warlords and warlord era, 10, 21, 27–30, 33, 34, 35, 39, 42, 51–53, 72, 103, 111, 124, 126

Washington Post, 158
weapons and weapons development: foreign, 19–20; German influence on, 41; Li Hongzhang and, 19–20; modernization of ROC forces, 163–64; U.S. arms transfers and sales, 59–60, 121–22, 127, 164, 165, 172
Wedemeyer, Albert, 65–66, 71, *82*, 85, 87, 108, 110
Wei Lihuang, 75
West Point. *See* U.S. Military Academy
Whampoa Academy, 13, 44, 47–48, 51; curriculum, 30–31; political training in, 33, 151; Soviet advisors at, 30, 35
Whampoa Monthly, 43–45, 50
"Why the Military Should Consider Themselves Dogs" (*Free China*), 163
Wilber, Martin, 13
Wood, Leonard, 57
Wood, Walter, 63
World War I, 101
World War II: American response to end of, 84–86; impact on military change, 94–95; Japanese surrender, 84–85; scholarship on, 12; study of German operations in, 120; U.S. partnership with China in, 55–56
Wu, K. C., 158, 163
Wuchang Military Academy, 24, 28
Wuchang Uprising, 27
Wu Peifu, 22, 35
Wu Xu, 19

X Force, 61, 64
Xiandai Junshi journal, 102, 105; on American and Soviet power, 95–99; on mobility, 100–101

Xiang Army, 19
Xian Military Academy, 24, 28, 103
Xinhua news service, 114
Xue Yue, 71–72
Xu Peigen, 95–96, 97, 99–100, 101
Xu Xiaoquin, *Chinese Professionals and the Republican State: The Rise of Professional Associations in Shanghai, 1912–1937*, 10

Yang, Y. C., *81*
Yang Jie, 99
Yangtze River valley, 35
Ye Du, 102–3
Yenangyaung battle, 72–73, 91
Y Force, 61, 62–64, 64, 90
You Fengchi, 101
"Your Money Is Building a Police State in Taiwan" (Wu), 163
Youth Party, 109
Yuan Shikai, 20–21, 27, 29
Yu Kuo-hwa, 170
Yunnan Military Academy, 28
Yunnan Military Science Journal, 28

Zeng Guofan, 19
Zhang Zhidong, 27
Zhang Zhizhong, 40, 45, 49, 109, 111–12
Zhang Zuolin, 27, 28
Zhejiang chao journal, 24
Zhou Enlai, 109; on military nationalization, 114; in military nationalization talks, 111–12
Zhu De, 99
zizhi, 125
Zunghars, 16, 17

www.ingramcontent.com/pod-product-compliance
Lightning Source LLC
Chambersburg PA
CBHW020834160426
43192CB00007B/651